Lecture Notes in Computer Science 13075

T0171837

More information about this subseries at https://link.springer.com/bookseries/7410

Rodrigo Roman · Jianying Zhou (Eds.)

Security and Trust Management

17th International Workshop, STM 2021
Darmstadt, Germany, October 8, 2021
Proceedings

Springer

Editors
Rodrigo Roman 🆔
University of Málaga
Málaga, Spain

Jianying Zhou 🆔
Singapore University of Technology
and Design
Singapore, Singapore

ISSN 0302-9743   ISSN 1611-3349   (electronic)
Lecture Notes in Computer Science
ISBN 978-3-030-91858-3   ISBN 978-3-030-91859-0   (eBook)
https://doi.org/10.1007/978-3-030-91859-0

LNCS Sublibrary: SL4 – Security and Cryptology

Preface

These proceedings contain the papers selected for presentation at the 17th International Workshop on Security and Trust Management (STM 2021) held as an online event on October 8, 2021, in conjunction with the 26th European Symposium on Research in Computer Security (ESORICS 2021). As in the previous year, due to the ongoing COVID-19 situation ESORICS 2021 and the associated workshops – including STM 2021 – ran as an all-digital conference experience.

This year we initiated two rounds of the call for papers, the first in July 2021 and the second in August 2021, which in total attracted 26 high-quality submissions. Each submission was assigned to three referees for review and, as in previous years, reviewing was double-blind. The review process resulted in ten full papers – an acceptance rate of 38% – being accepted for presentation and included in the proceedings. These contributions cover topics related to applied cryptography; privacy; formal methods for security and trust; and systems security.

As in previous editions, the program of the STM 2021 workshop also featured an invited talk by the recipient of the 2021 ERCIM STM Best PhD Award. The laureate of this year was Jo Van Bulck for his thesis "Microarchitectural Side-Channel Attacks for Privileged Software Adversaries," written at the Katholieke Universiteit Leuven (KU Leuven), Belgium.

This year we also introduced the Best Paper Award. The selection was based on review comments from Program Committee (PC) members as well as the paper's overall quality. The award went to Korbinian Spielvogel, Henrich C. Pöhls, and Joachim Posegga for their paper "TLS beyond the broker: Enforcing fine-grained security and trust in publish/subscribe environments for IoT".

We would like to thank all the people that helped us in the organization of this event. In no particular order, thanks to Pierangela Samarati, chair of the Security and Trust Management Working Group, for her support and advice during the organization of the workshop; to Weizhi Meng, publicity chair, to help us bring this workshop to the eyes of all contributors; to all the members of the Program Committee and external reviewers, who endured two rounds of submissions and provided the authors with excellent feedback; to all the authors who submitted papers; and to all the attendees for contributing to the workshop discussions.

We also want to thank you, the reader, for picking up this volume. We hope that the contents of these proceedings will inspire you and help you in your future research.

October 2021

Rodrigo Roman
Jianying Zhou

Organization

Program Chairs

Rodrigo Roman   University of Málaga, Spain
Jianying Zhou   SUTD, Singapore

Publicity Chair

Weizhi Meng   Technical University of Denmark, Denmark

Program Committee

Cristina Alcaraz	University of Malaga, Spain
Pasquale Annicchino	Archimede Solutions, Switzerland
Joonsang Baek	University of Wollongong, Australia
Mauro Conti	University of Padua, Italy
Said Daoudagh	ISTI-CNR, Italy
Sabrina De Capitani di Vimercati	Università degli Studi di Milano, Italy
Roberto Di Pietro	Hamad Bin Khalifa University, Qatar
Carmen Fernandez Gago	University of Malaga, Spain
Olga Gadyatskaya	Leiden University, The Netherlands
Dieter Gollmann	TUHH, Germany
Jinguang Han	Queen's University Belfast, UK
Marko Hölbl	University of Maribor, Slovenia
Chenglu Jin	Centrum Wiskunde & Informatica, The Netherlands
Panayiotis Kotzanikolaou	University of Piraeus, Greece
Giovanni Livraga	Università degli Studi di Milano, Italy
Bo Luo	University of Kansas, USA
Xiapu Luo	The Hong Kong Polytechnic University, Hong Kong
Fabio Martinelli	IIT-CNR, Italy
Daisuke Mashima	ADSC, Singapore
Sjouke Mauw	University of Luxembourg, Luxembourg
Keith Mayes	Royal Holloway, University of London, UK
Weizhi Meng	Technical University of Denmark, Denmark
Chuadhry Mujeeb Ahmed	University of Strathclyde, UK
Surya Nepal	Data 61, Australia
Liliana Pasquale	University College Dublin, Ireland
Joachim Posegga	University of Passau, Germany
Davy Preuveneers	KU Leuven, Belgium
Pierangela Samarati	Università degli Studi di Milano, Italy
Qingni Shen	Peking University, China

Marco Squarcina	TU Wien, Austria
Chunhua Su	University of Aizu, Japan
Yangguang Tian	Osaka University, Japan
Hiroshi Tsunoda	Tohoku Institute of Technology, Japan
Zheng Yang	SUTD, Singapore
Chia-Mu Yu	National Chiao Tung University, Taiwan

External Reviewers

Sergiu Bursuc
Maryam Ehsanpour
Alzubair Hassan
Gulshan Kumar
Eleonora Losiouk
Elizabeth Quaglia
Korbinian Spielvogel
Utku Tefek
Pengfei Wu

Contents

x   Contents

Applied Cryptography

An Aggregate Signature with Pre-communication in the Plain Public Key Model

Masayuki Fukumitsu[1(✉)] and Shingo Hasegawa[2(✉)]

[1] Faculty of Information Media, Hokkaido Information University,
Nishi-Nopporo 59-2, Ebetsu, Hokkaido 069–8585, Japan
`fukumitsu@do-johodai.ac.jp`
[2] Graduate School of Information Sciences, Tohoku University,
41 Kawauchi, Aoba-ku, Sendai, Miyagi 980–8576, Japan
`shingo.hasegawa.b7@tohoku.ac.jp`

Abstract. Aggregate signatures without the bilinear map is a challenging and important problem in aspects of practical and theoretical cryptology. There exists only one aggregate signature which does not use the bilinear map, however, the scheme requires a non-standard cryptographic assumption in the security proof. In ProvSec 2020, Takemure *et al.* proposed a new variant of aggregate signatures, the aggregate signature with the pre-communication (ASwPC), to realize the security proof from a standard assumption. The ASwPC requires signers to interact with each other to share a temporary randomness before deciding their messages to be signed. After the pre-communication, each signer can start the signing process individually. They gave an instantiation of ASwPC based on the discrete logarithm (DL) assumption, and its security is proven in the random oracle and the knowledge of secret key (KOSK) model.

Although the previous construction achieved the provable security from the standard assumption, it requires a slightly stronger security model, the KOSK model. Thus we aim to construct a new ASwPC scheme whose security is proven in the plain public key (PPK) model which is the standard security notion of the aggregate signature. We employ the DDH assumption rather than the DL assumption and the property of the decisional assumption helps us to apply the lossy key technique to construct a security proof in the PPK model.

Keywords: Aggregate signature with pre-communication · Plain public key model · DDH assumption · Pairing-free

1 Introduction

The aggregate signature can compress multiple signatures for different messages into a single signature. The resulting aggregated signature ensures that each message is signed by the corresponding secret key and public key. Boneh, Gentry,

© Springer Nature Switzerland AG 2021
R. Roman and J. Zhou (Eds.): STM 2021, LNCS 13075, pp. 3–19, 2021.
https://doi.org/10.1007/978-3-030-91859-0_1

Lynn, and Shacham [7] proposed the notion of the aggregate signature with its first construction. Their scheme uses the bilinear map in the verification step, and its security is proven under the coDH assumption.

There are many instantiations of aggregate signatures. As well as the first construction by [7], many constructions employ the bilinear map, e.g., [3,7,10]. However, the usage of the bilinear map makes the implementation of the schemes less efficient. There also exist some constructions without the bilinear map, however, they are subject to some restrictions, such as sequential aggregation [14,16], interactive signing protocol [4] and synchronized aggregation [1,11].

Zhao [21] proposed the first aggregate signature with no restriction on the signing process or the aggregation process, without the usage of the bilinear map. His construction is based on the Γ-signature [20], a variant of the Fiat-Shamir signature [8]. Although Zhao's scheme has the provable security in the random oracle model [5], it requires a non-standard assumption, called the non-malleable discrete logarithm (NMDL) assumption. In the paper [21], the NMDL assumption is justified in the generic group model [15] with the random oracles. However, there is no other evidence that guarantees the hardness of the NMDL assumption so far.

The known works suggest that constructing efficient aggregate signatures without restrictions on the protocol of scheme or the usage of the bilinear map is difficult unless we use a non-standard cryptographic assumption. Takemura, Sakai, Santoso, Hanaoka, and Ohta [18] reconsidered what reasonable restrictions are on the design of practical aggregate signatures which do not use the bilinear map. They focused on the notion of interactive aggregate signatures. The existing interactive aggregate signatures such as [4] are realized under a standard assumption without the bilinear map by imposing the interaction during the signing and aggregation processes. On the interactive aggregate signature, each signer runs an interactive signing protocol to issue an aggregated signature. However, one can find that the singing protocol of the interactive aggregate signatures can be divided into the interactive phase and the non-interactive phase.

[18] proposed the notion of the *aggregate signature with the pre-communication* (ASwPC) from the observation above. In the ASwPC, the signing process consists of *the pre-communication phase* and *the signing phase*, and the former is interactive, and the latter is non-interactive, respectively. In the pre-communication phase, the signers interact with each other to share temporary randomness. Then, each signer chooses his message in the signing phase and signs it using his secret key and the shared randomness. The shared randomness enables us to realize that the signing phase requires no interaction among signers. Thus, each signer can decide the timing of running the signing phase individually. The generated signatures are sent to a specific signer called the *aggregator*, who computes the aggregated signature from all signatures.

Compared to the ordinary aggregate signature, the ASwPC requires signers to communicate in the pre-communication phase. On the other hand, such interactions are no longer required in the signing phase, unlike the interactive aggregate signature and the multisiganture [4] which need some interactions at the signing phase. Namely, the ASwPC can be considered as the intermediate notion between the ordinary aggregate signature and the interactive aggregate signature. The ASwPC can be substituted for the interactive aggregate signature and the multisiganture with more flexibility by its feature. Moreover, the ASwPC can also play the same role as the aggregate signature in the case where the pre-communication phase is naturally performed. For example, consider the situation that a central server periodically collects data from other nodes. The central server plays the role of the aggregator and computes the aggregated signature from all signatures sent from all nodes with data. Since the transactions between the central server and nodes are periodic, the pre-communication phase can be naturally added to the transactions. Moreover, the ASwPS has an advantage than the synchronized aggregate signature. The ASwPC does not need to determine the total number of generable signatures at the setup phase, while the synchronized aggregate signature requires us to determine it. Thus the ASwPC seems to have a reasonable restriction in practice.

In [18], the authors gave a concrete construction of the ASwPC. Their scheme is based on the discrete logarithm (DL) assumption, one of the most standard cryptographic assumptions. They proved the security of their construction under the DL assumption in the random oracle model and the *knowledge of secret key* (KOSK) model [6,13]. Namely, the ASwPC can achieve the provable security from the standard cryptographic assumption, which is the purpose of the ASwPC.

Although the existing ASwPC scheme achieves the security under the standard cryptographic assumption, the security proof requires a slightly stronger security model, namely the KOSK model. In the KOSK model, the adversary in the security reduction is forced to output secret keys with corresponding public keys and forgery. However, as mentioned in [4], realizing the KOSK model in practice causes an additional cost in the key generation. Intuitively, the KOSK model states that the adversary must prove the possession of the secret keys of public keys with which he computes the forgery. One method of implementing it is employing the proof of possession (PoP) [17] and the zero-knowledge proof of knowledge (ZKoK) [2]. Thus the KOSK model helps us to construct the security proof, however it requires additional computation costs in practice. This means that the KOSK model spoils the advantage of the ASwPC, namely the high efficiency rather than the bilinear map-based schemes from the standard cryptographic assumption.

In order to address the problem on the KOSK model above, the *plain public key* (PPK) model [4] is proposed in the context of the multisignature scheme. The adversary can choose public keys with no restriction in the PPK model, unlike the KOSK model. Especially, the adversary has not to prove the possession of secret keys which correspond to public keys that he uses in producing a forgery. Thus when we implement the schemes in the PPK model in practice, we do not have to employ PoP and ZKoK. Moreover, the adversary in the PPK model has a stronger power in computing a forgery rather than the one in the KOSK model. This implies that the security in the PPK model is superior to that in the KOSK model in an aspect of security and efficiency in practice. Therefore the PPK model is the standard security notion of the aggregate signatures and the multisignatures.

1.1 Contribution

In this paper, we aim to construct an ASwPC scheme whose security is proven in the PPK model. Before describing our strategy, we briefly recall the security proof of [18] under the DL assumption in order to see the reason why it requires the KOSK model than the PPK model.

The ASwPC scheme of [18] is based on the DL assumption. In the security proof, the reduction aims to solve the DL problem by using a forgery of the ASwPC scheme. For a given instance of the DL assumption, the reduction embeds it into the challenge public key. Then the adversary generates a forgery for public keys he chooses arbitrarily but including the challenge public key. However, the reduction cannot directly compute a solution of the DL instance from the forgery because the forgery is *aggregated* one. In order to extract a DL solution from the forgery, the reduction must eliminate the parts corresponding to other public keys from the forgery. The reduction requires the secret keys of them to realize it. This is the reason why the security proof under the DL assumption needs the KOSK model.

As we have seen above, it seems unavoidable to employ the KOSK model as long as we consider the reduction from the DL assumption. The main reason is that the constructed reduction is required to find the correct solution of the given DL instance exactly. This difficulty is inherent in computational assumptions, including the DL assumption. Thus our main idea to consider the security in the PPK model is applying other cryptographic assumptions, especially deterministic assumptions. We employ the DDH assumption instead of the DL assumption. The DDH assumption enables us to use the *lossy key technique* [12] in the setting of aggregate signatures, and then we can complete the security proof in the PPK model.

The basic strategy of our security proof is to apply the lossy key technique in the case of aggregate signatures. The lossy key technique considers two types of public keys, the *regular* public key and the *lossy* public key. The regular public key is an ordinary public key of the scheme which has a corresponding secret key. On the other hand, the lossy public key does not have a secret key. Moreover, when a lossy public key is given to the adversary as the challenge public key, the adversary cannot compute a forgery even if it runs in unbounded polynomial time. This is because we can show that there exist at most negligibly many challenges for which the adversary can produce a forgery with respect to a lossy public key. Since every challenge is computed by the random oracle, the probability that such *desirable* challenges are chosen to the adversary can be negligible. Thus the adversary cannot compute a forgery when a lossy public key is given.

Let us consider our case of the DDH-based scheme. The regular public key of our scheme consists of a DDH tuple (g, h, g^a, h^a), where g and h are generators

Table 1. Summary of aggregate signature without bilinear maps

	Assumption	PreCom	Security	Model	Reduction	# of parties
[21]	NMDL	No	PPK	ROM	Loose	Poly
[18]	DL	Yes	KOSK	ROM	Loose	Poly
[ours]	DDH	Yes	PPK	ROM	Tight	Log

The column Assumption means the cryptographic assumption used in each scheme. The column PreCom shows whether or not the scheme requires the pre-communication phase in the signing process. [18] and our scheme require the pre-communication phase while [21] does not need it. The column Security means the security model that each scheme uses in the security proof. All schemes are proven secure in the PPK or KOSK model with the random oracle model (ROM). The column Reduction means that the security proofs are loose or tight. The last column means the number of signers that each scheme can support.

of the underlying group, and a is an integer. The lossy public key is of the form (g, h, g^a, h^b) for another integer b. Then the DDH assumption implies that the regular public keys and the lossy public keys are indistinguishable by the polynomial-time adversary. We can also show that when lossy public keys are used as the challenge public key, the adversary cannot produce a forgery even for the aggregated signature. This can be done by using the similar technique of [9] in which the lossy key technique succeeds in the aggregated *multisignature* case and the PPK model. We show that there is at most one hash value related to the challenge public key that derives the acceptance when the challenge public key is replaced with a lossy one. In the random oracle model, any hash value is obtained by the reduction. Since the reduction chooses the hash value uniformly at random from the exponentially large set, the adversary has a chance to meet the hash value that derives the acceptance with only negligible probability. Thus we complete the security proof in the PPK model by using the DDH assumption.

Employing the DDH assumption brings an additional advantage to the security proof. Our security proof achieves tight security in which the success probability of breaking the DDH assumption is almost the same as the probability of computing a forgery. This is because we do not use the general forking lemma [4]. The (general) forking lemma is typically used for the reduction of computational assumptions and causes an inherent security loss. We can avoid the usage of the general forking lemma by employing the decisional assumption, the DDH assumption, then succeed in constructing the tight security reduction.

1.2   Comparison

Zhao [21] proposed the aggregate signature, which does not use the bilinear map and does not pose any restriction on the signing process or the aggregation process. This scheme is constructed based on the Γ-signature [20]. Although Zhao's scheme has the provable security, it requires the NMDL assumption,

Table 2. Comparison of component and communication size

	Public parameter	Component size		Signature size		PreCom size
		pk	sk	Each sig.	Aggregated sig.	
[21]	$(\mathbb{G}, p, g)$	$|\mathbb{G}|$	$|\mathbb{Z}_p|$	$2|\mathbb{Z}_p|$	$|\mathbb{Z}_p| + N|\mathbb{G}|$	–
[18]	$(\mathbb{G}, p, g)$	$|\mathbb{G}|$	$|\mathbb{Z}_p|$	$|\mathbb{Z}_p| + \lambda$	$|\mathbb{Z}_p| + N\lambda + |\mathbb{G}|$	$2|\mathbb{G}|$
[ours]	$(\mathbb{G}, p, g, h)$	$2|\mathbb{G}|$	$|\mathbb{Z}_p|$	$|\mathbb{Z}_p| + \lambda$	$|\mathbb{Z}_p| + N\lambda + 2|\mathbb{G}|$	$4|\mathbb{G}|$

The column Public Parameter displays a public parameter of each scheme. The public parameter of DL-based scheme [18, 21] consists of the group description $\mathbb{G}$ of prime order p and its generator g. Since our scheme is based on the DDH assumption, the additional generator h is appended. The column Component size displays the storage of each component. $|\mathbb{G}|$ and $|\mathbb{Z}_p|$ mean the size of one element in $\mathbb{G}$ and $\mathbb{Z}_p$, respectively. The column Signature size displays the size of the signature. In this column, Each sig. shows the size of the signature that each signer computes and Aggregated sig. shows the size of the aggregated signature. N means the number of involved signers, and λ is the security parameter. The column PreCom size displays the traffic expended in the pre-communication phase of the signing protocol.

which is considered as a non-standard cryptographic assumption at the present time.

The notion of aggregate signature with the pre-communication is introduced by [18] in order to address the problem on [21] concerning the cryptographic assumption. Their scheme has the security proof from the ordinary DL assumption, instead of employing the interaction among signers in the signing process.

The summary of these two schemes with ours is given in Table 1. Each scheme has advantages and disadvantages, respectively. The advantage of the first scheme [21] is the security in the PPK model and it does not require the pre-communication phase, however, it uses the NMDL assumption. The second scheme [18] can prove its security from the DL assumption. On the other hand, the disadvantage of the second scheme is employing the KOSK model and the use of the pre-communication. Our scheme has the advantage such as the tight security proof in the PPK model. However, our scheme requires the pre-communication and the DDH assumption in the security proof. Moreover, our scheme has to restrict the number of signers to be log in the security parameter. This restriction is due to the sub-exponential attack using the k-sum algorithm described in [19].

We compare the efficiency of our proposed scheme with the other two schemes. The result is given in Table 2. This table shows that the size of public keys of ours is twice that of other schemes, however, the size of secret keys is the same. On the size of individual signatures, that of [21] is constant. On the other hand, those of [18] and ours are proportional to the number of signers. The size of aggregated signatures grows with the group size of signers in all three schemes. The communication complexity in the pre-communication phase of our scheme is twice that of [18].

In conclusion, the DL-based scheme of [21] is the most efficient although it employs a strong cryptographic assumption. Moreover, an aggregated signature

GGen(1^λ). For input 1^λ, returns a tuple $(\mathbb{G}, p, g, h)$ such that

- p is a prime of bit length λ,
- $\mathbb{G}$ is the group of prime order p,
- g and h are generators of $\mathbb{G}$.

Fig. 1. Group generator GGen.

$\text{Gen}_{\text{reg}}^{\text{DDH}}(\mathbb{G}, p, g, h)$. For input $(\mathbb{G}, p, g, h)$, returns a tuple $(x, (Y_1, Y_2))$ as follows:

1. $x \xleftarrow{\$} \mathbb{Z}_p$.
2. $(Y_1, Y_2) = (g^x, h^x)$.
3. returns $(x, (Y_1, Y_2))$.

$\text{Gen}_{\text{los}}^{\text{DDH}}(\mathbb{G}, p, g, h)$. For input $(\mathbb{G}, p, g, h)$, returns a tuple $((x_1, x_2), (Y_1, Y_2))$ as follows:

1. $x_1, x_2 \xleftarrow{\$} \mathbb{Z}_p$.
2. $(Y_1, Y_2) = (g^{x_1}, h^{x_2})$.
3. returns $((x_1, x_2), (Y_1, Y_2))$.

Fig. 2. Instance generators $\text{Gen}_{\text{reg}}^{\text{DDH}}$ and $\text{Gen}_{\text{los}}^{\text{DDH}}$.

is polynomial-size in the number of involved signers in all schemes. It is an important open question to construct an aggregate signature scheme which does not use the bilinear map and has the constant-size aggregated signature.

2   Preliminaries

Let $\mathbb{Z}$ denote the ring of integers. For a natural number q, $\mathbb{Z}_q$ is the quotient ring $(\mathbb{Z}/q\mathbb{Z})$, and $\mathbb{Z}_q^*$ is the group of units of $\mathbb{Z}_q$. For a finite set X, $x \xleftarrow{\$} X$ means that x is chosen uniformly at random from the set X. For a probabilistic algorithm $\mathcal{A}$, $y \leftarrow \mathcal{A}(x)$ denotes that $\mathcal{A}$ outputs y on input x. $\mathcal{A}(x)$ means the random variable for $\mathcal{A}$'s output on input x, where the probability is taken over the internal coin flips of $\mathcal{A}$. $P\langle \mathcal{A}_1(x_1), \ldots, \mathcal{A}_N(x_N) \rangle$ denotes an interactive protocol P executed by $\mathcal{A}_1, \ldots, \mathcal{A}_N$, where each $\mathcal{A}_i$ takes x_i as input and outputs their individual output.

2.1   DDH Assumption

We recall the *decisional Diffie-Hellman* (DDH) assumption. Consider the group generator GGen which outputs a tuple $(\mathbb{G}, p, g, h)$, where p is a prime of bit length λ, $\mathbb{G}$ is a multiplicative group of order p, and g and h are generators of $\mathbb{G}$, on input security parameter λ. The formal description of GGen is given in Fig. 1.

We then consider two instance generators $\text{Gen}_{\text{reg}}^{\text{DDH}}$ and $\text{Gen}_{\text{los}}^{\text{DDH}}$ defined in Fig. 2. Intuitively, $\text{Gen}_{\text{reg}}^{\text{DDH}}$ outputs a *regular* DDH tuple, and $\text{Gen}_{\text{los}}^{\text{DDH}}$ outputs a *non-regular* one, respectively. A pair $(x, (Y_1, Y_2))$ is said to *follow the DDH distribution with respect to* $(\mathbb{G}, p, g, h)$ if the distribution of $(x, (Y_1, Y_2))$ is identical to the one returned by $\text{Gen}_{\text{reg}}^{\text{DDH}}(\mathbb{G}, p, g, h)$.

For an algorithm $\mathcal{D}$, we consider the following two probabilities:

$$P_{\text{reg}}^{\text{DDH}}(\lambda) = \Pr[\mathcal{D}(1^\lambda, (\mathbb{G}, p, g, h), (Y_1, Y_2)) = 1 \mid (\mathbb{G}, p, g, h) \leftarrow \text{GGen}(1^\lambda),$$
$$(x, (Y_1, Y_2)) \leftarrow \text{Gen}_{\text{reg}}^{\text{DDH}}(\mathbb{G}, p, g, h)],$$
$$P_{\text{los}}^{\text{DDH}}(\lambda) = \Pr[\mathcal{D}(1^\lambda, (\mathbb{G}, p, g, h), (Y_1, Y_2)) = 1 \mid (\mathbb{G}, p, g, h) \leftarrow \text{GGen}(1^\lambda),$$
$$((x_1, x_2), (Y_1, Y_2)) \leftarrow \text{Gen}_{\text{los}}^{\text{DDH}}(\mathbb{G}, p, g, h)].$$

The DDH assumption states that there exists no probabilistic polynomial-time algorithm that can distinguish whether a given instance is generated from $\text{Gen}_{\text{reg}}^{\text{DDH}}$ or $\text{Gen}_{\text{los}}^{\text{DDH}}$. The formal definition of the DDH assumption is as follows.

Definition 1. *Let $\mathcal{D}$ be a probabilistic algorithm. The advantage $\text{Adv}_{\mathcal{D}}^{\text{DDH}}$ of $\mathcal{D}$ on the DDH assumption is defined by*

$$\text{Adv}_{\mathcal{D}}^{\text{DDH}}(\lambda) = \left| P_{\text{reg}}^{\text{DDH}}(\lambda) - P_{\text{los}}^{\text{DDH}}(\lambda) \right|.$$

Then, we say that $\mathcal{D}$ (T, ϵ)-breaks the DDH assumption if $\text{Adv}_{\mathcal{D}}^{\text{DDH}}(\lambda) \geq \epsilon(\lambda)$ when $\mathcal{D}$ runs in time T. We also say that the (T, ϵ)-DDH assumption holds if there no probabilistic algorithm which (T, ϵ)-breaks the DDH assumption.

3 Aggregate Signature with Pre-communication

3.1 Syntax

We recall the notion of the aggregate signature with pre-communication (ASwPC) [18]. In ASwPC, each signer communicates the aggregator to share the temporary randomness used in the signature generation. The randomness is shared among all the signers and the aggregator before signers decide their messages to be signed. After each signer signs his message, the message and its signature are sent to the aggregator. Then the aggregator aggregates all signatures into a single signature.

Algorithms. We now give the formal definition of ASwPC. ASwPC consists of the six components (Setup, KeyGen, PreCom, Sign, Agg, AggVer). Setup is a probabilistic algorithm for a public parameter generation. KeyGen(pp) is a probabilistic algorithm which generates a pair of public key pk_i and its secret key sk_i for each signer $\mathcal{S}_i$. PreCom is an interactive protocol executed between N signers $\mathcal{S}_1, \ldots, \mathcal{S}_N$ and the aggregator $\mathcal{AG}$. Sign($pp, pk_i, sk_i, st_i, m_i$) is a probabilistic algorithm that computes a signature of each signer $\mathcal{S}_i$. Agg($pp, st_A, \{(pk_i, m_i, \sigma_i)\}_{i=1}^N$) is a probabilistic or deterministic algorithm to aggregate signatures into a single aggregated signature by $\mathcal{AG}$. AggVer($pp, \{(pk_i, m_i)\}_{i=1}^N, \sigma_A$) is a deterministic algorithm for the verification of the signature. The description of each algorithm and protocol is given as follows:

Setup(1^λ) outputs a public parameter pp on a security parameter λ.

KeyGen(pp) outputs a pair (pk_i, sk_i) of a public key pk_i and a secret key sk_i on pp for each signer S_i.

PreCom$\langle S_1(pk_1, sk_1), \ldots, S_N(pk_N, sk_N), \mathcal{AG}(\{pk_i\})\rangle$ outputs a state information st_i for S_i and st_A for $\mathcal{AG}$.

Sign($pp, pk_i, sk_i, st_i, m_i$) outputs a signature σ_i of the signer S_i on a message m_i.

Agg($pp, st_A, \{(pk_i, m_i, \sigma_i)\}_{i=1}^N$) outputs an aggregate signature σ_A of $\{(pk_i, m_i, \sigma_i)\}_{i=1}^N$ on pp.

AggVer($pp, \{(pk_i, m_i)\}_{i=1}^N, \sigma_A$) outputs 1 if σ_A is a valid signature for $\{(pk_i, m_i)\}_{i=1}^N$, or 0 otherwise.

On the signature generation, the signers $S_1, \ldots, S_N$ and the aggregator $\mathcal{AG}$ run PreCom first to share temporary randomness used as the state information. Note that PreCom is executed between each signer S_i and the aggregator $\mathcal{AG}$ in a one-to-one manner. Namely, the signers S_i do not communicate with each other S_j during the execution of PreCom. After each signer S_i decides his message and computes his signature by Sign, they send their signature to the aggregator $\mathcal{AG}$. $\mathcal{AG}$ computes the aggregated signature by Agg.

Completeness. The completeness states that it holds that

$$\Pr[\mathsf{AggVer}(pp, \{(pk_i, m_i)\}, \sigma_A) = 1] = 1,$$

for any messages $\{m_i\}$, if all signers $S_1, \ldots, S_N$ and the aggregator $\mathcal{AG}$ behaves honestly along with the description of each algorithm and protocol.

3.2   Security Model

We introduce the security model for ASwPC in the plain public key model. We follow the definition of the KOSK security game in [18]. However, we consider the plain public key security. Namely, in our security model, the forger can choose his public keys in the output arbitrary with no restriction, while the forger must add secret keys corresponding to public keys to the output in the KOSK security.

The security game, the *plain public key (PPK) game*, is defined between the challenger C and the forger $\mathcal{F}$. The description of the game is as follows:

Setup The challenger C generates $pp \leftarrow$ Setup(1^λ) and the challenge key pair $(pk^*, sk^*) \leftarrow$ KeyGen(pp). Then C sends (pp, pk^*) to the forger $\mathcal{F}$.

Sign This phase is separated into the following two parts:

First Part On a new index j as a query to **First part**, C and $\mathcal{F}$ run PreCom first with (pk^*, sk^*) as input for C, then C obtains a state information st_j.

Second Part $\mathcal{F}$ queries a pair (j, m_j) of an index j, which is already queried to **First Part**, and a message m_j to **Second Part**. C computes the corresponding signature σ_j by using (pk^*, sk^*) and st_j with Sign algorithm, and consequently C answers σ_j to $\mathcal{F}$ and discards st_j. Namely, the state information is used only once through **Sign** phase.

Challenge $\mathcal{F}$ outputs a forgery σ_A^* with the set of public keys and messages $\{(pk_i^*, m_i^*)\}$. $\mathcal{F}$ *wins the PPK game* if the output satisfies the following conditions:

1. $pk_1^* = pk^*$.
2. all pk_i^* are distinct.
3. m_1^* is not queried in **Sign** phase.
4. $\mathsf{AggVer}(pp, \{(pk_i^*, m_i^*)\}, \sigma_A^*) = 1$.

In this game, the challenger $\mathcal{C}$ is supposed to play the role of the first signer $\mathcal{S}_1$ in the group without loss of generality.

In this paper, we consider the random oracle model. Therefore, the following definition of the security in the PPK model involves the random oracle.

Definition 2. *Let T be a polynomial and ϵ be a function. An aggregate signature with pre-communication ASwPC for N signers is $(T, \epsilon, q_S, q_H, N)$-secure in PPK and random oracle model if for any forger $\mathcal{F}$ which runs in at most time T and makes at most q_S queries in* **Sign** *phase and q_H queries to the random oracle, the probability that $\mathcal{F}$ wins the PPK game is ϵ.*

4 DDH-based Aggregate Signature with Pre-communication

We propose an aggregate signature with pre-communication based on the DDH assumption. The proposed scheme is secure in PPK and the random oracle model under the DDH assumption.

4.1 Protocol Description

We give the description of our DDH-based scheme DHASP. Let $H : \{0, 1\}^* \to \mathbb{Z}_p$ be a hash function with a prime p. The description of DHASP is as follows:

$\mathsf{Setup}(1^\lambda)$ generates $(\mathbb{G}, p, g, h) \leftarrow \mathsf{GGen}(1^\lambda)$ and outputs it as a public parameter pp.

$\mathsf{KeyGen}(pp)$ is run by each signer $\mathcal{S}_i$. $\mathcal{S}_i$ computes $(x_i, (Y_{i,1}, Y_{i,2})) \leftarrow \mathsf{Gen}_{\mathsf{reg}}^{\mathsf{DDH}}(pp)$ with $pp = (\mathbb{G}, p, g, h)$ and outputs $(Y_{i,1}, Y_{i,2})$ as pk_i and x_i as sk_i.

$\mathsf{PreCom}\langle \mathcal{S}_1(pk_1, sk_1), \ldots, \mathcal{S}_N(pk_N, sk_N), \mathcal{AG}(\{pk_i\}_{i=1}^N)\rangle$ outputs a state information st_i for the signer $\mathcal{S}_i$ and st_A for $\mathcal{AG}$ according to the following protocol:

(PC-1) $\mathcal{S}_i$ computes $(W_{i,1}, W_{i,2}) = (g^{w_i}, h^{w_i})$ for $w_i \leftarrow \mathbb{Z}_p$.

(PC-2) $\mathcal{S}_i$ sends $(W_{i,1}, W_{i,2})$ to $\mathcal{AG}$.

(PC-3) $\mathcal{AG}$ computes $(W_1, W_2) = (\prod_{i=1}^N W_{i,1}, \prod_{i=1}^N W_{i,2})$.

(PC-4) $\mathcal{AG}$ sends (W_1, W_2) to each signer.

(PC-5) $\mathcal{S}_i$ stores the state information $st_i = (w_i, (W_1, W_2))$ and $\mathcal{AG}$ stores his state information $st_A = (W_1, W_2)$.

$\mathsf{Sign}(pp, pk_i, sk_i, st_i, m_i)$ outputs a signature σ_i on message m_i as follows:

(S-1) $\mathcal{S}_i$ chooses $t_i \xleftarrow{\$} \{0, 1\}^\lambda$.

(S-2) $\mathcal{S}_i$ computes $c_i \leftarrow H((Y_{i,1}, Y_{i,2}), (W_1, W_2), t_i, m_i)$.

(S-3) $\mathcal{S}_i$ computes $s_i = w_i + c_i x_i \bmod p$.

(S-4) $\mathcal{S}_i$ outputs the signature $\sigma_i = (s_i, t_i)$.

$\mathsf{Agg}(pp, st_A, \{(pk_i, m_i, \sigma_i)\}_{i=1}^N)$ outputs the aggregated signature $\sigma_A = (s, \{t_i\}_{i=1}^N, (W_1, W_2))$ with $s = \sum_{i=1}^N s_i$.

$\mathsf{AggVer}(pp, \{(pk_i, m_i)\}_{i=1}^N, \sigma_A)$ outputs 1 if the input $(pp, \{(pk_i, m_i)\}_{i=1}^N, \sigma_A)$ satisfies the following conditions:

(V-1) all pk_i are distinct.

(V-1) $g^s = W_1 \prod_{i=1}^N Y_{i,1}^{c_i}$ and $h^s = W_2 \prod_{i=1}^N Y_{i,2}^{c_i}$ for the public keys $pk_i = (Y_{i,1}, Y_{i,2})$, the aggregated signature $\sigma_A = (s, \{t_i\}_{i=1}^N, (W_1, W_2))$ and the hash values $c_i \leftarrow H((Y_{i,1}, Y_{i,2}), (W_1, W_2), t_i, m_i)$.

Theorem 1. DHASP *satisfies the correctness.*

Proof. Fix the number N of signers. Let $pp = (\mathbb{G}, p, g, h) \leftarrow \mathsf{GGen}(1^\lambda)$ be a public parameter and $(x_i, (Y_{i,1}, Y_{i,2})) \leftarrow \mathsf{Gen}_{\mathsf{reg}}^{\mathsf{DDH}}(pp)$ be a pair of a public key and a secret key for the signer $\mathcal{S}_i$. Suppose that each signer $\mathcal{S}_i$ belonging to a group generates an individual signature $\sigma_i = (s_i, t_i)$ for a message m_i, respectively, and then the aggregator $\mathcal{AG}$ computes $\sigma_A = (s, \{t_i\}_{i=1}^N, (W_1, W_2))$, by using PreCom, Sign and Agg. Then, we have

$$g^s = g^{\sum_{i=1}^N (w_i + c_i x_i)} = g^{\sum_{i=1}^N w_i} g^{\sum_{i=1}^N c_i x_i} = \prod_{i=1}^N g^{w_i} \prod_{i=1}^N g^{c_i x_i} = \prod_{i=1}^N W_{i,1} \prod_{i=1}^N Y_{i,1}^{c_i}$$

$$= W_1 \prod_{i=1}^N Y_{i,1}^{c_i},$$

$$h^s = h^{\sum_{i=1}^N (w_i + c_i x_i)} = h^{\sum_{i=1}^N w_i} h^{\sum_{i=1}^N c_i x_i} = \prod_{i=1}^N h^{w_i} \prod_{i=1}^N h^{c_i x_i} = \prod_{i=1}^N W_{i,2} \prod_{i=1}^N Y_{i,2}^{c_i}$$

$$= W_2 \prod_{i=1}^N Y_{i,2}^{c_i},$$

where $c_i \leftarrow H((Y_{i,1}, Y_{i,2}), (W_1, W_2), t_i, m_i)$. Thus the verification formulas in AggVer are satisfied. $\qquad\square$

4.2   Security Proof

Theorem 2. *Let T, q_S, q_H be polynomials in a security parameter λ, and let ϵ be a funciton in λ, respectively. N is a some fixed parameter at most $\log(\lambda)$. Assume that (T, ϵ)-DDH assumption holds. Then DHASP is $(T', \epsilon', q_S, q_H, N)$-secure in PPK and random oracle model, where*

$$T' = T - O(q_S + q_H),$$

$$\epsilon' \leq \epsilon + \frac{q_H + q_S}{2^\lambda} + \frac{2}{p},$$

and p is the order of the underlying group $\mathbb{G}$.

Proof. We prove the theorem by the hybrid argument. We consider the sequence of games $\mathsf{Game}_0, \ldots, \mathsf{Game}_2$. Let $\mathcal{C}$ be a challenger and let $\mathcal{F}$ be a forger in each game, respectively. Win_k denotes the event that $\mathcal{F}$ wins the game Game_k for $0 \leq k \leq 2$.

Game_0. Game_0 is identical to the PPK game of DHASP between $\mathcal{C}$ and $\mathcal{F}$. The formal description of Game_0 is given as follows:

Setup $\mathcal{C}$ computes $pp = (\mathbb{G}, p, g, h) \leftarrow \mathsf{GGen}(1^\lambda)$ and $(sk^*, pk^*) = (x^*, (Y_1^*, Y_2^*)) \leftarrow \mathsf{Gen}_{\mathsf{reg}}^{\mathsf{DDH}}(pp)$. Then $\mathcal{C}$ sends (pp, pk^*) to $\mathcal{F}$.

H On a j-th hash query $(pk^{(j)}, (W_1^{(j)}, W_2^{(j)}), t^{(j)}, m^{(j)})$ from $\mathcal{F}$, $\mathcal{C}$ sets its hash value $H(pk^{(j)}, (W_1^{(j)}, W_2^{(j)}), t^{(j)}, m^{(j)}) \xleftarrow{\$} \mathbb{Z}_p$, if it is not defined. $\mathcal{C}$ answers $c^{(j)} = H(pk^{(j)}, (W_1^{(j)}, W_2^{(j)}), t^{(j)}, m^{(j)})$.

Sign This phase consists of two parts.

    First Part On a new index j as a query to **First Part** of **Sign** phase, $\mathcal{C}$ proceeds as follows:

      – $\mathcal{C}$ first computes $(W_{1,1}^{(j)}, W_{1,2}^{(j)}) = (g^{w_1^{(j)}}, h^{w_1^{(j)}})$ with $w_1^{(j)} \xleftarrow{\$} \mathbb{Z}_p$.

      – $\mathcal{C}$ sends $(W_{1,1}^{(j)}, W_{1,2}^{(j)})$ to $\mathcal{F}$.

      – After receiving $(W_1^{(j)}, W_2^{(j)})$, $\mathcal{C}$ sets $st_1^{(j)} = (w_1^{(j)}, (W_1^{(j)}, W_2^{(j)}))$.

    Second Part On a pair $(j, m_1^{(j)})$ of an index j, which is already queried to **First Part**, and a message $m_1^{(j)}$ as a query to **Second Part** of **Sign** phase, $\mathcal{C}$ proceeds as follows:

      – $\mathcal{C}$ chooses $t_1^{(j)} \xleftarrow{\$} \{0,1\}^\lambda$.

      – $\mathcal{C}$ computes $c_1^{(j)} \leftarrow H((Y_1^*, Y_2^*), (W_1^{(j)}, W_2^{(j)}), t_1^{(j)}, m_1^{(j)})$.

      – $\mathcal{C}$ computes $s_1^{(j)} = w_1^{(j)} + c_1^{(j)} x^* \bmod p$.

      – $\mathcal{C}$ outputs $\sigma_1^{(j)} = (s_1^{(j)}, t_1^{(j)})$, and finally discards $st_1^{(j)}$.

Challenge $\mathcal{F}$ outputs the forgery $\sigma_A^* = (s^*, \{t_i^*\}_{i=1}^N, (W_1^*, W_2^*))$ with $\{(pk_i^*, m_i^*)\}_{i=1}^N$. $\mathcal{F}$ wins the game if σ_A^* and $\{(pk_i^*, m_i^*)\}_{i=1}^N$ satisfy the following conditions:

1. $pk_1^* = pk^*$.
2. all pk_i^* are distinct.
3. m_1^* is not queried in **Sign** phase.
4. $g^{s^*} = W_1^* \prod_{i=1}^N Y_{i,1}^{*c_i^*}$ and $h^{s^*} = W_2^* \prod_{i=1}^N Y_{i,2}^{*c_i^*}$ for $pk_i^* = (Y_{i,1}^*, Y_{i,2}^*)$ and $c_i^* \leftarrow H((Y_{i,1}^*, Y_{i,2}^*), (W_1^*, W_2^*), t_i^*, m_i^*)$.

DHASP is $(T', \epsilon', q_S, q_H, N)$-secure in PPK and random oracle model. Then we have the following lemma.

Lemma 1.
$$\Pr[\mathsf{Win}_0] = \epsilon'. \tag{1}$$

Proof. By the description of Game_0, Game_0 coincides with the PPK game correctly. Then the probability Win_0 that $\mathcal{F}$ wins Game_0 equals the probability ϵ' that $\mathcal{F}$ wins the PPK game. $\qquad\square$

Game$_1$. Game$_1$ is identical to Game$_0$ except the processes of **Sign** phase. In this game, $\mathcal{C}$ answers queries by $\mathcal{F}$ without the secret key. Namely, the signing protocol in Game$_1$ is replaced with the simulated one. The description of **Sign** phase in Game$_1$ is as follows:

Sign This phase consists of two parts.

First Part On a new index j as a query to **First Part** of **Sign** phase, $\mathcal{C}$ proceeds as follows:

- $\mathcal{C}$ first chooses $s_1^{(j)}, c_1^{(j)} \xleftarrow{\$} \mathbb{Z}_p$.
- $\mathcal{C}$ computes $(W_{1,1}^{(j)}, W_{1,2}^{(j)}) = (g^{s_1^{(j)}} (Y_1^*)^{-c_1^{(j)}}, h^{s_1^{(j)}} (Y_2^*)^{-c_1^{(j)}})$.
- $\mathcal{C}$ sends $(W_{1,1}^{(j)}, W_{1,2}^{(j)})$ to $\mathcal{F}$.
- After receiving $(W_1^{(j)}, W_2^{(j)})$, $\mathcal{C}$ sets $st_1^{(j)} = ((s_1^{(j)}, c_1^{(j)}), (W_1^{(j)}, W_2^{(j)}))$.

Second Part On a pair $(j, m_1^{(j)})$ of an index j, which is already queried to **First Part**, and a message $m_1^{(j)}$ as a query to **Second Part** of **Sign** phase, $\mathcal{C}$ proceeds as follows:

- $\mathcal{C}$ chooses $t_1^{(j)} \xleftarrow{\$} \{0,1\}^\lambda$.
- If the following two conditions hold, then $\mathcal{C}$ aborts the game:
  - $H((Y_1^*, Y_2^*), (W_1^{(j)}, W_2^{(j)}), t_1^{(j)}, m_1^{(j)})$ is already defined; and
  - $c_1^{(j)} \neq H((Y_1^*, Y_2^*), (W_1^{(j)}, W_2^{(j)}), t_1^{(j)}, m_1^{(j)})$.
- Otherwise, $\mathcal{C}$ sets $H((Y_1^*, Y_2^*), (W_1^{(j)}, W_2^{(j)}), t_1^{(j)}, m_1^{(j)}) \leftarrow c_1^{(j)}$.
- $\mathcal{C}$ outputs $\sigma_1^{(j)} = (s_1^{(j)}, t_1^{(j)})$ and finally discards $st_1^{(j)}$.

Lemma 2.

$$\Pr[\mathsf{Win}_1] = \Pr[\mathsf{Win}_0] - (q_H + q_S)/2^\lambda. \tag{2}$$

Proof. We first show that the simulation is correct. Since we now set $(W_{1,1}^{(j)}, W_{1,2}^{(j)})$ as $(g^{s_1^{(j)}} (Y_1^*)^{-c_1^{(j)}}, h^{s_1^{(j)}} (Y_2^*)^{-c_1^{(j)}})$, the following equations hold obviously:

$$(W_{1,1}^{(j)} (Y_1^*)^{c_1^{(j)}}, W_{1,2}^{(j)} (Y_2^*)^{c_1^{(j)}}) = (g^{s_1^{(j)}}, h^{s_1^{(j)}}).$$

This satisfies the "$\mathcal{C}$'s part" of the verification formulas of AggVer.

We next consider the distribution of outputs of $\mathcal{C}$ in replaced **Sign** phase. At **First Part**, $\mathcal{C}$ sends $(W_{1,1}^{(j)}, W_{1,2}^{(j)}) = (g^{s_1^{(j)}} (Y_1^*)^{-c_1^{(j)}}, h^{s_1^{(j)}} (Y_2^*)^{-c_1^{(j)}})$ generated by using $s_1^{(j)}, c_1^{(j)} \xleftarrow{\$} \mathbb{Z}_p$. As in **Setup** phase, $pk^* = (Y_1^*, Y_2^*)$ is set as $(Y_1^*, Y_2^*) = (g^{x^*}, h^{x^*})$ for the randomly chosen element $x^* \xleftarrow{\$} \mathbb{Z}_p$. By letting $w_1^{(j)'} = s_1^{(j)} - x^* \cdot c_1^{(j)} \bmod p$, the uniform choice of $s_1^{(j)}$ from $\mathbb{Z}_p$ implies that $w_1^{(j)'}$ is also uniformly distributed over $\mathbb{Z}_p$. It follows that $(W_{1,1}^{(j)}, W_{1,2}^{(j)}) = (g^{s_1^{(j)}} (Y_1^*)^{-c_1^{(j)}}, h^{s_1^{(j)}} (Y_2^*)^{-c_1^{(j)}}) = (g^{w_1^{(j)'}}, h^{w_1^{(j)'}})$ such that $(w_1^{(j)'}, (W_{1,1}^{(j)}, W_{1,2}^{(j)}))$ follows the DDH distribution with respect to $(\mathbb{G}, p, g, h)$. On the other hand, in Game$_0$, $(W_{1,1}^{(j)}, W_{1,2}^{(j)})$ is computed by $(W_{1,1}^{(j)}, W_{1,2}^{(j)}) = (g^{w_1^{(j)}}, h^{w_1^{(j)}})$ with

$w_1^{(j)} \xleftarrow{\$} \mathbb{Z}_p$. This means that $(w_1^{(j)}, (W_{1,1}^{(j)}, W_{1,2}^{(j)}))$ also follows the DDH distribution with respect to $(\mathbb{G}, p, g, h)$. Thus the distribution of $(W_{1,1}^{(j)}, W_{1,2}^{(j)})$ equals in both games.

At **Second Part**, $\mathcal{C}$ sends his signature $\sigma_1^{(j)} = (s_1^{(j)}, t_1^{(j)})$ to $\mathcal{F}$. The way of drawing $t_1^{(j)}$ is not changed in Game_1 from the way in Game_0. $s_1^{(j)}$ in Game_1 is already determined at **First Part** by uniformly choosing it from $\mathbb{Z}_p$. In Game_0, $s_1^{(j)}$ is computed as $s_1^{(j)} = w_1^{(j)} + x^* c_1^{(j)} \bmod p$ with the value $w_1^{(j)}$ fixed at **First Part**. Since $w_1^{(j)}$ is uniformly chosen from $\mathbb{Z}_p$, $s_1^{(j)}$ in Game_0 is also distributed uniformly over $\mathbb{Z}_p$. That is, the distribution of $s_1^{(j)}$ equals in both games.

We finally evaluate the probability that $\mathcal{C}$ aborts Game_1. In Game_1, $\mathcal{C}$ aborts the game if the hash value $H((Y_1^*, Y_2^*), (W_1^{(j)}, W_2^{(j)}), t_1^{(j)}, m_1^{(j)})$ is already defined by $\mathcal{F}$ when $\mathcal{C}$ aims to set $H((Y_1^*, Y_2^*), (W_1^{(j)}, W_2^{(j)}), t_1^{(j)}, m_1^{(j)}) = c_1^{(j)}$. Since $\mathcal{C}$ chooses $t_1^{(j)}$ from $\{0,1\}^\lambda$ uniformly at random, $\mathcal{F}$ can guess $t_1^{(j)}$ with probability at most $1/2^\lambda$. The number of hash queries is at most $q_H + q_S$. This implies that the probability of aborting the game is $(q_H + q_S)/2^\lambda$. Then Eq. (2) follows. $\square$

Game_2. Game_2 is identical to Game_1 except the process of **Setup** phase. In this game, the public key of $\mathcal{C}$ is generated by $\mathsf{Gen}_{\mathsf{los}}^{\mathsf{DDH}}$ instead of $\mathsf{Gen}_{\mathsf{reg}}^{\mathsf{DDH}}$, and the secret key of $\mathcal{C}$ no longer exists. This change does not affect the signing protocol, because the signing protocol is replaced by the one which does not require a secret key in Game_1. The description of **Setup** phase in Game_2 is as follows:

Setup $\mathcal{C}$ computes $pp = (\mathbb{G}, p, g, h) \leftarrow \mathsf{GGen}(1^\lambda)$ and $((x_1^*, x_2^*), (Y_1^*, Y_2^*)) \leftarrow \mathsf{Gen}_{\mathsf{los}}^{\mathsf{DDH}}(pp)$. Then $\mathcal{C}$ sets $pk^* = (Y_1^*, Y_2^*)$ and sends (pp, pk^*) to $\mathcal{F}$.

Lemma 3.
$$\Pr[\mathsf{Win}_2] = \Pr[\mathsf{Win}_1] - \epsilon. \tag{3}$$

Proof. The difference between Game_1 and Game_2 is the way of generating the public key pk^* of $\mathcal{C}$. Each distribution of the public key coincides with the corresponding distribution in the DDH assumption defined in Definition 1. Moreover, the total running times of $\mathcal{C}$ and $\mathcal{F}$ on Game_2 is $T = O(q_S + q_H) + T'$. Then the statement follows from the (T, ϵ)-DDH assumption. $\square$

Evaluation of Win_2. We finally evaluate the upper bound of Win_2, the winning probability of $\mathcal{F}$ in Game_2. Let $\sigma_A^* = (s^*, \{t_i^*\}_{i=1}^N, (W_1^*, W_2^*))$ and $\{(pk_i^*, m_i^*)\}_{i=1}^N$ be the final output of $\mathcal{F}$ in Game_2, where $pk_1^* = (Y_{1,1}^*, Y_{1,2}^*) = (Y_1^*, Y_2^*) = pk^*$. Each c_i^* is computed as $c_i^* = H((Y_{i,1}^*, Y_{i,2}^*), (W_1^*, W_2^*), t_i^*, m_i^*)$ for $1 \le i \le N$. Then the verification formulas of AggVer are written as follows:

$$g^{s^*} = W_1^* \cdot (Y_1^*)^{c_1^*} \prod_{i=2}^N (Y_{i,1}^*)^{c_i^*},$$

$$h^{s^*} = W_2^* \cdot (Y_2^*)^{c_1^*} \prod_{i=2}^N (Y_{i,2}^*)^{c_i^*}.$$

We show that there do not exist two distinct hash values that satisfy the formulas above and hence make $\mathcal{F}$ win by considering the opposite situation. Let the elements $x_1^*, x_2^* \in \mathbb{Z}_p$ be $Y_1^* = g^{x_1^*}$, $Y_2^* = h^{x_2^*}$ and $x_1^* \neq x_2^*$. Fix a pair $(W_1^*, W_2^*) \in \mathbb{G}^2$ and a set $\{pk_i^* = (Y_{i,1}^*, Y_{i,2}^*), c_i^*\}_{i=2}^N$. We suppose that there exist distinct hash values $c, c' \in \mathbb{Z}_p$ such that both of them derive the acceptance. Then, for some $s, s' \in \mathbb{Z}_p$, we have

$$W_1^* = g^s \cdot (Y_1^*)^{-c} \prod_{i=2}^N (Y_{i,1}^*)^{-c_i^*} = g^{s'} \cdot (Y_1^*)^{-c'} \prod_{i=2}^N (Y_{i,1}^*)^{-c_i^*},$$

$$W_2^* = h^s \cdot (Y_2^*)^{-c} \prod_{i=2}^N (Y_{i,2}^*)^{-c_i^*} = h^{s'} \cdot (Y_2^*)^{-c'} \prod_{i=2}^N (Y_{i,2}^*)^{-c_i^*}.$$

It follows from the above equations that

$$Y_1^* = g^{(s-s')/(c-c')},$$
$$Y_2^* = h^{(s-s')/(c-c')}.$$

Then we have

$$Y_1^* = g^{(s-s')/(c-c')} = g^{x_1^*},$$
$$Y_2^* = h^{(s-s')/(c-c')} = h^{x_2^*}.$$

Since g and h are generators of $\mathbb{G}$, $Y_1^* = g^{x_1^*}$ and $Y_2^* = h^{x_2^*}$, these equations imply $x_1^* = (s - s')/(c - c') = x_2^*$. This contradicts the assumption that $x_1^* \neq x_2^*$ above. Thus we can show that there exist no distinct hash values $c, c' \in \mathbb{Z}_p$ such that both of them derive the acceptance under the assumption that $x_1^* \neq x_2^*$.

We consider the probability of Win_2 under the assumption that $x_1^* \neq x_2^*$. Since the hash value c_1^* is uniformly chosen from $\mathbb{Z}_p$, $\mathcal{F}$ has the chance to obtain the hash value c_1^* that derives the acceptance under the assumption $x_1^* \neq x_2^*$ with the probability at most $1/p$. Therefore, the considered probability is $1/p$.

In Game_2, Y_1^* and Y_2^* are generated by $\mathsf{Gen}_{los}^{\mathsf{DDH}}$, that is $x_1^*, x_2^* \xleftarrow{\$} \mathbb{Z}_p$. Let DDH be the event that $\mathsf{Gen}_{los}^{\mathsf{DDH}}$ returns $x_1^*, x_2^* \in \mathbb{Z}_p$ such that $x_1^* = x_2^*$. Then the probability of DDH is evaluated by $1/p$. Thus, we finally have

$$\begin{aligned}
\Pr[\mathsf{Win}_2] &= \Pr[\mathsf{Win}_2 \wedge \mathsf{DDH}] + \Pr[\mathsf{Win}_2 \wedge \neg\mathsf{DDH}] \\
&\leq \Pr[\mathsf{DDH}] + \Pr[\neg\mathsf{DDH}] \cdot \Pr[\mathsf{Win}_2 \mid \neg\mathsf{DDH}] \\
&= \frac{1}{p} + \left(1 - \frac{1}{p}\right) \cdot \frac{1}{p} \leq \frac{2}{p}.
\end{aligned} \tag{4}$$

From Eqs. (1), (2), (3), (4), We have

$$\epsilon' \leq \epsilon + \frac{q_H + q_S}{2^\lambda} + \frac{2}{p}.$$

$\square$

Acknowledgements. We would like to thank anonymous reviewers for their valuable comments and suggestions. A part of this work is supported by JSPS KAKENHI Grant Numbers 18K11288 and 19K20272.

References

1. Ahn, J.H., Green, M., Hohenberger, S.: Synchronized aggregate signatures: new definitions, constructions and applications. In: Proceedings of the 17th ACM Conference on Computer and Communications Security, CCS 2010, pp. 473–484. Association for Computing Machinery, New York (2010). https://doi.org/10.1145/1866307.1866360
2. Bellare, M., Goldreich, O.: On defining proofs of knowledge. In: Brickell, E.F. (ed.) CRYPTO 1992. LNCS, vol. 740, pp. 390–420. Springer, Heidelberg (1993). https://doi.org/10.1007/3-540-48071-4_28
3. Bellare, M., Namprempre, C., Neven, G.: Unrestricted aggregate signatures. In: Arge, L., Cachin, C., Jurdziński, T., Tarlecki, A. (eds.) ICALP 2007. LNCS, vol. 4596, pp. 411–422. Springer, Heidelberg (2007). https://doi.org/10.1007/978-3-540-73420-8_37
4. Bellare, M., Neven, G.: Multi-signatures in the plain public-key model and a general forking lemma. In: Proceedings of the 13th ACM Conference on Computer and Communications Security, CCS 2006, pp. 390–399. ACM, New York (2006). https://doi.org/10.1145/1180405.1180453
5. Bellare, M., Rogaway, P.: Random oracles are practical: a paradigm for designing efficient protocols. In: Proceedings of the 1st ACM Conference on Computer and Communications Security, CCS 1993, pp. 62–73. Association for Computing Machinery, New York (1993). https://doi.org/10.1145/168588.168596
6. Boldyreva, A.: threshold signatures, multisignatures and blind signatures based on the gap-Diffie-Hellman-group signature scheme. In: Desmedt, Y.G. (ed.) PKC 2003. LNCS, vol. 2567, pp. 31–46. Springer, Heidelberg (2003). https://doi.org/10.1007/3-540-36288-6_3
7. Boneh, D., Gentry, C., Lynn, B., Shacham, H.: Aggregate and verifiably encrypted signatures from bilinear maps. In: Biham, E. (ed.) EUROCRYPT 2003. LNCS, vol. 2656, pp. 416–432. Springer, Heidelberg (2003). https://doi.org/10.1007/3-540-39200-9_26
8. Fiat, A., Shamir, A.: How to prove yourself: practical solutions to identification and signature problems. In: Odlyzko, A.M. (ed.) CRYPTO 1986. LNCS, vol. 263, pp. 186–194. Springer, Heidelberg (1987). https://doi.org/10.1007/3-540-47721-7_12
9. Fukumitsu, M., Hasegawa, S.: A tightly secure DDH-based multisignature with public-key aggregation. In: 2020 Eighth International Symposium on Computing and Networking Workshops (CANDARW), pp. 321–327 (2020). https://doi.org/10.1109/CANDARW51189.2020.00069
10. Gentry, C., Ramzan, Z.: Identity-based aggregate signatures. In: Yung, M., Dodis, Y., Kiayias, A., Malkin, T. (eds.) PKC 2006. LNCS, vol. 3958, pp. 257–273. Springer, Heidelberg (2006). https://doi.org/10.1007/11745853_17
11. Hohenberger, S., Waters, B.: Synchronized aggregate signatures from the RSA assumption. In: Nielsen, J.B., Rijmen, V. (eds.) EUROCRYPT 2018. LNCS, vol. 10821, pp. 197–229. Springer, Cham (2018). https://doi.org/10.1007/978-3-319-78375-8_7

12. Katz, J., Wang, N.: Efficiency improvements for signature schemes with tight security reductions. In: Proceedings of the 10th ACM Conference on Computer and Communications Security, CCS 2003, pp. 155–164. ACM, New York (2003). https://doi.org/10.1145/948109.948132
13. Lu, S., Ostrovsky, R., Sahai, A., Shacham, H., Waters, B.: Sequential aggregate signatures and multisignatures without random oracles. In: Vaudenay, S. (ed.) EUROCRYPT 2006. LNCS, vol. 4004, pp. 465–485. Springer, Heidelberg (2006). https://doi.org/10.1007/11761679_28
14. Lysyanskaya, A., Micali, S., Reyzin, L., Shacham, H.: Sequential aggregate signatures from trapdoor permutations. In: Cachin, C., Camenisch, J.L. (eds.) EUROCRYPT 2004. LNCS, vol. 3027, pp. 74–90. Springer, Heidelberg (2004). https://doi.org/10.1007/978-3-540-24676-3_5
15. Maurer, U.: Abstract models of computation in cryptography. In: Smart, N.P. (ed.) Cryptography and Coding 2005. LNCS, vol. 3796, pp. 1–12. Springer, Heidelberg (2005). https://doi.org/10.1007/11586821_1
16. Neven, G.: Efficient sequential aggregate signed data. In: Smart, N. (ed.) EUROCRYPT 2008. LNCS, vol. 4965, pp. 52–69. Springer, Heidelberg (2008). https://doi.org/10.1007/978-3-540-78967-3_4
17. Ristenpart, T., Yilek, S.: The power of proofs-of-possession: securing multiparty signatures against rogue-key attacks. In: Naor, M. (ed.) EUROCRYPT 2007. LNCS, vol. 4515, pp. 228–245. Springer, Heidelberg (2007). https://doi.org/10.1007/978-3-540-72540-4_13
18. Takemure, K., Sakai, Y., Santoso, B., Hanaoka, G., Ohta, K.: Achieving pairing-free aggregate signatures using pre-communication between signers. In: Nguyen, K., Wu, W., Lam, K.Y., Wang, H. (eds.) ProvSec 2020. LNCS, vol. 12505, pp. 65–84. Springer, Cham (2020). https://doi.org/10.1007/978-3-030-62576-4_4
19. Takemure, K., Sakai, Y., Santoso, B., Hanaoka, G., Ohta, K.: Achieving pairing-free aggregate signatures using pre-communication between signers. IEICE Trans. Fundam. Electron. Commun. Comput. Sci. **advpub** (2021). https://doi.org/10.1587/transfun.2020DMP0023
20. Yao, A.C.C., Zhao, Y.: Online/offline signatures for low-power devices. Trans. Inf. Forensics Secur. **8**(2), 283–294 (2013). https://doi.org/10.1109/TIFS.2012.2232653
21. Zhao, Y.: Practical aggregate signature from general elliptic curves, and applications to blockchain. In: Proceedings of the 2019 ACM Asia Conference on Computer and Communications Security, Asia CCS 2019, pp. 529–538. Association for Computing Machinery, New York (2019). https://doi.org/10.1145/3321705.3329826

The Adversary Capabilities in Practical Byzantine Fault Tolerance

Yongge Wang[✉]

College of Computing and Informatics, UNC Charlotte, Charlotte, NC 28223, USA
yonwang@uncc.edu

Abstract. The problem of Byzantine Fault Tolerance (BFT) has received a lot of attention in the last 30 years. The seminal work by Fisher, Lynch, and Paterson (FLP) shows that there does not exist a deterministic BFT protocol in complete asynchronous networks against a single failure. In order to address this challenge, researchers have designed randomized BFT protocols in asynchronous networks and deterministic BFT protocols in partial synchronous networks. For both kinds of protocols, a basic assumption is that there is an adversary that controls at most a threshold number of participating nodes and that has a full control of the message delivery order in the network. Due to the popularity of Proof of Stake (PoS) blockchains in recent years, several BFT protocols have been deployed in the large scale of Internet environment. We analyze several popular BFT protocols such as Capser FFG/CBC-FBC for Ethereum 2.0 and GRANDPA for Polkadot. Our analysis shows that the security models for these BFT protocols are slightly different from the models commonly accepted in the academic literature. For example, we show that, if the adversary has a full control of the message delivery order in the underlying network, then none of the BFT protocols for Ethereum blockchain 2.0 and Polkadot blockchain could achieve liveness even in a synchronized network. Though it is not clear whether a practical adversary could *actually* control and re-order the underlying message delivery system (at Internet scale) to mount these attacks, it raises an interesting question on security model gaps between academic BFT protocols and deployed BFT protocols in the Internet scale. With these analysis, this paper proposes a Casper CBC-FBC style binary BFT protocol and shows its security in the traditional academic security model with complete asynchronous networks. Finally, we propose a multi-value BFT protocol XP for complete asynchronous networks and show its security in the traditional academic BFT security model.

Keywords: Byzantine fault tolerance · Security models · Blockchain

1 Introduction

Consensus is hard to achieve in open networks such as partial synchronous networks or complete asynchronous networks. Several practical protocols such as Paxos [10] and Raft [12] have been designed to tolerate $\lfloor \frac{n-1}{2} \rfloor$ non-Byzantine faults. For example, Google, Microsoft, IBM, and Amazon have used Paxos in their storage or cluster

© Springer Nature Switzerland AG 2021
R. Roman and J. Zhou (Eds.): STM 2021, LNCS 13075, pp. 20–39, 2021.
https://doi.org/10.1007/978-3-030-91859-0_2

management systems. Lamport, Shostak, and Pease [11] and Pease, Shostak, and Lamport [13] initiated the study of reaching consensus in face of Byzantine failures and designed the first synchronous solution for Byzantine agreement. Dolev and Strong [6] proposed an improved protocol in a synchronous network with $O(n^3)$ communication complexity. By assuming the existence of digital signature schemes and a public-key infrastructure, Katz and Koo [9] proposed an expected constant-round BFT protocol in a synchronous network setting against $\lfloor \frac{n-1}{2} \rfloor$ Byzantine faults.

Fischer, Lynch, and Paterson [8] showed that there is no deterministic protocol for the BFT problem in face of a single failure. Several researchers have tried to design BFT consensus protocols to circumvent the impossibility. The first category of efforts is to use a probabilistic approach to design BFT consensus protocols in completely asynchronous networks. This kind of work was initiated by Ben-Or [2] and Rabin [14] and extended by others such as Cachin, Kursawe, and Shoup [5]. The second category of efforts was to design BFT consensus protocols in partial synchronous networks which was initiated by Dwork, Lynch, and Stockmeyer [7]. Though the network communication model could be different for these protocols, the assumption on the adversary capability is generally same. That is, there is a threshold t such that the adversary could coordinate the activities of the malicious t participating nodes. Furthermore, it is also assumed that the adversary could re-order messages on communication networks.

In recent years, many practical BFT protocols have been designed and deployed at the Internet scale. For example, Ethereum foundation has designed a BFT finality gadget for their Proof of Stake (PoS) blockchain. The current Ethereum 2.0 beacon network uses Casper Friendly Finality Gadget (Casper FFG) [4] and Ethereum foundation has been advocating the "Correct-by-Construction" (CBC) family consensus protocols [17,18] for their future release of Ethereum blockchain. Similarly, the Polkadot blockchain deployed their home-brew BFT protocol GRANDPA [16]. The analysis in this paper shows that these protocols have an assumption that the adversary cannot control the message delivery order in the underlying networks. Our examples show that if the adversary could control the the message delivery order, then these blockchains could not achieve liveness property. This brings up an interesting question to the research community: what kind of models are appropriate for the Internet scale BFT protocols? Does an adversary have the capability to co-ordinate/control one-third of the participating nodes and to reschedule message delivery order for a blockchain at Internet scale?

Before we have a complete understanding about the impact of the new security assumptions for these blockchain BFT protocols (i.e., the adversary cannot control the message delivery order on the underlying networks), we should still design practical large-scale BFT protocols that are robust in the traditional academic security model. For complete asynchronous networks, we present an Casper CBC-FBC style binary BFT protocol and a multi-value BFT protocol XP and prove their security in the traditional security model.

The structure of the paper is as follows. Section 2 introduces system models and Byzantine agreement. Section 3 shows that Ethereum blockchain 2.0's BFT protocol Casper FFG could not achieve liveness if the adversary can re-order messages in the network. Section 4 shows that Ethereum blockchain's candidate BFT protocol Casper FBC for future deployment could not achieve liveness if the adversary can re-order messages in the network. Section 4 also proposes a Casper FBC style binary BFT protocol that achieves both safety and liveness in the traditional academic security model for complete asynchronous networks. Section 5 reviews the Polkadot's GRANDPA BFT protocol and shows that it cannot achieve liveness if the adversary is allowed to reschedule the message delivery order in the underlying networks. Section 6 proposes a multi-value BFT protocol XP for complete asynchronous networks and proves its security.

2   System Model and Byzantine Agreement

For the Byzantine general problem, there are n participants and an adversary that is allowed to corrupt up to t of them. The adversary model is a static one wherein the adversary must decide whom to corrupt at the start of the protocol execution. For the network setting, we consider three kinds of networks: synchronous networks, partial synchronous networks by Dwork, Lynch, and Stockmeyer [7], and complete asynchronous networks by Fischer, Lynch, and Paterson [8].

1. In a synchronous network, the time is divided into discrete units called slots T_0, $T_1, T_2, \cdots$ where the length of the time slots are equal. Furthermore, we assume that: (1) the current time slot is determined by a publicly-known and monotonically increasing function of current time; and (2) each participant has access to the current time. In a synchronous network, if an honest participant P_1 sends a message m to a participant P_2 at the start of time slot T_i, the message m is guaranteed to arrive at P_2 at the end of time slot T_i.
2. In partial synchronous networks, the time is divided into discrete units as in synchronous networks. The adversary can selectively delay or re-order any messages sent by honest parties. In other words, if an honest participant P_1 sends a message m to an honest participant P_2 at the start of time slot T_{i_1}, P_2 will receive the message m eventually at time T_{i_2} where $i_2 = i_1 + \Delta$. Based on the property of Δ, we can distinguish the following two scenarios:
   - Type I partial synchronous network: $\Delta < \infty$ is unknown. That is, there exists a Δ but participants do not know the exact (or even approximate) value of Δ.
   - Type II partial synchronous network: $\Delta < \infty$ holds eventually. That is, the participant knows the value of Δ. But this Δ only holds after an unknown time slot $T = T_i$. Such a time T is called the Global Stabilization Time (GST).
   For Type I partial synchronous networks, the protocol designer supplies the consensus protocol first, then the adversary chooses her Δ. For Type II partial synchronous networks, the adversary picks the Δ and the protocol designer (knowing Δ) supplies the consensus protocol, then the adversary chooses the GST.
3. In a complete asynchronous network, we make no assumptions about the relative speeds of processes or about the delay time in delivering a message. We also assume that processes do not have access to synchronized clocks. Thus algorithms based on time-outs cannot be used.

In all of the network models, we assume that the adversary has *complete control of the network*. That is, the adversary may schedule/reorder the delivery of messages as he wishes, and may insert messages as he wishes. The honest participants are completely passive: they simply follow the protocol steps and maintain their internal state between protocol steps.

The computations made by the honest participants and the adversary are modeled as polynomial-time computations. We assume that public key cryptography is used for message authentications. In particular, each participant should have authentic public keys of all other participants. This means that if two participants P_i and P_j are honest and P_j receives a message from P_i over the network, then this message must have been generated by P_i at some prior point in time. A Byzantine agreement protocol must satisfy the following properties:

- **Safety:** If an honest participant decides on a value, then all other honest participants decides on the same value. That is, it is computationally infeasible for an adversary to make two honest participants to decide on different values.
- **Liveness (termination):** There exists a function $B(\cdot)$ such that all honest participants should decide on a value after the protocol runs at most $B(n)$ steps. It should be noted that $B(n)$ could be exponential in n. In this case, we should further assume that 2^n is significantly smaller than 2^κ where κ is the security parameter for the underlying authentication scheme. In other words, one should not be able to break the underlying authentication scheme within $O(B(n))$ steps.
- **Non-triviality (Validity):** If all honest participants start the protocol with the same initial value, then all honest participants that decide must decide on this value.

3   Casper the Friendly Finality Gadget (FFG)

Buterin and Griffith [4] proposed the BFT protocol Casper the Friendly Finality Gadget (Casper FFG) as an overlay atop a block proposal mechanism. Casper FFG has been deployed in the Proof of Stake Based Ethereum 2.0. In Casper FFG, weighted participants validate and finalize blocks that are proposed by an existing proof of work chain or other mechanisms. To simplify our discussion, we assume that there are $n = 3t + 1$ validators of equal weight. The Casper FFG works on the checkpoint tree that only contains blocks of height $100 * k$ in the underlying block tree. Each validator P_i can broadcast a signed vote $\langle P_i : s, t \rangle$ where s and t are two checkpoints and s is an ancestor of t on the checkpoint tree. For two checkpoints a and b, we say that $a \to b$ is a supermajority link if there are at least $2t + 1$ votes for the pair. A checkpoint a is justified if there are supermajority links $a_0 \to a_1 \to \cdots \to a$ where a_0 is the root. A checkpoint a is finalized if there are supermajority links $a_0 \to a_1 \to \cdots \to a_i \to a$ where a_0 is the root and a is the direct son of a_i. In Casper FFG, an honest validator P_i should not publish two distinct votes

$$\langle P_i : s_1, t_1 \rangle \quad \text{AND} \quad \langle P_i : s_2, t_2 \rangle$$

such that either

$$h(t_1) = h(t_2) \quad \text{OR} \quad h(s_1) < h(s_2) < h(t_2) < h(t_1)$$

where $h(\cdot)$ denotes the height of the node on the checkpoint tree. In other words, *an honest validator should neither publish two distinct votes for the same target height nor publish a vote strictly within the span of its other votes.* Otherwise, the validator's deposit will be slashed. The authors [4] claimed that Casper FFG achieves accountable safety and plausible liveness where

1. achieve accountable safety means that two conflicting checkpoints cannot both be finalized (assuming that there are at most t malicious validators), and
2. plausible liveness means that supermajority links can always be added to produce new finalized checkpoints, provided there exist children extending the finalized chain.

In order to achieve the liveness property, [4] proposed to use the "correct by construction" fork choice rule: the underlying block proposal mechanism should *"follow the chain containing the justified checkpoint of the greatest height"*.

The authors in [4] proposed to defeat the long-range revision attacks by a fork choice rule to never revert a finalized block, as well as an expectation that each client will "log on" and gain a complete up-to-date view of the chain at some regular frequency (e.g., once per month). In order to defeat the catastrophic crashes where more than t validators crash-fail at the same time (i.e., they are no longer connected to the network due to a network partition, computer failure, or the validators themselves are malicious), the authors in [4] proposed to slowly drains the deposit of any validator that does not vote for checkpoints, until eventually its deposit sizes decrease low enough that the validators who are voting are a supermajority. Related mechanism to recover from related scenarios such as network partition is considered an open problem in [4].

No specific network model is provided in [4]. In the implementation of the Casper FFG (see GO-Ethereum implementation), a participating node broadcasts his message as soon as he receives a sufficient number of messages to move forward. In other words, even if the network is a synchronized network, a participant may just make his decision on the first $2t + 1$ messages and ignore the remaining messages if these first $2t + 1$ messages are sufficient for him to move forward. This is reasonable and necessary since the remaining t nodes could be malicious ones and will never send any message at all. Based on this observation, we show that if the adversary could reschedule the message delivery order on the underlying networks, Casper FFG cannot achieve liveness property even in synchronized networks.

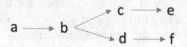

Fig. 1. Casper FFG cannot achieve liveness

As an example, assume that, at time T, the checkpoint a is finalized where there is a supermajority link from a to its direct child b (that is, b is justified) and no vote for b's descendant checkpoint has been broadcast by any validator yet (see Fig. 1). Now assume that the underlying block production mechanism produces a fork starting from b. That is, b has two descendant checkpoints c and d. The adversary who controls the network can arrange t honest validators to receive c first and $t + 1$ honest validators to receive d first where $h(c) = h(d)$. Thus t honest validators vote for $b \rightarrow c$, $t + 1$ honest validators vote for $b \rightarrow d$, and t malicious validators vote randomly so that both $b \rightarrow c$ and $b \rightarrow d$ receives same number of votes. This means that c and d could not be finalized since neither the link $b \rightarrow c$ nor the link $b \rightarrow d$ could get a supermajority vote. It should be noted that by the two slashing rules in Casper FFG, an honest validator who voted for $b \rightarrow c$ is allowed to vote for $b \rightarrow f$ later since the two votes on $b \rightarrow c$ and $b \rightarrow f$ are not slashable. Next assume that the adversary schedules the message delivery order so that t honest validators receive e first and $t + 1$ honest validators receive f first (without loss of generality, we may assume that $h(e) = h(f)$). Thus t honest validators vote for $b \rightarrow e$, $t + 1$ honest validators vote for $b \rightarrow f$, and t malicious validators vote randomly so that both $b \rightarrow e$ and $b \rightarrow f$ receives same number of votes. Thus e and f could not be finalized since neither the link $b \rightarrow e$ nor the link $b \rightarrow f$ could get a supermajority vote. This process continues forever and no checkpoint after a could be finalized. That is, Casper FFG could not achieve liveness with this kind of message delivery schedule by the adversary.

4 CBC Casper the Friendly Binary Consensus (FBC)

The network model for Casper FFG is not clearly defined. In order to make Ethereum blockchain robust in complete asynchronous networks, Ethereum foundation has been advocating the "Correct-by-Construction" (CBC) family of Casper blockchain consensus protocols [17, 18] for their future release of Ethereum blockchain. The CBC Casper the Friendly Ghost emphasizes the safety property. But it does not try to address the liveness requirement for the consensus process. Indeed, it explicitly says that [17] "*liveness considerations are considered largely out of scope, and should be treated in future work*". Thus in order for CBC Casper to be deployable, a lot of work needs to be done since the Byzantine Agreement Problem becomes challenging only when both safety and liveness properties are required to be satisfied at the same time. It is simple to design BFT protocols that only satisfy one of the two requirements (safety or liveness). The Ethereum foundation community has made several efforts to design safety oracles for CBC Casper to help participants to make a decision when an agreement is reached (see, e.g., [15]). However, this problem is at least as hard as coNP-complete problems. So no satisfactory solution has been proposed yet.

CBC Casper has received several critiques from the community. For example, Ali et al. [1] concluded that "*the definitions and proofs provided in [18] result in neither a theoretically sound nor practically useful treatment of Byzantine fault-tolerance. We believe that considering correctness without liveness is a fundamentally wrong approach. Importantly, it remains unclear if the definition of the Casper protocol family provides any meaningful safety guarantees for blockchains*". Though CBC Casper is not a deployable solution yet and it has several fundamental issues yet to be addressed, we think these critiques as in [1] may not be fair enough. Indeed, CBC Casper provides an interesting framework for consensus protocol design. In particular, the algebraic approach proposed by CBC Casper has certain advantages for describing Byzantine Fault Tolerance (BFT) protocols. The analysis in this section shows that the current formulation of CBC Casper could not achieve liveness property. However, if one revises the

CBC Casper's algebraic approach to include the concept of "waiting" and to enhance participant's capability to identify more malicious activities (that is, to consider general malicious activities in addition to equivocating activities), then one can design efficiently constructive liveness concepts for CBC Casper even in complete asynchronous networks.

4.1 Casper FBC Protocol Description

CBC Casper contains a binary version and an integer version. In this paper, we only consider Casper the Friendly Binary Consensus (FBC). Our discussion can be easily extended to general cases. For the Casper FBC protocol, each participant repeatedly sends and receives messages to/from other participants. Based on the received messages, a participant can infer whether a consensus has been achieved. Assume that there are n participants $P_1, \cdots, P_n$ and let $t < n$ be the Byzantine-fault-tolerance threshold. The protocol proceeds from step to step (starting from step 0) until a consensus is reached. Specifically the step s proceeds as follows:

– Let $\mathcal{M}_{i,s}$ be the collection of valid messages that P_i has received from all participants (including himself) from steps $0, \cdots, s-1$. P_i determines whether a consensus has been achieved. If a consensus has not been achieved yet, P_i sends the message

$$m_{i,s} = \langle P_i, e_{i,s}, \mathcal{M}_{i,s} \rangle \tag{1}$$

to all participants where $e_{i,s}$ is P_i's estimated consensus value based on the received message set $\mathcal{M}_{i,s}$.

In the following, we describe how a participant P_i determines whether a consensus has been achieved and how a participant P_i calculates the value $e_{i,s}$ from $\mathcal{M}_{i,s}$.

For a message $m = \langle P_i, e_{i,s}, \mathcal{M}_{i,s} \rangle$, let $J(m) = \mathcal{M}_{i,s}$. For two messages m_1, m_2, we write $m_1 \prec m_2$ if m_2 depends on m_1. That is, there is a sequence of messages $m_1', \cdots, m_v'$ such that

$$m_1 \in J(m_1')$$
$$m_1' \in J(m_2')$$
$$\cdots$$
$$m_v' \in J(m_2)$$

For a message m and a message set $\mathcal{M} = \{m_1, \cdots, m_v\}$, we say that $m \prec \mathcal{M}$ if $m \in \mathcal{M}$ or $m \prec m_j$ for some $j = 1, \cdots, v$. The *latest message* $m = L(P_i, \mathcal{M})$ by a participant P_i in a message set $\mathcal{M}$ is a message $m \prec \mathcal{M}$ satisfying the following condition:

– There does not exist another message $m' \prec \mathcal{M}$ sent by participant P_i with $m \prec m'$.

It should be noted that the "latest message" concept is well defined for a participant P_i if P_i has not equivocated, where a participant P_i equivocates if P_i has sent two messages $m_1 \neq m_2$ with the properties that "$m_1 \not\prec m_2$ and $m_2 \not\prec m_1$".

For a binary value $b \in \{0, 1\}$ and a message set $\mathcal{M}$, the score of a binary estimate for b is defined as the number of non-equivocating participants P_i whose latest message voted for b. That is,

$$\text{score}(b, \mathcal{M}) = \sum_{L(P_i, \mathcal{M})=(P_i, b, *)} \lambda(P_i, \mathcal{M}) \tag{2}$$

where

$$\lambda(P_i, \mathcal{M}) = \begin{cases} 0 \text{ if } P_i \text{ equivocates in } \mathcal{M}, \\ 1 \text{ otherwise.} \end{cases}$$

To Estimate Consensus Value: Now we are ready to define P_i's estimated consensus value $e_{i,s}$ based on the received message set $\mathcal{M}_{i,s}$ as follows:

$$e_{i,s} = \begin{cases} 0 \text{ if } \text{score}(0, \mathcal{M}_{i,s}) > \text{score}(1, \mathcal{M}_{i,s}) \\ 1 \text{ if } \text{score}(1, \mathcal{M}_{i,s}) > \text{score}(0, \mathcal{M}_{i,s}) \\ b \text{ otherwise, where } b \text{ is coin-flip output} \end{cases} \tag{3}$$

To Infer Consensus Achievement: For a protocol execution, it is required that for all i, s, the number of equivocating participants in $\mathcal{M}_{i,s}$ is at most t. A participant P_i determines that a consensus has been achieved at step s with the received message set $\mathcal{M}_{i,s}$ if there exists $b \in \{0, 1\}$ such that

$$\forall s' > s : \text{score}(b, \mathcal{M}_{i,s'}) > \text{score}(1 - b, \mathcal{M}_{i,s'}). \tag{4}$$

4.2 Efforts to Achieve Liveness for CBC Casper FBC

From CBC Casper protocol description, it is clear that CBC Casper is guaranteed to be correct against equivocating participants. However, the "inference rule for consensus achievement" requires a mathematical proof that is based on infinitely many message sets $\mathcal{M}_{i,s'}$ for $s' > s$. This requires each participant to verify that for each potential set of t Byzantine participants, their malicious activities will not overturn the inequality in (4). This problem is at least co-NP hard. Thus even if the system reaches a consensus, the participants may not realize this fact. In order to address this challenge, Ethereum community provides three "safety oracles" (see [15]) to help participants to determine whether a consensus is obtained. The first "adversary oracle" simulates some protocol execution to see whether the current estimate will change under some Byzantine attacks. As mentioned previously, this kind of problem is co-NP hard and the simulation cannot be exhaustive generally. The second "clique oracle" searches for the biggest clique of participant graph to see whether there exist more than 50% participants who agree on current estimate and all acknowledge the agreement. That is, for each message, the oracle checks to see if, and for how long, participants have seen each other agreeing on the value of that message. This kind of problem is equivalent to the complete bipartite graph problem which is NP-complete. The third "Turan oracle" uses Turan's Theorem to find the minimum size of a clique that must exist in the participant edge graph. In a summary, currently there is no satisfactory approach for CBC Casper participants to determine whether finality has achieved. Thus no liveness is guaranteed for CBC Casper. Indeed, we can show that it is impossible to achieve liveness in CBC Casper.

4.3   Impossibility of Achieving Liveness in CBC Casper

In this section, we use a simple example to show that without a protocol revision, no liveness could be achieved in CBC Casper. Assume that there are $3t + 1$ participants. Among these participants, $t - 1$ of them are malicious and never vote. Furthermore, assume that $t + 1$ of them hold value 0 and $t + 1$ of them hold value 1. Since the message delivery system is controlled by the adversary, the adversary can let the first $t+1$ participants to receive $t+1$ voted 0 and t voted 1. On the other hand, the adversary can let the next $t + 1$ participants to receive $t + 1$ voted 1 and t voted 0. That is, at the end of this step, we still have that $t + 1$ of them hold value 0 and $t + 1$ of them hold value 1. This process can continue forever and never stop.

In CBC Casper FBC [17, 18], a participant is identified as malicious only if he equivocates. This is not sufficient to guarantee liveness (or even safety) of the protocol. For example, if no participant equivocates and no participant follows the Eq. (3) for consensus value estimation, then the protocol may never make a decision (that is, the protocol cannot achieve liveness property). However, the protocol execution satisfies the valid protocol execution condition of [17, 18] since there is zero equivocating participant.

4.4   Revising CBC Casper FBC

CBC Casper does not have an in-protocol fault tolerance threshold and does not have any timing assumptions. Thus the protocol works well in complete asynchronous settings. Furthermore, it does not specify when a participant P_i should broadcast his step s protocol message to other participants. That is, it does not specify when P_i should stop waiting for more messages to be included $\mathcal{M}_{i,s}$. We believe that CBC Casper authors do not specify the time for a participant to send its step s protocol messages because they try to avoid any timing assumptions. In fact, there is a simple algebraic approach to specify this without timing assumptions. First, we revise the message set $\mathcal{M}_{i,s}$ as the collection of messages that P_i receives from all participants (including himself) during step $s - 1$. That is, the message set $\mathcal{M}_{i,s}$ is a subset of E_s where E_s is defined recursively as follows:

$$E_0 = \emptyset$$
$$E_1 = \{\langle P_j, b, \emptyset \rangle : j = 1, \cdots, n; b = 0, 1\}$$
$$E_2 = \{\langle P_j, b, \mathcal{M}_{j,1} \rangle : j = 1, \cdots, n; b = 0, 1; \mathcal{M}_{j,1} \subset E_1\}$$
$$\cdots$$
$$E_s = \{\langle P_j, b, \mathcal{M}_{j,s-1} \rangle : j = 1, \cdots, n; b = 0, 1; \mathcal{M}_{j,s-1} \subset E_{s-1}\}$$
$$\cdots$$

Then we need to revise the latest message definition $L(P_j, \mathcal{M}_{i,s})$ accordingly:

$$L(P_j, \mathcal{M}_{i,s}) = \begin{cases} m \text{ if } \langle P_j, b, m \rangle \in \mathcal{M}_{i,s} \\ \emptyset \text{ otherwise} \end{cases} \tag{5}$$

As we have mentioned in the preceding section, CBC Casper FBC [17, 18] only considers equivocating as malicious activities. This is not sufficient to guarantee protocol liveness against Byzantine faults. In our following revised CBC Casper model, we consider any participant that does not follow the protocol as malicious and exclude their messages:

- For a message set $\mathcal{M}_{i,s}$, let $I(\mathcal{M}_{i,s})$ be the set of identified malicious participants from $\mathcal{M}_{i,s}$. Specifically, let

$$I(\mathcal{M}_{i,s}) = E(\mathcal{M}_{i,s}) \cup F(\mathcal{M}_{i,s})$$

where $E(\mathcal{M}_{i,s})$ is the set of equivocating participants within $\mathcal{M}_{i,s}$ and $F(\mathcal{M}_{i,s})$ is the set of participants that does not follow the protocols within $\mathcal{M}_{i,s}$. For example, $F(\mathcal{M}_{i,s})$ includes participants that do not follow the consensus value estimation process properly or do not wait for enough messages before posting his own protocol messages.

With the definition of $I(\mathcal{M}_{i,s})$, we should also redefine the score function (2) by revising the definition of $\lambda(P_i, \mathcal{M})$ accordingly:

$$\lambda(P_i, \mathcal{M}) = \begin{cases} 0 \text{ if } P_i \in I(\mathcal{M}), \\ 1 \text{ otherwise.} \end{cases}$$

4.5 Secure BFT Protocol in the Revised CBC Casper

With the revised CBC Casper, we are ready to introduce the "waiting" concept and specify when a participant P_i should send his step s protocol message:

- A participant P_i should wait for at least $n - t + |I(\mathcal{M}_{i,s})|$ valid messages $m_{j,s-1}$ from other participants before he can broadcast his step s message $m_{i,s}$. That is, P_i should wait until $|\mathcal{M}_{i,s}| \geq n - t + |I(\mathcal{M}_{i,s})|$ to broadcast his step s protocol message.
- In case that a participant P_i receives $n - t + |I(\mathcal{M}_{i,s})|$ valid messages $m_{j,s-1}$ from other participants (that is, he is ready to send step s protocol message) before he could post his step $s - 1$ message, he should wait until he finishes sending his step $s - 1$ message.
- After a participant P_i posts his step s protocol message, it should discard all messages from steps $s - 1$ or early except decision messages that we will describe later.

It is clear that these specifications does not have any restriction on the timings. Thus the protocol works in complete asynchronous networks.

In Ben-Or's BFT protocol [2], if consensus is not achieved yet, the participants autonomously toss a coin until more than $\frac{n+t}{2}$ participant outcomes coincide. For Ben-Or's maximal Byzantine fault tolerance threshold $t \leq \lfloor \frac{n}{5} \rfloor$, it takes exponential steps of coin-flipping to converge. It is noted that, for $t = O(\sqrt{n})$, Ben-Or's protocol takes constant rounds to converge. Bracha [3] improved Ben-Or's protocol to defeat $t < \frac{n}{3}$ Byzantine faults. Bracha first designed a reliable broadcast protocol with the following properties (Bracha's reliable broadcast protocol is briefly reviewed in the Appendix): If an honest participant broadcasts a message, then all honest participants will receive the same message in the end. If a dishonest participants P_i broadcasts a message, then either all honest participants accept the identical message or no honest participant accepts any value from P_i. By using the reliable broadcast primitive and other validation primitives, Byzantine participants can be transformed to fail-stop participants. In the following, we assume that a reliable broadcast primitive such as the one by Bracha is used in our protocol execution and present Bracha's style BFT protocol in the CBC Casper framework. At the start of the protocol, each participant P_i holds an initial value in his variable $x_i \in \{0, 1\}$. The protocol proceeds from step to step. The step s consists of the following sub-steps.

1. Each participant P_i reliably broadcasts $\langle P_i, x_i, \mathcal{M}_{i,s,0} \rangle$ to all participants where $\mathcal{M}_{i,s,0}$ is the message set that P_i has received during step $s - 1$. Then P_i waits until it receives $n - t$ valid messages in $\mathcal{M}_{i,s,1}$ and computes the estimate $e_{i,s}$ using the value estimation function (3).
2. Each participant P_i reliably broadcasts $\langle P_i, e_{i,s}, \mathcal{M}_{i,s,1} \rangle$ to all participants and waits until it receives $n - t$ valid messages in $\mathcal{M}_{i,s,2}$. If there is a b such that $\texttt{score}(b, \mathcal{M}_{i,s,2}) > \frac{n}{2}$, then let $e'_{i,s} = b$ otherwise, let $e'_{i,s} = \perp$.
3. Each participant P_i reliably broadcasts $\langle P_i, e'_{i,s}, \mathcal{M}_{i,s,2} \rangle$ to all participants and waits until it receives $n - t$ valid messages in $\mathcal{M}_{i,s,3}$. P_i distinguishes the following three cases:
   - If $\texttt{score}(b, \mathcal{M}_{i,s,2}) > 2t + 1$ for some $b \in \{0, 1\}$, then P_i decides on b and broadcasts his decision together with justification to all participants.
   - If $\texttt{score}(b, \mathcal{M}_{i,s,2}) > t + 1$ for some $b \in \{0, 1\}$, then P_i lets $x_i = b$ and moves to step $s + 1$.
   - Otherwise, P_i flips a coin and let x_i to be coin-flip outcome. P_i moves to step $s + 1$.

Assume that $n = 3t + 1$. The security of the above protocol can be proved be establishing a sequence of lemmas.

Lemma 1. *If all honest participants hold the same initial value b at the start of the protocol, then every participant decides on b at the end of step $s = 0$.*

Proof. At sub-step 1, each honest participant receives at least $t + 1$ value b among the $2t + 1$ received values. Thus all honest participants broadcast b at sub-step 2. If a malicious participant P_j broadcasts $1 - b$ during sub-step 2, then it cannot be justified since P_j could not receive $t + 1$ messages for $1 - b$ during sub-step 1. Thus P_j will be included in $I(\mathcal{M})$. That is, each honest participant receives $2t + 1$ messages for b at the end of sub-step 2 and broadcasts b during sub-step 3. Based on the same argument, all honest participants decide on b at the end of sub-step 3. $\square$

Lemma 2. *If an honest participant P_i decides on a value b at the end of step s, then all honest participants either decide on b at the end of step s or at the end of step $s + 1$.*

Proof. If an honest participant P_i decides on a value b at the end of sub-step 3, then P_i receives $2t + 1$ valid messages for the value b. Since the underlying broadcast protocol is reliable, each honest participant receives at least $t + 1$ these valid messages for the value b. Thus if a participant P_i does not decide on the value b at the end of sub-step 3, it would set $x_i = b$. That is, all honest participants will decide during step $s + 1$. $\square$

The above two Lemmas show that the protocol is a secure Byzantine Fault Tolerance protocol against $\lfloor \frac{n-1}{3} \rfloor$ Byzantine faults in complete asynchronous networks. The above BFT protocol may take exponentially many steps to converge. However, if a common coin such as the one in Rabin [14] is used, then the above protocol converges in constant steps. It should be noted that Ethereum 2.0 provides a random beacon which could be used as a common coin for the above BFT protocol. Thus the above BFT protocol could be implemented with constant steps on Ethereum 2.0.

5   Polkadot's BFT Protocol GRANDPA

The project Polkadot (https://github.com/w3f) proposed an algebraic approach based BFT finality gadget protocol GRANDPA which is similar to Casper FBC in some sense. There are different versions of GRANDPA protocol. In this paper, we refer to the most recent one [16] dated on June 19, 2020. Specifically, Polkadot implements a nominated proof-of-stake (NPoS) system. At certain time period, the system elects a group of validators to serve for block production and the finality gadget. Nominators also stake their tokens as a guarantee of good behavior, and this stake gets slashed whenever their nominated validators deviate from their protocol. On the other hand, nominators also get paid when their nominated validators play by the rules. Elected validators get equal voting power in the consensus protocol. Polkadot uses BABE as its block production mechanism and GRANDPA as its BFT finality gadget. Here we are interested in the finality gadget GRANDPA (GHOST-based Recursive ANcestor Deriving Prefix Agreement) that is implemented for the Polkadot relay chain. GRANDPA contains two protocols, the first protocol works in partially synchronous networks and tolerates 1/3 Byzantine participants. The second protocol works in full asynchronous networks (requiring a common random coin) and tolerates 1/5 Byzantine participants. The first GRANDPA protocol assumes that underlying network is a Type I partial synchronous network. In the following paragraphs, we will show that GRANDPA cannot achieve liveness property in partial synchronous networks if the adversary is allowed to reschedule the message delivery order.

Assume that there are $n = 3t + 1$ participants $P_0, \cdots, P_{n-1}$ and at most t of them are malicious. Each participant stores a tree of blocks produced by the block production mechanism with the genesis block as the root. A participant can vote for a block on the tree by digitally signing it. For a set S of votes, a participant P_i equivocates in S if P_i has more than one vote in S. A set S of votes is called safe if the number of participants who equivocate in S is at most t. A vote set S has supermajority for a block B if

$$|\{P_i : P_i \text{ votes for } B*\} \cup \{P_i : P_i \text{ equivocates}\}| \geq 2t + 1$$

where P_i votes for $B*$ mean that P_i votes for B or a descendant of B.

In GRANDPA, the 2/3-GHOST function $g(S)$ returns the block B of the maximal height such that S has a supermajority for B or a "nil" if no such block exists. If a safe vote set S has a supermajority for a block B, then there are at least $t + 1$ voters who do vote for B or its descendant but do not equivocate. Based on this observation, it is easy to check that if $S \subseteq T$ and T is safe, then $g(S)$ is an ancestor of $g(T)$.

The authors in [16] defined the following concept of *possibility* for a vote set to have a supermajority for a block: "We say that it is *impossible* for a set S to have a supermajority for a block B if at least $2t + 1$ voters either equivocate or vote for blocks who are not descendant of B. Otherwise it is *possible* for S to have a supermajority for B". Then they claimed (the second paragraph above Lemma 2.6 in [16]) that "a vote set S is possible to have a supermajority for a block B if and only if there exists a safe vote set $T \supseteq S$ such that T has a supermajority for B". Unfortunately, this claim is not true in practice if the adversary selects a non-equivocating strategy which may introduce deadlock to the system (on the other hand, this claim is true if all t malicious voters MUST equivocate).

Example 1. Assume that blocks C and D are inconsistent (that is, C is not an ancestor of D and D is not an ancestor of C) and the vote set S contains the following votes which could be achieved by letting the adversary re-order the messages to be delivered on the network (this could also happen before GST in partial synchronous networks).

1. $t + 1$ voters vote for C.
2. $2t$ voters vote for D.
3. no voters equivocate.

Since only $2t$ votes in S that "either equivocate or vote for blocks who are not descendant of C", by the above definition, S is NOT *impossible* to have a supermajority for C. Thus, by the above definition, S is *possible* to have a supermajority for a block C. If malicious voters choose not to equivocate (we cannot force a malicious voter to equivocate), there does not exist a semantically valid safe vote set $T \supseteq S$ such that T has a supermajority for C. Similarly, by the above definition, S is NOT *impossible* to have a supermajority for D and is *possible* to have a supermajority for a block D. If malicious voters choose not to equivocate, there does not exist a semantically valid safe vote set $T \supseteq S$ such that T has a supermajority for D. On the other hand, if a malicious voter submits another vote (either for C or D) to S, then D has a supermajority vote in S.

In the following sections, we will use Example 1 to show that the GRANDPA protocol will enter deadlock and cannot achieve the liveness property if the adversary is allowed to reschedule the message delivery order.

5.1   GRANDPA Protocol

The GRANDPA protocol starts from round 1. For each round, one participant is designated as the primary and all participants know who is the primary. Each round consists of two phases: *prevote* and *precommit*. Let $V_{r,i}$ and $C_{r,i}$ be the sets of prevotes and precommits received by P_i during round r respectively. Let $E_{0,i}$ be the genesis block and $E_{r,i}$ be the last ancestor block of $g(V_{r,i})$ that is possible for $C_{r,i}$ to have a supermajority. If either $E_{r,i} < g(V_{r,i})$ or it is impossible for $C_{r,i}$ to have a supermajority for any children of $g(V_{r,i})$, then we say that P_i sees that round r is *completable*. Let Δ be a time bound such that it suffices to send messages and gossip them to everyone. The protocol proceeds as follows.

1. P_i starts round $r > 1$ if round $r - 1$ is completable and P_i has cast votes in all previous rounds. Let $t_{r,i}$ be the time P_i starts round r.
2. The primary voter P_i of round r broadcasts $E_{r-1,i}$.

3. **prevote:** P_i waits until either it is at least time $t_{r,i} + 2\Delta$ or round r is completable. P_i *prevotes* for the head of the best chain containing $E_{r-1,i}$ unless P_i receives a block B from the primary with $g(V_{r-1}, i) \geq B > E_{r-1,i}$. In this case, P_i uses the best chain containing B.
4. **precommit:** P_i waits until $g(V_{r,i}) \geq E_{r-1,i}$ and one of the following holds
   (a) it is at least time $t_{r,i} + 4\Delta$
   (b) round r is completable
   Then P_i broadcasts a precommit for $g(V_{r,i})$

At any time after the precommit step of round r, if P_i sees that $B = g(C_{r,i})$ is descendant of the last finalized block and $V_{r,i}$ has a supermajority, then P_i finalizes B.

5.2 GRANDPA Cannot Achieve Liveness in Partial Synchronous Networks

In this section, we show that GRANDPA BFT protocol cannot achieve liveness property in partial synchronous networks. Assume that $E_{r-1,0} = \cdots = E_{r-1,n-1} = A$ and all $3t + 1$ voters prevote and precommit to A during round $r - 1$ and A is finalized by all voters during round $r - 1$. Also assume that no voter will ever equivocate. During round $\dot{r}$, the block production mechanisms produces a fork of A. That is, we get two children blocks C and D of A.

Counter-Example 1: By adjusting the message delivery schedule (this could happen before GST in partial synchronous networks), $t + 1$ voters only receive the block C before time $t_{r,i} + 2\Delta$ and $2t$ voters only receive the block D before time $t_{r,i} + 2\Delta$. However, all voters will receive both blocks C and D before time $t_{r,i} + 3\Delta$.

At step 2 of round r, the primary voter broadcasts $A = E_{r-1,i}$. At step 3, both $V_{r,i}$ and $C_{r,i}$ are empty initially, the round r cannot be completable until time $t_{r,i} + 2\Delta$. Thus voter P_i waits until time $t_{r,i} + 2\Delta$ to submit its prevote. The $t + 1$ voters that received block C would prevote for C and the other $2t$ voters that received block D would prevote for D. The adversary allows all prevotes of Step 3 to be delivered to all voters synchronously before time $t_{r,i} + 4\Delta$. During Step 4, each voter P_i receives $t + 1$ prevotes for C and $2t$ prevotes for D. Since $C_{r,i}$ is empty until it receives any precommit, round r is not completable until time $t_{r,i} + 4\Delta$. That is, each voter P_i waits until $t_{r,i} + 4\Delta$ to precommit $g(V_{r,i}) = A$. The adversary allows all voters to receive all precommit votes for A. Now each voter P_i estimates $E_{r,i} = g(V_{r,i}) = A$. By the fact that $C_{r,i} = \{3t+1 \text{ precommit votes for } A\}$, we have $g(C_{r,i}) = A$. Since A has already been finalized, P_i will not finalize any block during round r.

In order for the round r to be completable, we need "either $E_{r,i} < g(V_{r,i})$ or it is impossible for $C_{r,i}$ to have a supermajority for any children of $g(V_{r,i})$". However, we have $E_{r,i} = g(V_{r,i}) = A$ and $C_{r,i} = \{3t + 1 \text{ precommit votes for } A\}$. That is, by definition of "*possibility*", it is "**possible**" for $C_{r,i}$ to have a supermajority for both children C and D of $g(V_{r,i}) = A$. In order words, the round r is NOT "completable" and GRANDPA cannot start Step 1 of round $r + 1$.

Counter-Example 2: This example is more involved than counter-example 1 and an example with $t = 1$ is shown in Fig. 2. By adjusting the message delivery schedule (this could happen before GST in partial synchronous networks), by time $t_{r,i} + 2\Delta$, we have

$P_1 \longrightarrow$ prevote C $\quad\quad P_1 \longrightarrow$ precommit A $\quad\quad P_1 \longrightarrow E_{r,1} = A$

$P_2 \longrightarrow$ prevote D $\quad\quad P_2$

$P_3 \longrightarrow$ prevote D $\quad\quad P_3 \longrightarrow$ precommit A $\quad\quad P_3 \longrightarrow E_{r,3} = A$

$P_4 \longrightarrow$ prevote D $\quad\quad P_4 \longrightarrow$ precommit D $\quad\quad P_4 \longrightarrow E_{r,4} = D$

Fig. 2. Counter-example 2 for GRANDPA

t voters received block C and $2t + 1$ voters received block D. Furthermore, all voters will receive both blocks C and D before time $t_{r,i} + 3\Delta$.

At step 2 of round r, the primary voter broadcasts $A = E_{r-1,i}$. At step 3, both $V_{r,i}$ and $C_{r,i}$ are empty initially, the round r cannot be completable until time $t_{r,i} + 2\Delta$. Thus voter P_i waits until time $t_{r,i} + 2\Delta$ to submit its prevote. The t voters that received block C would prevote for C and the other $2t + 1$ voters that received block D would prevote for D. Durng Step 4, the adversary schedules the message delivery in such a way that, by time $t_{r,i} + 4\Delta$, t voters receive "$2t + 1$ prevotes for D" and $2t + 1$ voters receive "t prevotes for C and $t + 1$ prevotes for D". Since $C_{r,i}$ is empty until it receives any precommit, round r is not completable until time $t_{r,i} + 4\Delta$. That is, each voter P_i waits until $t_{r,i} + 4\Delta$ to precommit $g(V_{r,i})$. At time $t_{r,i} + 4\Delta$, t voters precommit for $D = g(V_{r,i})$, $2t$ voters precommit for $A = g(V_{r,i})$, and one malicious voter does not precommit. The adversary let all precommit messages to be delivered to all voters synchronously.

Now t voters estimates $E_{r,i} = g(V_{r,i}) = D$ and $2t + 1$ voters P_i estimates $E_{r,i} = g(V_{r,i}) = A$. By the fact that

$$C_{r,i} = \{t \text{ precommit votes for } D \text{ and } 2t \text{ precommit votes for } A\},$$

we have $g(C_{r,i}) = A$. Since A has already been finalized, P_i will not finalize any block during round r. In order for the round r to be completable, we need "either $E_{r,i} < g(V_{r,i})$ or it is impossible for $C_{r,i}$ to have a supermajority for any children of $g(V_{r,i})$". However, we have $E_{r,i} = g(V_{r,i})$ for all voters and, by Example 1, it is **"possible"** for $C_{r,i}$ to have a supermajority for all children of $g(V_{r,i})$. In order words, the round r is NOT "completable" and GRANDPA cannot start Step 1 of round $r + 1$.

Paper [16, p. 7] mentions that "$C_{r,i}$ and $V_{r,i}$ may change with time and also that $E_{r-1,i}$, which is a function of $V_{r-1,i}$ and $C_{r-1,i}$, can also change with time if P_i sees more votes from the previous round". However, this has no impact on our preceding examples since after an honest voter prevotes/precommits, the honest voter cannot change his prevote/prevommit votes anymore (otherwise, it will be counted as equivocation).

6   Multi-value BFT Protocols for Asynchronous Networks

Section 4.5 proposed a binary BFT finality gadget in complete asynchronous networks. Furthermore, the BFT protocol in Sect. 4.5 requires a strongly reliable broadcast channel. In this section, we present a constant round multi-value BFT protocol XP for complete asynchronous networks that does not require strongly reliable broadcast channels.

The XP protocol is motivated by the probabilistic binary BFT protocol in Cachin, Kursawe, and Shoup [5] and requires a shared common random beacon which could be implemented using the Ethereum random beacon.

We assume that there is a partial order on the list of candidate blocks to be finalized: $\mathcal{B} = \{B_j : 1 \leq j \leq \tau\}$ where $B_1 \prec B_2 \prec \cdots \prec B_\tau$. During the protocol run, each participant P_i maintains a list of known candidate blocks in its local variable $X_i \subseteq \mathcal{B}$. At the start of the protocol run, X_i contains the list of candidate blocks that the participant P_i has learned and could be empty. During the protocol run, we assume that there is a random coin shared by all participants. For example, for the Ethereum 2.0, one may use the existing random beacon protocol as a common coin. Let σ be the random string shared by all participants for step s. Then participant P_i sets the "common" block X_i^σ as a block $B_j \in X_i$ such that $H(B_j, s)$ and $H(\sigma, s)$ has the maximal common prefix within X_i, where $H(\cdot)$ is a hash function. If there are two candidate blocks $B_{j_1} \prec B_{j_2}$ such that

$$\text{commonPrefix}(H(B_{j_1}, s), H(\sigma, s)) = \text{commonPrefix}(H(B_{j_2}, s), H(\sigma, s)),$$

then P_i sets $X_i^\sigma = B_{j_2}$. It is easy to observe that if $X_{i_1} = X_{i_2}$, then $X_{i_1}^\sigma = X_{i_2}^\sigma$. However, if $X_{i_1} \neq X_{i_2}$, then $X_{i_1}^\sigma$ and $X_{i_2}^\sigma$ may be different.

The protocol proceeds from step to step until an agreement is achieved and the protocol does not have any assumption on the time setting. Each participant waits for at least $n - t$ justified messages from participants (including himself) to proceed to the next sub-step. The step $s \geq 0$ for a participant P_i consists of the following sub-steps:

- **lock:** If $s = 0$, then let B be the maximal element in X_i. If $s > 0$ then wait for $n - t$ justified commit-votes from step $s - 1$ and let

$$B = \begin{cases} B' & P_i \text{ receives a commit-vote for } B' \text{ in step } s - 1 \\ X_i^\sigma & P_i \text{ receives } 2t + 1 \text{ commit-votes for } \perp \text{ and } \sigma \text{ is common coin} \end{cases} \quad (6)$$

Then P_i sends the following message to all participants.

$$\langle P_i, \texttt{lock}, s, B, \texttt{justification} \rangle \quad (7)$$

where justification consists of messages to justify the selection of the value B.
- **commit:** P_i collects $n - t$ justified lock messages (7) and lets

$$\bar{B} = \begin{cases} B & \text{if there are } n - t \text{ locks for } B \,. \\ \perp & \text{otherwise} \end{cases} \quad (8)$$

Then P_i sends the following message to all participants

$$\langle P_i, \texttt{commit}, s, \bar{B}, X_i, \texttt{justification} \rangle \quad (9)$$

where justification consists of messages to justify the selection of the value $\bar{B}$.
- **check-for-decision:** Collect $n - t$ properly justified commit votes (9) and lets $X_i = X_i \cup (\cup_j X_j)$ where X_j are from messages (9). Furthermore, if these are $n - t$ commit-votes for a block $\bar{B}$, then P_i decides the block $\bar{B}$ and continues for one more step (up to commit sub-step). Otherwise, simply proceed.

Assume that $n = 3t + 1$. The security of the above protocol can be proved by establishing a sequence of lemmas.

Lemma 3. *If an honest participant P_i decides on the value $\bar{B}$ at the end of step s (but no honest participant has ever decided before step s), then all honest participants either decide on $\bar{B}$ at the end of step s or at the end of step $s + 1$.*

Proof. If an honest participant P_i decides on the value $\bar{B}$ at the end of step s, then at least $t + 1$ honest participants commit-vote for $\bar{B}$. Thus each participant (including malicious participant) receives at least one commit-vote for $\bar{B}$ at the end of step s. This means that a malicious participant cannot create a justification that she has received a commit-vote for another block $B \neq \bar{B}$ or has received $2t+1$ commit-votes for $\perp$ during step s. In other words, if a participant broadcasts a lock message for a block $B \neq \bar{B}$ during step $s+1$, it cannot be justified and will be discarded by honest participants. This means that, all honest participants will commit-vote for the block $\bar{B}$ during step $s + 1$ and any commit-vote for other blocks cannot be justified. Thus, all honest participants will collect $n - t$ justified commit-vote for the block $\bar{B}$ and decide on block $\bar{B}$ at the end of step $s + 1$. $\square$

Lemma 4. *Block B in Eq. (6) is uniquely defined for each honest participant.*

Proof. It is sufficient to show that each participant P_i (including both honest and dishonest participants) can not receive commit-votes for two different blocks $\bar{B}_1$ and $\bar{B}_2$ during step s. For a contradiction, assume that P_i receives commit-vote for both $\bar{B}_1$ and $\bar{B}_2$ during step s. Then there are $2t + 1$ participants who submit `lock` messages for $\bar{B}_1$ and $2t + 1$ participants who submit `lock` messages for $\bar{B}_2$. This means that at least $t + 1$ participants (thus at least one honest participant) submit `lock` messages for both $\bar{B}_1$ and $\bar{B}_2$ which is impossible. $\square$

Lemma 5. *During step s, if participants P_i and P_j receive commit votes for $\bar{B}_1$ and $\bar{B}_2$ respectively, then $\bar{B}_1 = \bar{B}_2$.*

Proof. For a contradiction, assume that $\bar{B}_1 \neq \bar{B}_2$. Then there are $2t + 1$ lock messages for $\bar{B}_1$ and $2t + 1$ lock messages for $\bar{B}_2$ during step s. This means that at least $t + 1$ participants (thus at least one honest participant) submit `lock` messages for both $\bar{B}_1$ and $\bar{B}_2$ which is impossible. $\square$

Lemma 6. *If all honest participants hold the the same local value $X_i = \mathcal{B}$ at the start of step s, then with high probability, every participant decides by the end of step $s + \tau$.*

Proof. The Lemma is proved by distinguishing the following two cases:

1. $s = 0$: At step 0, each honest participant broadcasts the lock for B_τ though dishonest participant may broadcast a lock for another block. At the commit phase, each honest participant P_i broadcasts $\mathcal{B}$ and a commit message for $\perp$ or B_τ depending on what he receives. If some participant decides at the end of Step 0, by Lemma 3, all honest participants decide by the end of Step 1. Assume that no participant

decides by the end of Step 0. During Step 1, when a participant broadcasts a lock for a block, he needs to include $2t+1$ commit messages from Step 0 as the justification. Among these $2t+1$ commit messages, at least $t+1$ come from honest participants which contain $\mathcal{B}$. Thus from now on, each participant must include its local variable $X_i = \mathcal{B}$ in its justification message. In other words, if a participant broadcast a lock for a block based on the common coin, this locked block must be identical for all participants who use the common coin. Therefore, from Step 1 on, a participant can only broadcast a lock for a block committed in the immediate previous step (cf. Lemma 5) or a lock for a block determined by the common coin. With probability $\frac{1}{\tau}$, the block determined by the common coin is identical to the committed block from the previous step. Thus all honest participants are expected to decide by Step τ.

2. $s > 0$: for this case, we distinguish the following three cases:
   (a) By the end of step $s-1$, at least one participant (including dishonest participant) can legally decide on a block (this means at least one honest participant receives a commit-vote for a block $B \neq \perp$ during step $s-1$): By Lemma 3, all honest participants decides by the end of step s.
   (b) By the end of step $s-1$, no participant (including dishonest participant) can legally decide on a block: From Step s and on, each honest participant broadcasts a lock message for the unique block X_i^σ determined by the common coin or a unique block that was committed in the immediate previous Step (cf. Lemma 5). With probability $\frac{1}{\tau}$, the block determined by the common coin is identical to the committed block from the immediate previous Step. Thus all honest participants are expected to decide by Step $s + \tau$.

This completes the proof of the Lemma.   □

Lemma 7. *All honest participant decides in constant steps.*

Proof. If no participant decides by the end of Step $s + \tau$, then, by Lemma 6, with high probability, at least one honest participant P_i revises its local variable X_i to include at least one more element during the Steps from s to $s + \tau$. Since there are at most τ candidate blocks, this process continues until no honest participant revises its local variable X_i. Then, by Lemma 6, all honest participants hold the same candidate block and the consensus will be reached.   □

The above five Lemmas show that the protocol XP is a secure Byzantine Fault Tolerance protocol against $\lfloor \frac{n-1}{3} \rfloor$ Byzantine faults in complete asynchronous networks.

A   Bracha's Strongly Reliable Broadcast Primitive

Assume $n > 3t$. Bracha [3] designed a broadcast protocol for asynchronous networks with the following properties:

- If an honest participant broadcasts a message, then all honest participants accept the message.
- If a dishonest participant P_i broadcasts a message, then either all honest participants accept the same message or no honest participant accepts any value from P_i.

Bracha's broadcast primitive runs as follows:

1. The transmitter P_i sends the value $\langle P_i, initial, v \rangle$ to all participants.
2. If a participant P_j receives a value v with one of the following messages
   - $\langle P_i, \texttt{initial}, v \rangle$
   - $\frac{n+t}{2}$ messages of the type $\langle \texttt{echo}, P_i, v \rangle$
   - $t + 1$ message of the type $\langle \texttt{ready}, P_i, v \rangle$
   then P_j sends the message $\langle \texttt{echo}, P_i, v \rangle$ to all participants.
3. If a participant P_j receives a value v with one of the following messages
   - $\frac{n+t}{2}$ messages of the type $\langle \texttt{echo}, P_i, v \rangle$
   - $t + 1$ message of the type $\langle \texttt{ready}, P_i, v \rangle$
   then P_j sends the message $\langle \texttt{ready}, P_i, v \rangle$ to all participants.
4. If a participant P_j receives $2t + 1$ messages of the type $\langle \texttt{ready}, P_i, v \rangle$, then P_j accepts the message v from P_i.

Assume that $n = 3t + 1$. The intuition for the security of Bracha's broadcast primitive is as follows. First, if an honest participant P_i sends the value $\langle P_i, initial, v \rangle$, then all honest participant will receive this message and echo the message v. Then all honest participants send the ready message for v and all honest participants accept the message v.

Secondly, if honest participants P_{j_1} and P_{j_2} send ready messages for u and v respectively, then we must have $u = v$. This is due to the following fact. A participant P_j sends a $\langle \texttt{ready}, P_j, u \rangle$ message only if it receives $t + 1$ ready messages or $2t + 1$ echo messages. That is, there must be an honest participant who received $2t + 1$ echo messages for u. Since an honest participant can only send one message of each type, this means that all honest participants will only sends ready message for the value u.

In order for an honest participant P_j to accept a message u, it must receive $2t + 1$ ready messages. Among these messages, at least $t + 1$ ready messages are from honest participants. An honest participant can only send one message of each type. Thus if honest participants P_{j_1} and P_{j_2} accept messages u and v respectively, then we must have $u = v$. Furthermore, if a participant P_j accepts a message u, we just showed that at least $t + 1$ honest participants have sent the ready message for u. In other words, all honest participants will receive and send at least $t + 1$ ready message for u. By the argument from the preceding paragraph, each honest participant sends one ready message for u. That is, all honest participants will accept the message u.

References

1. Ali, M., Nelson, J., Blankstein, A.: Peer review: CBC Casper. https://medium.com/ @muneeb/peer-review-cbc-casper-30840a98c89a. Accessed 6 Dec 2018
2. Ben-Or, M.: Another advantage of free choice: Completely asynchronous agreement protocols (extended abstract). In: Proceedings of 2nd ACM PODC, pp. 27–30 (1983)
3. Bracha, G.: An asynchronous $[(n-1)/3]$-resilient consensus protocol. In: Proceedings of 3rd ACM PODC, pp. 154–162. ACM (1984)
4. Buterin, V., Griffith, V.: Casper the friendly finality gadget (2019)
5. Cachin, C., Kursawe, K., Shoup, V.: Random oracles in constantinople: practical asynchronous byzantine agreement using cryptography. J. Cryptol. **18**(3), 219–246 (2005)

6. Dolev, D., Strong, H.R.: Polynomial algorithms for multiple processor agreement. In: Proceedings of 14th ACM STOC, pp. 401–407. ACM (1982)
7. Dwork, C., Lynch, N., Stockmeyer, L.: Consensus in the presence of partial synchrony. JACM **35**(2), 288–323 (1988)
8. Fischer, M.J., Lynch, N.A., Paterson, M.S.: Impossibility of distributed consensus with one faulty process. JACM **32**(2), 374–382 (1985)
9. Katz, J., Koo, C.Y.: On expected constant-round protocols for byzantine agreement. J. Comput. Syst. Sci. **75**(2), 91–112 (2009)
10. Lamport, L.: The part-time parliament. ACM Trans. Comput. Syst. (TOCS) **16**(2), 133–169 (1998)
11. Lamport, L., Shostak, R., Pease, M.: The Byzantine generals problem. ACM Trans. Program. Lang. Syst. (TOPLAS) **4**(3), 382–401 (1982)
12. Ongaro, D., Ousterhout, J.: In search of an understandable consensus algorithm. In: 2014 USENIX Annual Technical Conference, pp. 305–319
13. Pease, M., Shostak, R., Lamport, L.: Reaching agreement in the presence of faults. JACM **27**(2), 228–234 (1980)
14. Rabin, M.O.: Randomized byzantine generals. In: 24th IEEE FOCS, pp. 403–409. IEEE (1983)
15. Research, E.: CBC Casper FAQ. https://github.com/ethereum/cbc-casper/wiki/FAQ. Acceesed 27 Nov 2018
16. Stewart, A., Kokoris-Kogia, E.: GRANDPA: a byzantine finality gadge. https://github.com/w3f/consensus/blob/master/pdf/grandpa.pdf. Accessed 19 June 2020
17. Zamfir, V.: Casper the friendly ghost: a correct by construction blockchain consensus protocol, https://github.com/ethereum/research/tree/master/papers. Accessed 18 Dec 2017
18. Zamfir, V., Rush, N., Asgaonkar, A., Piliouras, G.: Introducing the minimal CBC Casper family of consensus protocols. https://github.com/cbc-casper/. Accessed 5 Feb 2019

Privacy

Where to Meet a Driver Privately: Recommending Pick-Up Locations for Ride-Hailing Services

Yifei Chen[1,2,3,4], Meng Li[1,2,3,4]([✉]), Shuli Zheng[1,2,3,4], Chhagan Lal[5], and Mauro Conti[6]

[1] Key Laboratory of Knowledge Engineering with Big Data (Hefei University of Technology), Ministry of Education, Hefei, China
`yifeichen@mail.hfut.edu.cn, mengli@hfut.edu.cn`
[2] School of Computer Science and Information Engineering, Hefei University of Technology, Hefei, China
[3] Anhui Province Key Laboratory of Industry Safety and Emergency Technology, Hefei University of Technology, Hefei, China
[4] Intelligent Interconnected Systems Laboratory of Anhui Province, Hefei University of Technology, Hefei, China
[5] Delft University of Technology, Delft, Netherlands
`c.lal@tudelft.nl`
[6] Department of Mathematics, University of Padua, 35131 Padua, Italy
`conti@math.unipd.it`

Abstract. Ride-Hailing Service (RHS) has motivated the rise of innovative transportation services. It enables riders to hail a cab or private vehicle at the roadside by sending a ride request to the Ride-Hailing Service Provider (RHSP). Such a request collects rider's real-time locations, which incur serious privacy concerns for riders. While there are many location privacy-preserving mechanisms in the literature, few of them consider *mobility patterns* or *location semantics* in RHS. In this work, we propose a pick-up location recommendation scheme with location indistinguishability and semantic indistinguishability for RHS. Specifically, we give formal definitions of location indistinguishability and semantic indistinguishability. We model the rider mobility as a time-dependent first-order Markov chain and generates a rider's mobility profile. Next, it calculates the geographic similarity between riders by using the Mallows distance and classifies them into different geographic groups. To comprehend the semantics of a location, it extracts such information through user-generated content from two popular social networks and obtains the semantic representations of locations. Cosine similarity and unified hypergraph are used to compute the semantic similarities between locations. Finally, it outputs a set of recommended pick-up locations. To evaluate the performance, we build our mobility model over the real-world dataset GeoLife, analyze the computational costs of a rider, show the utility, and implement it on an Android smartphone. The experimental results show that it costs less than 0.12 ms to recommend 10 pick-up locations within 500 m of walking distance.

© Springer Nature Switzerland AG 2021
R. Roman and J. Zhou (Eds.): STM 2021, LNCS 13075, pp. 43–61, 2021.
https://doi.org/10.1007/978-3-030-91859-0_3

Keywords: Ride-hailing service · Location privacy · Mobility pattern · Location semantics · Android

1   Introduction

Ride-hailing service [19,20,25] (RHS) is now a ubiquitous application in vehicular networks [22,23,31]. It enables riders to be matched with available drivers in their vicinity [10]. A rider meets a driver at a pick-up location and they drive toward the rider's destination. To complete the matching between riders and drivers, a Ride-Hailing Service Provider (RHSP) is required and successful RHSPs include Uber and Didi. According to a report from Statista, RHSs enable 78 million people to enjoy rides using the Uber app on a monthly basis [24].

To find a driver, the rider has to upload a pick-up location to the RHSP for notifying the drivers in the area covering this location. However, location is highly related to rider's sensitive locations, e.g., home and work, and it calls for proper sanitation before sharing it with the RHSP. Furthermore, there are attacks against riders' location privacy, such as location inference attack [27] and membership inclusion attack [8].

Among all the ride activities, riders tend to hail a ride from the same location frequently as shown in Fig. 1. For example, Alice takes a cab to work every morning on weekdays. This observation is also supported by two latest works which call it spatiotemporal activity [9] and similar query [18]. There has been a large body of work on designing a Location Privacy-Preserving Mechanism (LPPM) [21]. In this work, we aim to protect riders' location privacy in such a setting, i.e., we protect the *true location* that could be masked by possible pick-up locations recommended via different LPPMs.

Fig. 1. A rider Alice frequently hails a ride near her home when using a RHS.

Existing LPPMs are mainly Differential Privacy (DP)-based approach [5,9,27,30] and cryptography-based approach [4,7,18]. The first one samples a random noise from a distribution (e.g., Laplace) and adds it to the location. This approach can be proven to be differentially private. The second one utilizes homomorphic encryption [7], private set intersection [4], and secure searchable encryption [18] to process locations, such that adversaries only have a negligible advantage on differentiating locations. Unfortunately, they cannot be applied to protect the true locations of riders in RHS. First, the DP-based schemes may output an odd location for the user to reach and they did not capture the mobility similarity between different users. Second, the cryptography schemes enforce too many computational burdens on users or server. Third, they did not consider the *semantic meanings* of locations for RHSs. It is shown that revealing information about the semantic type of locations can reduce geographical location privacy by 50% [6].

1.1 Motivations

Our motivation arises from achieving *location indistinguishability* and *semantic indistinguishability* of pick-up locations while defending the location inference attacks and the membership inclusion attack. Location indistinguishability refers to the new objective that a user's true location is indistinguishable from a group of nearby riders who share a similar mobility pattern. Semantic indistinguishability indicates that submitted locations from the same rider do not leak semantic information of the true location. We note that the semantic indistinguishability where is different from the one in modern cryptography [16] that applies to encryption domain.

1.2 Technical Challenges and Proposed Solution

To achieve our goals, we have two technical challenges to solve. **Challenge 1.** We should consider the mobility pattern of users who hail rides in the same area and find the ones who share the same mobility pattern with the target rider. How to calculate the mobility similarity of users is the first challenge. **Challenge 2.** We should define a specific region covering the riders above make the recommended location semantically different from the true location. How to calculate semantic distance between two locations is the second challenge. In summary, we need to make sure that a recommended location is indeed location indistinguishable as well as semantically dissimilar.

Intuitively, we recommend a set of pick-up locations in the following steps. First, we model the rider mobility (which reflects how a user moves in a city) as a time-dependent first-order Markov chain [26,28] on a set of locations. This is because users have a certain pattern of moving and it correlates with time. A rider's mobility profile is a transition probability matrix of the Markov chain related to the rider's mobility and visiting probability distribution over locations [8]. Second, we calculate the geographic similarity between riders by using the Mallows distance [17] and classify them into different geographic groups. We assume that there are at least k riders in each ride-hailing area, which constitutes k-anonymity (an adversary cannot distinguish a target user from other $k - 1$ users), but with stronger protection for absorbing their similar mobility pattern. We calculate the overlapping area of each alternative rider and the current rider. The resulted set of areas is prepared for finding semantically dissimilar locations later. Third, we extract location semantics through user generated contents (UGCs) from social networks and obtain the semantic representations of locations. The UGCs include business time, rating, and type. All the contents are collected from Gaode Map [1] and Google Maps [3] are preprocessed. We use cosine similarity [14, 29] to compute individual semantic similarities between locations from heterogeneous cues and fusion them in a unified hypergraph framework [15] to compute the semantic similarities between locations. Finally, we output a set of recommended pick-up locations. Riders can choose one location from the set to request their ride. To evaluate the performance of the proposed scheme, we build our mobility model upon a real-world dataset GeoLife [2, 11], and leverage the walking distance function and waiting time to show its utility.

1.3   Paper Organization

The remaining of this paper proceeds as below. We review some related work in Sect. 2. We elaborate on the system model, threat model, and design objectives in Sect. 3. We present the proposed scheme in Sect. 4. We formally analyze the privacy of the scheme in Sect. 5. In Sect. 6, we implement the system and analyze its performance. Lastly, we provide some discussions in Sect. 7 and conclude this paper in Sect. 8.

2   Related Work

2.1   General LPPMs

Shokri et al. [27] provided a formal framework for the analysis of LPPMs. Specifically, they provide a generic model to formalize inference attacks on location-information and evaluate the performance of such attacks. Next, they design and justify the metric to quantify location privacy. A location-privacy meter is proposed to evaluate the effectiveness of various LPPMs. They also show the inappropriateness of entropy and k-anonymity. Andrés et al. [5] proposed a formal definition of location privacy geo-indistinguishability, to protect users' locations, while enabling approximate information to be collected for obtaining location-based services. Such a definition formalizes the concept of preserving users' locations within a radius R with a privacy level. Its core idea is that, for any $R > 0$, the user has ϵR privacy within R, i.e., the privacy level is proportional to R. Cao et al. [9] extend differential privacy to ϵ-spatiotemporal event privacy by formally defining spatiotemporal event as Boolean expressions between location and time predicates. They design a framework to transform an existing LPPM into one preserving spatiotemporal event privacy against adversaries with any prior knowledge.

2.2   LPPM for Meeting Location Determination

There is some related work on protecting locations when a meeting location is to be determined. Bilogrevic et al. [7] formulate the Fair Rendez-Vous Point (FRVP) problem for a group of users as an optimization problem and propose two algorithms based on homomorphic cryptosystems for solving the FRVP problem in a privacy-preserving way. Each user provides only a single location preference to a server. However, this approach brings extra communication costs to users and computational costs to the server. Aïvodji et al. [4] utilized privacy-enhancing technologies and multimodal shortest path algorithms to compute meeting points for both drivers and riders in ride-sharing services. Rider and drivers identify potential locations locally and collaboratively compute common pick-up locations via a private information retrieval method. However, it requires too much computation and communication burden onto users. Zhang et al. [30] designed a location privacy protection scheme ShiftRoute for navigation services. It enables users to query a route without disclosing any meaningful location information. Its main idea is to selectively shift the start point/endpoint to the ones close-by and guarantee that the semantic meanings of the two points change much but preserve service usability. However, ShiftRoute only defines a simple semantic distance function with two outputs 0 and 1, which are far from enough.

3   Problem Formulation

3.1   System Model

Different from a typical system model of RHS, which consists of rider, driver, and RHSP, our system model mainly focuses on the rider. We aim to recommend pick-up locations locally on the rider side, and we do not rely on another party to compute the locations. The rider is a user requesting a ride on the roadside by sending a ride request via a smartphone application to the RHSP. The original ride request includes a true (current) location and a destination. The true location is assumed to be a frequently visited location of the rider, e.g., home and work. Each rider has an acceptable walking distance $wDis$ and an acceptable waiting time wt of location recommendation. Here, the $wDis()$ is computed by invoking a walking distance computing function from Gaode. After the rider inputs a true location tl and a destination de, the application will automatically calculate a set of recommended locations for the rider to choose from. The key notations are listed in Table 1.

3.2   Threat Model

The privacy threat is raised from the honest-but-curious RHSP and passive adversaries observing from outside of the system. It is against the users whose trajectories are sampled in our algorithm. In this case, the adversary knows that all submitted locations are generated. His attack agenda is to extract location or semantic information about the true locations of users.

3.3   Design Objectives

We have three design objectives for recommending a pick-up location: location indistinguishability and semantic indistinguishability, while not sacrificing utility.

Table 1. Key notations

Notations	Meaning
tl, de	True location, destination
rl	Recommended location
$\mathcal{ML}$	Set of marked locations on the map
$\mathcal{RL}$	Set of recommended locations
K	Number of locations in $\mathcal{RL}$
$\mathcal{C}$	Textual description repository
$wDis$	Walking distance between two locations
wt	Waiting time of location recommendation
Sim_g	Geographic similarity between two riders
Sim_s	Semantic similarity between two locations
α	Required minimum of geographic similarity
β	Required maximum of semantic similarity

- **Location indistinguishability.** We need to guarantee location indistinguishability between (1) the current rider and his/her nearby $k-1$ riders and (2) the recommended locations and their true location underneath. We use a function $\mathsf{Sim}_g(l_i, l_j)$ to measure the geographic similarity between two locations l_i, l_j. We require that the geographic distance between the recommended location rl and the true location tl is bigger than α, i.e., $\mathsf{Dis}(rl, tl) > \alpha$. We give a formal definition of location indistinguishability as follows.

Definition 1 (Location indistinguishability). *Given k riders with a similar mobility pattern, an adversary $\mathcal{A}$ cannot distinguish 1) a rider r_i from the other $k-1$ riders, and 2) a recommended location l from the true location tl, i.e.,*

$$|\Pr[\mathcal{A}(l_{r_i}) = r_i] - \Pr[\mathcal{A}(l_{r_j}) = r_i]| \leq \mathrm{negl}(k), j \in [1, i-1] \wedge [i, k],$$
$$|\Pr[\mathcal{A}(l) = tl] - \Pr[\mathcal{A}(tl) = tl]| \leq \mathrm{negl}(k).$$

- **Semantic indistinguishability.** Besides the location indistinguishability, we have to consider the semantic meaning of pick-up locations such that the semantic of true location cannot be acquired from one of recommended locations. We define a function $\mathsf{Sim}_s(l_i, l_j)$ to measure the semantic similarity between two locations l_i, l_j. We require that the semantic similarity between the recommended location rl and the true location tl is small than β, i.e., $\mathsf{Dis}(rl, tl) < \beta$. We give a formal definition of semantic indistinguishability as follows.

Definition 2 (Semantic indistinguishability). *Given a recommended location l, its true location tl, and a semantic function $Sim()$, an adversary $\mathcal{A}$ cannot distinguish l from tl, i.e.,*

$$|\Pr[\mathcal{A}(l, Sim(l)) = tl] - \Pr[\mathcal{A}(tl, Sim(tl)) = tl]| \leq \mathrm{negl}(k).$$

- **Utility.** Even though we aim to protect the location privacy of riders, we cannot ignore utility. We do not want riders to walk too far away from their true locations, which is the walking distance $wDis(rl, tl)$ between the recommended location rl and the true location tl. In addition, to guarantee user experience, we also have to control the local computational costs so that the recommendation process does not incur too much waiting time wt for riders. Given that different users may have different requirements on utility, $wDis$ and wt can vary according to their own choices.

4   Proposed Scheme

In this section, we first give an overview of our proposed scheme and then present the detailed steps.

4.1   Overview

We now provide an overview of our scheme in Fig. 2. In step 1, we model the rider mobility as a time-dependent first-order Markov chain [26, 28] on a set of locations. In step 2, we obtain the mobility models of all riders. In step 3, we compute the mobility similarity between riders and build a location similarity graph of riders. In step 4, we compute the location distance between riders and choose $k - 1$ riders. Till here, we have acquired the geographic similarity between riders. In step 5, we comprehend the location semantics from heterogeneous UGCs. In step 6, we compute the semantic similarity between marked locations on the map and build a similarity graph of locations. In step 7, we compute the semantic distance between locations and choose from dissimilar locations. Finally, we recommend a set of locations to the rider. We provide the details of our recommendation scheme in Algorithm 1.

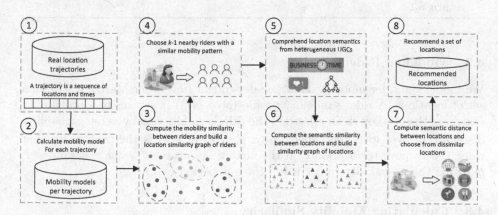

Fig. 2. Overview of recommendation algorithm.

Algorithm 1: Recommendation Algorithm

Input: r_i, tl, de

Output: $\mathcal{RL}$

//Read Riders' Trajectories

Store a rider's trajectory as a sequence of locations and times;

//Calculating Mobility Model

for $(j = 1; j \leq n; j++)$ **do**

   Model the rider mobility as a time-dependent first-order Markov chain;

   Compute the r_i's mobility profile $\langle p(r_i), g(r_i) \rangle$;

//Computing Mobility Similarity

for $(j = 1; j \leq n \land j \neq i; j++)$ **do**

   Compute $\mathbb{E}[M_d(p_{l,t}^{l',t'}(r_i), p_{l,t}^{l'',t'}(r_j))]$;

   Compute $\mathsf{Sim}_g(r_i, r_j) = 1 - \frac{\mathbb{E}[M_d(p_{l,t}^{l',t'}(r_i), p_{l,t}^{l'',t'}(r_j))]}{con}$;

//Rider Section

Select $k - 1$ riders with the smallest Sim_g with r_i;

//Comprehending Location Semantics

Form a minimum circle $\mathcal{C}$ covering the k users;

Collect a location set $\mathcal{ML}$ of all the marked locations in $\mathcal{C}$;

for $(i = 1; i \leq |\mathcal{ML}|; i++)$ **do**

   Compute three semantic vectors for l_i from $\mathcal{B}, \mathcal{R}, \mathcal{T}$;

//Computing Semantic Similarity

for $(i = 1, j = 1; i, j \leq |\mathcal{ML}|, i \neq j; i++, j++, \mathcal{D} = \mathcal{B}, \mathcal{R}, \mathcal{T})$ **do**

   Compute $\mathsf{Sim}_s^{\mathcal{D}}(l_i, l_j) = \frac{\mathbf{v}_{l_i}^{\mathcal{D}} \cdot \mathbf{v}_{l_i}^{\mathcal{D}}}{||\mathbf{v}_{l_i}^{\mathcal{D}}|| ||\mathbf{v}_{l_j}^{\mathcal{D}}||}$;

//Computing Semantic Distance

Construct a hypergraph to compute $\mathsf{Sim}_s(l_i, l_j) = f[j]$;

Form K groups based on their semantic distances;

//Recommending Locations

Randomly choose K locations from K groups;

Insert the chosen locations to $\mathcal{RL}$;

return $\mathcal{RL}$;

4.2 Modeling Rider Mobility

We model the rider mobility as a time-dependent first-order Markov chain on a set of locations. A rider's mobility profile $\langle p(r), g(r) \rangle$ is a transition probability matrix of the Markov chain related to the rider's mobility and visiting probability distribution over locations. Specifically, $p_{l,t}^{l',t'}(r)$ of $p(r)$ is the probability that rider r will move to location l' in the next time instant t' when r is now at l. $g_{l,t}(r)$ is the probability that r is in l in time period t.

4.3 Calculating Mobility Similarity

Assume that now we are to recommend a set of pick-up locations for a current rider r at a true location tl. We compute the mobility similarity as follows.

- The geographic similarity captures the correlation between trajectories that are generated by two rider's mobility profiles. It indicates whether two riders visit similar locations over time with similar probabilities and if they move between those locations also with similar probabilities [8]. We compute the geographic similarity of two riders based on Mallows distance. The dissimilarity of two mobility profiles $\langle p(r), g(r) \rangle$ and $\langle p(s), g(s) \rangle$ is defined as the Mallows distance of the next random locations l' and l'':

$$\mathbb{E}[M_d(p_{l,t}^{l',t'}(r), p_{l,t}^{l'',t'}(s))], \tag{1}$$

where d is an arbitrary distance function and the expectation is calculated over random variable l and time periods l and l'.

- The geographic similarity between two mobility patterns of r and s is defined as:

$$\mathsf{Sim}_g(r,s) = 1 - \frac{\mathbb{E}[M_d(p_{l,t}^{l',t'}(r), p_{l,t}^{l'',t'}(s))]}{con}, \tag{2}$$

where con is a constant ensuring that the Sim_g stays between 0 and 1.

Next, we compute the geographic similarity between r and other riders, and select the nearby $k-1$ riders with a similar mobility pattern to the current rider as depicted in Fig. 3. As new riders and their trajectories join, we will update the circle and renew the location pool.

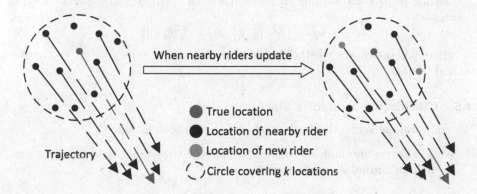

Fig. 3. Circling k riders with similar mobility pattern and updating the circle.

4.4 Comprehending Location Semantics

Given the other $k-1$ riders, we collect the $k-1$ locations from the $k-1$ users that are near tl and form a minimum circle that is covering all the k users. Next, we collect a location set of all the marked locations $\mathcal{ML}$ in the circle on the map, e.g., supermarket, shoe store, barber shop, and restaurant. Since the heterogeneous UGCs capture semantics of a location, we comprehend them in $\mathcal{ML}$ from four aspects: business time, rating, and type.

– Business time is shown for an open venue, e.g., "08:00-16:00" for a Tim Hortons coffee shop. Different business time indicates the type of a location to some extent. We quantize the business time into 48 time zones a day, i.e., half an hour for each time zone. For each location l_i, the business time is separated and put into the corresponding bin. The business time distribution vector of a location venue is the histogram of business time associated to the location

$$\mathbf{v}_{l_i}^{\mathcal{B}} = [f_{l_i}^{\mathcal{B}}(1), f_{l_i}^{\mathcal{B}}(2), ..., f_{l_i}^{\mathcal{B}}(48)], \tag{3}$$

where $f_{l_i}^{\mathcal{B}}(j)$ denotes the openness of the location at time j, i.e., 1 means open and 0 otherwise. However, we observe that not all locations are open to public, e.g., a commercial building/university that requires an entrance guard card/student ID card to enter. For these locations, we manually mark their business time distribution vector as $[0, 0, ..., 0]$.

– Rating r_{l_i} reveals customers' opinions toward a location. They are usually adopting the five-star rating mechanism on many social networks. We extract the ratings and generate a rating vector

$$\mathbf{v}_{l_i}^{\mathcal{R}} = [f_{l_i}^{\mathcal{R}}(1), f_{l_i}^{\mathcal{R}}(2), ..., f_{l_i}^{\mathcal{R}}(5)], \tag{4}$$

where $f_{l_i}^{\mathcal{R}}(5 - j) = 1$ for $0 \le j < 5$ if $j < r_{l_i}$ and $f_{l_i}^{\mathcal{R}}(5 - j) = 0$ otherwise. For example, $\mathbf{v}_{l_i}^{\mathcal{R}} = [0, 1, 1, 1, 1]$ when $r_{l_i} = 4$.

– Type shows the classification of a location. We use the POI classification method from Gaode Maps [1] and extract the ratings and generate a type vector

$$\mathbf{v}_{l_i}^{\mathcal{T}} = [f_{l_i}^{\mathcal{T}}(1), f_{l_i}^{\mathcal{T}}(2), ..., f_{l_i}^{\mathcal{T}}(23)], \tag{5}$$

where $f_{l_i}^{\mathcal{T}}(j)$ denotes whether the location belongs to type j, i.e., 1 means yes and 0 otherwise.

4.5   Calculating Semantic Similarity

We compute the semantic similarity between locations as follows.

– We use the cosine similarity metric to compute the similarity of two locations at each individual dimension

$$\mathsf{Sim}_s^D(l_i, l_j) = \frac{\mathbf{v}_{l_i}^{\mathcal{D}} \cdot \mathbf{v}_{l_i}^{\mathcal{D}}}{||\mathbf{v}_{l_i}^{\mathcal{D}}||||\mathbf{v}_{l_j}^{\mathcal{D}}||}, \tag{6}$$

where $\mathcal{D} = \mathcal{B}, \mathcal{R}, \mathcal{T}$. The semantic distance between two locations is denoted as $\mathsf{Dis}_s(l_i, l_j) = 1 - \mathsf{Sim}_s^D(l_i, l_j)$. $\overline{\mathsf{Dis}^{\mathcal{D}}}$ denotes the mean value of elements in the Dth distance matrix.

– Based on the hypergraph framework, we take each location venue as a centroid and collect the k-nearest neighbors. The hyperedge weight is calculated as

$$we(e) = \sum_{v_i, v_j \in e} \mathbf{A}_{ij}, \tag{7}$$

where $\mathbf{A}_{ij}$ is the affinity between vertex v_i and v_j. $\mathbf{A}_{ij} = \exp\left(-\sum_{D=1}^{3} \frac{\mathsf{Dis}_{ij}^D}{3\overline{\mathsf{Dis}^D}}\right)$.

- We construct the hypergraph for location semantics and compute the hypergraph Laplacian, then we select a query location l_i and use a query vector $y \in R^{|\mathcal{ML}|}$, only the entry corresponding to the query location is set to be 1 and all others are set to 0. After solving the linear system $(\mu I + \Delta)f = \mu y$ where Δ is the hypergraph Laplacian matrix, we obtain the ranking scores $f \in R^{|\mathcal{ML}|}$ [15].
- We perform an normalization method on ranking scores f. Finally, the similarity between the query location l_i and an other location l_j is

$$\mathsf{Sim}_s(l_i, l_j) = f[j]. \tag{8}$$

- Finally, we build a semantic similarity graph of all the marked locations and tl by classifying the locations into K groups according to their semantic similarity.

We note that we need to filter some noises when handling business time and ratings from UGCs. Some locations do not have the information of business time or rating. For these locations, we manually mark their business time as the one of the locations in their same classification that have the most probable business time. We also rate these locations as three stars as default.

4.6   Recommending a Set of Pick-Up Locations

After obtaining the semantic similarity graph, we randomly choose K locations from K different groups that have a low semantic similarity to tl and form a set of recommended locations $\mathcal{RL}$. Specifically, we set the business time of tl as "19:00-08:00" [12] and rating as the sequence of the unit price range in the city, which lays a foundation for semantic distance calculation. For example, we divide the unit prices of residence communities in Beijing into five ranges $[0, 50000]$, $[50001, 100000]$, $[150001, 200000]$, $[250001, 300000]$, and $[300001, \infty]$. If the unit price of a residence community is 120000 yuan, then it belongs to the second unit price range and its rating is $[0, 0, 0, 1, 1]$, which is similar to the rating mechanism. To satisfy the real demands of riders, we provide two metrics for them, i.e., walking distance between two locations $wDis$ and waiting time wt. We consider these two metrics during the selection of $k - 1$ riders as well as K marked locations.

5   Privacy and Security Analysis

5.1   Location Indistinguishability

We model the mobility patterns for riders and compute the geographic similarity between $k - 1$ nearby riders with the current rider r. Next, we classify the nearest $k - 1$ riders with r. A minimum circle covering the k riders is calculated as the potential area within which we recommend a pick-up location. By doing so, an adversary cannot differentiate r from other $k - 1$ riders within this circle since the users of these true locations inside the circle all share a similar mobility pattern. Thus location indistinguishability between the current rider and his/her nearby $k - 1$ riders is achieved, i.e., $|\Pr[\mathcal{A}(l_{r_i}) = r_i] - \Pr[\mathcal{A}(l_{r_j}) = r_i]| \leq \mathrm{negl}(k), j \in [1, i - 1] \wedge [i, k]$.

Instead of generating noise and adding it to the true location, we only recommend a marked locations on the map excluding the true location. Meanwhile, we update the circle with the trajectories such that new marked locations will be added to the location pool. More importantly, we do not leak any useful information of the true location by releasing the recommended location. In this way, an adversary cannot infer the true location from the recommended locations, thus achieving location indistinguishability between the recommended locations and its true location underneath, i.e., $|\Pr[\mathcal{A}(l) = tl] - \Pr[\mathcal{A}(tl) = tl]| \leq \mathrm{negl}(k)$.

5.2   Semantic Indistinguishability

Based on the circle we have calculated from users' mobility patterns, we comprehend the semantics of all the marked location on the map and classify them according to their semantic similarities. Locations with similar semantics are grouped and separated from the ones with dissimilar semantic meanings. Next, we only choose K locations from K different semantic groups. The semantic similarity between this group and the one to which the true location belongs to is less than a threshold β. Therefore, an adversary cannot acquire the semantic of the true location from the one observed from the recommended locations which have distant semantic meanings, achieving semantic indistinguishability, i.e., $|\Pr[\mathcal{A}(l, Sim(l)) = tl] - \Pr[\mathcal{A}(tl, Sim(tl)) = tl]| \leq \mathrm{negl}(k)$.

6   Performance Evaluation

6.1   Experimental Settings

We implement the recommendation algorithm on a desktop with AMD Ryzen5 3600 CPU, 16 GB memory, and Windows 10 professional operating system. The experimental parameters and their values are listed in Table 2.

Table 2. Experimental parameters

Parameters	Value
k	12
K	5
$wDis$ (meters)	[10, 500]
wt (millisecond)	(0, 100]
α	0.7
β	0.3

6.2 Dataset

The dataset is GeoLife 1.3 [2] collected in a Microsoft project which consists of 18, 760 trajectories with 24, 876, 978 locations and 50, 186 h. The mean number of points of each trajectory is 1,332, and the mean duration of the trajectories is 7.26 min. As it did not explicitly mark the home or work for users, we only choose a set of trajectories that resemble those covering home and work.

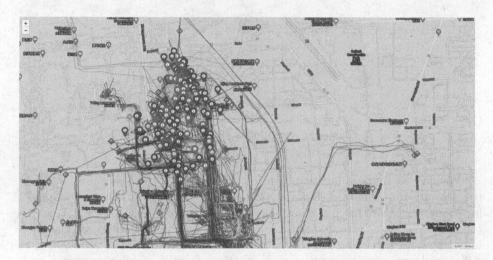

Fig. 4. Marking green start points, red endpoints, and trajectories for users. (Color figure online)

6.3 Computational Costs

Now we analyze the computational costs of processing trajectory dataset, finding $k-1$ riders with similar mobility pattern, and finding K locations with dissimilar semantic at the rider side. We first cluster the star points and endpoints of 182 users by using DBSCAN [13] to observe potentially similar trajectories, as shown in Fig. 4 and Fig. 5. It takes us 19.6 min to finish the clustering and obtain 581 trajectory groups. Since we need to define "same location", we cluster adjacent locations within each trajectory group. For example, we choose the #1 group with 12 users, which takes 360 ms to model their mobility patterns, i.e., computing their transition probability matrix.

Next, we compute all the 11 geographic similarities for all the 12 users. As shown in Fig. 6, the time of comparing with 11 users is approximately 7 s, i.e., it costs less than 1 s to compute one geographic similarity for one pair of users. Afterward, we compute a minimum circle with a radius of 500 m covering the obtained k locations and process the semantics of all the marked locations in the circle.

Fig. 5. Clustering start points and endpoints for users.

We find 83 marked locations within this circle. In the beginning, we need to compute the semantic similarity between the home and the remaining 82 locations. We show the time costs of 10 different home locations in Fig. 7, where the time cost is less than 0.03 ms. Automatically, the 82 locations are classified into 10 groups according to their similarity with the one of hl of a target rider. Afterwards, we can select the top K locations from K similarity groups with the smallest semantic similarity. It is to be noted that modeling the mobility patterns, computing geographic similarity, drawing the circle, and classifying locations, could be preprocessed locally for each rider, thus saving the time.

6.4   Utility

To analyze the utility, we consider two metrics for riders, namely walking distance $wDis$ and waiting time wt. We first compute the walking distance from tl to other 82 locations by querying the cloud server in the normal way. Each query takes an average of 103 ms which is considered as pre-processing time. We set the K and $wDis$ as variables and see how much time the rider has to wait for in average. If a recommended pick-up location does not coincide with the $wDis$, we select the next pick-up locations with less semantic dissimilarity. From Fig. 8, when K is fixed, the waiting time increases with $wDis$ because we will have more optional locations and it takes more time to compute the semantic similarity. When $wDis$ is fixed, the walking time also increases with K for processing more locations. The reason behind the existence of several odd points is that the corresponding two variables require more search in the location pool. Finally, the recommendation time of selecting 10 pick-up locations within 500 m of walking distance is less than 0.12 ms.

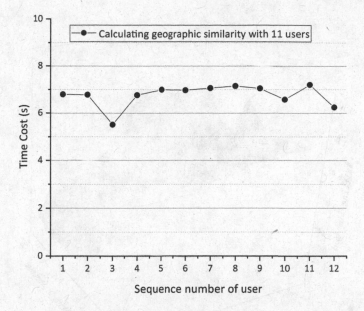

Fig. 6. Time cost in computing geographic similarity.

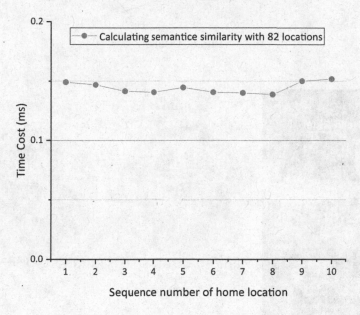

Fig. 7. Time cost in computing semantic similarity.

6.5   Android Implementation

We also implement our recommendation scheme on an Android smartphone. We perform preprocessing on the rider end, including modeling the mobility pat-

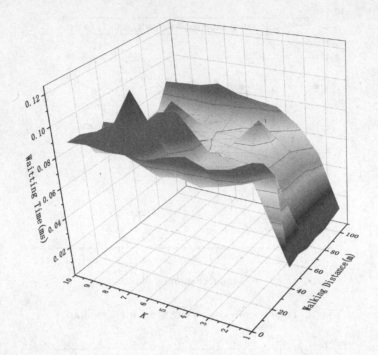

Fig. 8. Utility.

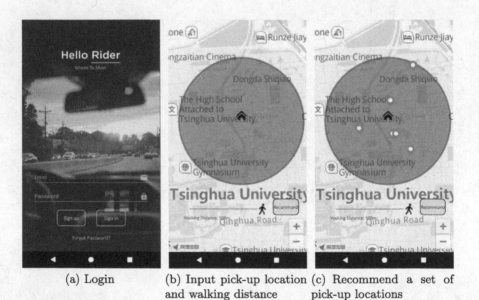

(a) Login   (b) Input pick-up location   (c) Recommend a set of
                  and walking distance   pick-up locations

Fig. 9. Android application

terns, computing geographic similarity, drawing the circle, classifying locations, and computing semantic similarity. As shown in Fig. 9, after logging in the ride-hailing app, the rider selects the home location and walking distance, and presses the recommendation button to obtain a set of pick-up locations.

7   Discussions

7.1 k-Anonymity

We assume that there are at least k riders in the ride-hailing area of the target rider, which constitutes k-anonymity. Meanwhile, we provide stronger protection for absorbing their similar mobility pattern. If this assumption does not hold, say there are not enough riders in the area, we can leverage the residence communities nearby as a backup approach.

7.2   Protection of Destination

Although the location recommendation scheme in this work is mainly designed for the pick-up location, it is also applicable to the protection of destinations. This is because the process of the two types of locations are the same since they have nearby riders and residence communities. All the considerations for pick-up locations are applicable to the destinations.

8   Conclusions and Future Work

In this work, we consider both mobility patterns and location semantics in choosing a pick-up location for ride-hailing services. A recommendation scheme with location indistinguishability and semantic indistinguishability is proposed. We model riders' mobility patterns as a time-dependent first-order Markov chain and compute the geographic similarity between riders by using the Mallows distance. We further comprehend the semantics of locations based on user generated contents from social networks and compute the semantic similarity between locations by using cosine similarity and a unified hypergraph. The experimental results over real-world dataset and an Android smartphone show that it only costs less than 0.12 ms to recommend 10 pick-up locations within 500 m of walking distance.

The future work is aimed at 1) further exploiting the theoretic aspects of the proposed scheme, and 2) experimenting on a large scale dataset to evaluate the efficacy and efficiency of the algorithm.

Acknowledgment. The work described in this paper was supported by National Natural Science Foundation of China (NSFC) under the grant No. 62002094 and Anhui Provincial Natural Science Foundation under the grant No. 2008085MF196. It is partially supported by EU LOCARD Project under Grant H2020-SU-SEC-2018-832735. This work was carried out during the tenure of an ERCIM 'Alain Bensoussan' Fellowship Programme granted to Dr. Meng Li.

References

1. Gaode Map. https://lbs.amap.com. Accessed 15 Apr 2021
2. GeoLife GPS Trajectories. https://www.microsoft.com/en-us/download/details.aspx?id=52367. Accessed 15 Apr 2021
3. Google Maps. https://developers.google.com/maps. Accessed 15 Apr 2021
4. Aïvodji, U.M., Gambs, S., Huguet, M.J., Killijian, M.O.: Meeting points in ridesharing: a privacy-preserving approach. Transp. Res. Part C **72**, 239–253 (2016)
5. Andrés, M.E., Bordenabe, N.E., Chatzikokolakis, K., Palamidessi, C.: Geo-indistinguishability: differential privacy for location-based systems. In: Proceedings of 20th ACM Conference on Computer and Communications Security (CCS), Germany, pp. 901–914, November 2013
6. Ağır, B., Huguenin, K., Hengartner, U., Hubaux, J.P.: On the privacy implications of location semantics. In: Proceedings of 16th Privacy Enhancing Technologies (PETS), pp. 165–183, October 2016
7. Bilogrevic, I., Jadliwala, M., Joneja, V., Kalkan, K., Hubaux, J.P., Aad, I.: Privacy-preserving optimal meeting location determination on mobile devices. IEEE Trans. Inf. Forensics Secur. (TIFS) **9**(7), 1141–1156 (2014)
8. Bindschaedler, V., Shorki, R.: Synthesizing plausible privacy-preserving location traces. In: Proceedings of 37th IEEE Symposium on Security and Privacy (S&P), pp. 546–563, May 2016
9. Cao, Y., Xiao, Y., Xiong, L., Bai, L., Yoshikawa, M.: Protecting spatiotemporal event privacy in continuous location-based services. IEEE Trans. Knowl. Data Eng. (TKDE) **99**, 1–13 (2019)
10. Chen, Y., Li, M., Zheng, S., Hu, D., Lai, C., Conti, M.: One-time, oblivious, and unlinkable query processing over encrypted data on cloud. In: Proceedings of 22nd International Conference on Information and Communications Security (ICICS), Copenhagen, Denmark, pp. 350–365, August 2020
11. Chen, Z., Shen, H.T., Zhou, X., Zheng, Y., Xie, X.: Searching trajectories by locations: an efficiency study. In: Proceedings of 29th ACM SIGMOD International Conference on Management of Data (SIGMOD), Indiana, USA, pp. 255–266, June 2010
12. Drakonakis, K., Ilia, P., Ioannidis, S., Polakis, J.: Please forget where i was last summer: the privacy risks of public location (meta)data. In: Proceedings of 26th Annual Network and Distributed System Security Symposium (NDSS), USA, February 2019
13. Ester, M., Kriegel, H.P., Sander, J., Xu, X.: A density-based algorithm for discovering clusters a density-based algorithm for discovering clusters in large spatial databases with noise. In: Proceedings of 2nd International Conference on Knowledge Discovery and Data Mining (KDD), Portland, USA, pp. 226–231, August 1996
14. Huang, A.: Similarity measures for text document clustering. In: Proceedings of Sixth New Zealand Computer Science Research Student Conference (NZCSRSC), Christchurch, New Zealand, pp. 49–56 (2008)
15. Huang, Y.: Hypergraph based visual categorization and segmentation. Ph.D. thesis, Rutgers Univ., New Brunswick, USA (2010)
16. Katz, J., Lindell, Y.: Introduction to Modern Cryptography, 2nd edn. Chapman and Hall/CRC (2014)
17. Levina, E., Bickel, P.: The earth mover's distance is the mallows distance: some insights from statistics. In: Proceedings of 8th IEEE International Conference on Computer Vision (ICCV), Vancouver, Canada, pp. 251–256 (2001)

18. Li, M., Chen, Y., Zheng, S., Hu, D., Lal, C., Conti, M.: Privacy-preserving navigation supporting similar queries in vehicular networks. IEEE Trans. Dependable Secure Comput. (TDSC) **99**, 1–16 (2020). https://doi.org/10.1109/TDSC.2020.3017534

19. Li, M., Gao, J., Chen, Y., Zhao, J., Alazab, M.: Privacy-preserving ride-hailing with verifiable order-linking in vehicular networks. In: Proceedings of 19th International Conference on Trust, Security and Privacy in Computing and Communications (TrustCom), Guangzhou, China, pp. 599–606, December 2020

20. Li, M., Zhu, L., Lin, X.: CoRide: a privacy-preserving collaborative-ride hailing service using blockchain-assisted vehicular fog computing. In: Proceedings of ACM 15th EAI International Conference on Security and Privacy in Communication Networks (SecureComm), Orlando, USA, pp. 408–422, October 2019

21. Li, M., Zhu, L., Lin, X.: Privacy-preserving traffic monitoring with false report filtering via fog-assisted vehicular crowdsensing. IEEE Trans. Serv. Comput. (TSC) **99**, 1–11 (2019). https://doi.org/10.1109/TSC.2019.2903060

22. Li, M., Zhu, L., Zhang, Z., Xu, R.: Differentially private publication scheme for trajectory data. In: Proceedings of 1st IEEE International Conference on Data Science in Cyberspace (DSC), Changsha, China, pp. 596–601, June 2016

23. Li, M., Zhu, L., Zhang, Z., Xu, R.: Achieving differential privacy of trajectory data publishing in participatory sensing. Inf. Sci. **400–401**, 1–13 (2017). https://doi.org/10.1016/j.ins.2017.03.015

24. Mazareanu, E.: Monthly number of uber's active users worldwide from 2017 to 2020, by quarter (in millions) (2020). https://www.statista.com/statistics/833743/us-users-ride-sharing-services. Accessed 15 Apr 2021

25. Pham, A., Dacosta, I., Endignoux, G., Troncoso-Pastoriza, J., Huguenin, K., Hubaux, J.P.: ORide: a privacy-preserving yet accountable ride-hailing service. In: Vancouver, C. (ed.) Proceedings of 26th USENIX Security Symposium (USENIX Security), pp. 1235–1252 (2017)

26. Sahina, A.D., Sen, Z.: First-order Markov chain approach to wind speed modelling. J. Wind Eng. Ind. Aerodyn. **89**, 263–269 (2001)

27. Shokri, R., Theodorakopoulos, G., Boudec, J.Y.L., Hubaux, J.P.: Quantifying location privacy. In: Proceedings of 32th IEEE Symposium on Security and Privacy (S&P), Oakland, USA, pp. 247–262, May 2011

28. Tan, C.C., Beaulieu, N.C.: On first-order Markov modeling for the Rayleigh fading channel. IEEE Trans. Commun. **48**(12), 2032–2040 (2000)

29. Wang, X., et al.: Semantic-based location recommendation with multimodal venue semantics. IEEE Trans. Multimed. (TMM) **17**(3), 409–419 (2015)

30. Zhang, P., Hu, C., Chen, D., Li, H., Li, Q.: ShiftRoute: achieving location privacy for map services on smartphones. IEEE Trans. Veh. Technol. (TVT) **67**(5), 4527–4538 (2018)

31. Zhu, L., Li, M., Zhang, Z., Qin, Z.: ASAP: an anonymous smart-parking and payment scheme in vehicular networks. IEEE Trans. Dependable Secure Comput. (TDSC) **17**(4), 703–715 (2020). https://doi.org/10.1109/TDSC.2018.2850780

Efficient Permutation Protocol for MPC in the Head

Peeter Laud$^{(\boxtimes)}$ (iD)

Cybernetica AS, Tartu, Estonia
`peeter.laud@cyber.ee`

Abstract. The *MPC-in-the-head* construction (Ishai et al., STOC'07) gives zero-knowledge proofs from secure multiparty computation (MPC) protocols. This paper presents an efficient MPC protocol for permuting a vector of values, making use of the relaxed communication model that can be handled by the MPC-in-the-head transformation. Our construction allows more efficient ZK proofs for relations expressed in the Random Access Machine (RAM) model. We benchmark our construction and compare it against other reasonable constructions of permutations under the MPC-in-the-head transformation and conclude that it significantly improves on efficiency and the range of applicability.

Keywords: Zero-knowledge proofs · MPC-in-the-head · Random Access Machine

1 Introduction

Zero-knowledge proofs (ZKP) are cryptographic protocols that allow one party—the Prover—to convince another party—the Verifier—in the correctness of a statement, with the Verifier learning nothing besides the fact that the statement holds. The language of statements and their truth values are given in terms of a specified relation $R \subseteq \{0,1\}^* \times \{0,1\}^*$. A statement is some $x \in \{0,1\}^*$, known both to the Prover and the Verifier. The Prover attempts to convince the Verifier that there exists some w (or: the Prover knows some w), such that $(x, w) \in R$.

There exist different techniques for turning the description of the relation R into a ZKP, based on various kinds of interactive proofs, or different secure multiparty computation techniques. They work best when R is represented as an arithmetic circuit, or a boolean circuit. In practice, we express R in some programming language; large parts of it may already be given to us in case we want to present a proof that a certain computer program behaves in a certain manner. Hence, we want to give zero-knowledge proofs for relations expressed in the *Random Access Machine* (RAM) model.

Translating the description of R given in the RAM model into a ZKP is less straightforward. Generic transformations from RAM to circuits incur at least quadratic overheads [37]. For smaller overheads, one separately translates the behaviour of the processing unit, and the behaviour of the memory. These two

R. Roman and J. Zhou (Eds.): STM 2021, LNCS 13075, pp. 62–80, 2021.
https://doi.org/10.1007/978-3-030-91859-0_4

behaviours have to be related to each other, and this requires showing that the load- and store-operations read and write the same values at both sides. Showing the equality of loaded and stored values requires us to sort these actions by the memory addresses; in ZKP, this amounts to proving that two vectors are permutations of each other, and to a sortedness check of one of the vectors.

A universal representation for permutations works by fixing a routing network [4,42], and giving the bits that state how each switching element must route its two incoming values. This representation is equally well usable with any ZKP technique. If there have been m memory operations in the program, then the size of the routing network is *linearithmic*—$O(m \log m)$. If m is close to the total number of operations that the relation R (expressed as a program) performs, then the size of the routing network may be the dominant component in the translation of R into a ZKP.

MPC-in-the-head [25] is a ZKP technique that internally makes use of secure multiparty computation protocols. In practical comparisons with other techniques, it has good running time for the Prover, a decent running time for the Verifier, but longer proofs. Nevertheless, there are a number of ZK proof systems built upon this technique [1,8,18]. The MPC-in-the-head technique is also expected to compose well with other ZKP techniques.

In this paper, we propose a $O(n)$-complexity MPC-in-the-head based method to verify the correctness of the application of a permutation to a vector of values. Our method, which is basically a secure multiparty computation protocol for a communication model that fits into the MPC-in-the-head technique, can be composed with other protocols in the same communication model, hence bringing down the complexity of ZKP protocols for relations represented in the RAM model. We present our construction in Sect. 4, after discussing related work in Sect. 2 and giving the preliminaries in Sect. 3.

To appreciate our result, its location deep down in the technology stack has to be recognized. We give a MPC subroutine, which can be composed with other MPC operations using the same data representations in order to build a MPC protocol in a particular communication model, that evaluates the relation R in a manner that small coalitions of parties do not learn anything about the witness w. Onto this MPC protocol, one can apply the MPC-in-the-head transformation of Ishai et al. [25] that turns it into a ZKP protocol for the relation R. Hence, our subroutine is not a standalone protocol; in particular, it is not a mix-net. Also, any complexity results of our subroutine have to be considered in the context of the MPC-in-the-head transformation.

2   Related Work

Zero-knowledge proofs were first proposed in [22]. In this section, we cannot hope to give an overview of all the advancements thereafter. Rather, we refer to the course notes [40] discussing interactive proofs and their zero-knowledge variants.

The MPC-in-the-head construction was proposed in [25,26]. A number of ZK proof systems have been built on top of this construction. The ZKBoo [18] and

ZKB++ [8] constructions are generic transformations from MPC protocols to ZKP protocols, carefully keeping track of bits that have to be included in the proof vs. can be generated from seeds included in the proof. The construction by Katz et al. [27] gives an improved transformation for MPC protocols that have a separate preprocessing phase. The Ligero transformation [1] applies only to MPC protocols of certain form, but gives proofs of size $O(\sqrt{n})$, where n is the size of the circuit describing R.

Privacy-preserving computations in the RAM model have been studied in the context of *garbled RAM*, which can be seen as RAM analogue for garbled circuits. A heuristic construction was proposed in [34], and constructions based on common hardness assumptions in [17]. Garg et al. [15] proposed a construction that made only black-box use of the underlying cryptographic primitives. Private RAM computation protocols have also been built on top of *oblivious RAM* [21], securely implementing the *client's* operations either on top of garbled circuits [33], or secret-sharing based MPC [28], or a combination of them [12,29].

For ZK proofs, practically most efficient constructions for relations expressed in the RAM model are based on showing that two vectors are permutations of each other. Permutations in ZK proofs and MPC protocols have received their share of attention and so have the means of connecting the processing unit and the memory unit in encoding RAM-based computations in both ZK proofs and MPC protocols. Laur et al. [32] were among the first to propose a composable MPC protocol for secret sharing based protocols; Laud [30] built oblivious reading and writing operations on top of it. For garbled circuits, Zahur and Evans [43] proposed similar constructions. For ZK proofs, Ben-Sasson et al. [2] used routing networks to connect the processing unit and the memory unit in a RAM-based computation. Bootle et al. [6] lifted a technique by Neff [35] for verifying that two encrypted vectors are permutations of each other, into the encodings of relations of ZK proofs; this technique is based on showing the equality of polynomials that have the elements of one of the vectors as its roots.

Making proofs of permutations in private fashion has also been an important component of electronic voting systems. In this context, the proofs— *cryptographic mix-nets* are full-fledged protocols for stating that two sets of ciphertexts encrypt the same bag of plaintexts. These proofs can use any ZKP techniques, and be very short, even down to a constant [23]. An overview of cryptographic mix-nets is given in [24]. There is no straightforward method for composing these protocols with ZKP protocols for an arbitrary relation R.

Current state of the art of oblivious permutations in ZK proofs is definitely not satisfactory. The approaches based on routing networks have linearithmic complexity, if we consider the size of the indices and/or permuted elements to be constant. The approaches based on comparing polynomials have linear complexity, but work only over large fields and introduce extra rounds of interaction into the proof. MPC-in-the-head techniques are more versatile with respect to the algebraic structures they support, and many interesting relations are not best expressed as computations over large fields. Hence we are looking for techniques with the versatility of routing networks, but with linear complexity.

3   Preliminaries

In this paper, $[n]$ denotes the set $\{1, \ldots, n\}$. We use bold font to denote vectors: $\boldsymbol{v} = (v_1, \ldots, v_n)$ is a vector of length n.

3.1   Secure Multiparty Computation

A secure multiparty computation (MPC) protocol allows n parties $P_1, \ldots, P_n$ to jointly evaluate a publicly-known function $f : (\{0,1\}^m)^n \rightarrow \{0,1\}^\ell$, where the i-th party supplies the i-th argument of the function. All parties learn the output. Passive security for MPC protocol sets is defined through the simulation paradigm [19]. The *view* of a party in a protocol consists of the inputs of this party, the randomness this party generates, and the messages this party receives from other parties; these values allow one to perform all computations of that party, in particular find the messages it sends to other parties, and the values it outputs at the end of the protocol. The protocol Π_f for n parties is passively secure against the coalition $P_{i_1}, \ldots, P_{i_k}$, if there exists an algorithm $\mathcal{S}$ (the simulator), such that for any $x_1, \ldots, x_n$, the joint view of $P_{i_1}, \ldots, P_{i_k}$ in Π_f, where the input of P_j is x_j, is indistinguishable from the output of $\mathcal{S}(x_{i_1}, \ldots, x_{i_k}, f(x_1, \ldots, x_n))$.

Let $\mathbb{A} \subseteq \{0,1\}^*$ be a finite set. Let $\mathbb{A}_\perp = \mathbb{A} \cup \{\perp\}$, where $\perp$ denotes the absence of a value. A (n, k)-*secret sharing scheme* for $\mathbb{A}$ consists of a randomized algorithm $\mathsf{Share} : \mathbb{A} \rightarrow \mathbb{A}^n$ and a deterministic algorithm $\mathsf{Combine} : \mathbb{A}_\perp^n \rightarrow \mathbb{A}_\perp$, such that the output of Share, when restricted to at most k positions, is independent from the input, and, for all $x \in \mathbb{A}$, for all $(x_1, \ldots, x_n)$ that can be output by $\mathsf{Share}(x)$, and for all $(x_1', \ldots, x_n') \in \mathbb{A}_\perp$, where $x_i' \in \{x_i, \perp\}$ and the number of non-$\perp$ elements x_i' is at least $(k+1)$, we have $\mathsf{Combine}(x_1', \ldots, x_n') = x$.

A (n, k)-secret sharing scheme may be a significant component of n-party MPC protocols secure against k parties. In this case, the private values are held by secret-sharing them among the n parties. For operations with private values, one needs cryptographic protocols that take the shares of the inputs of the operation as the input, and return to the parties the shares of the output [16,20]. Typically, the function f is given by an arithmetic circuit that implements it. The inputs and outputs of f, as well as the intermediate values computed in the circuit are elements of $\mathbb{A}$, which is required to be an algebraic structure, typically a ring (or, more strongly, a field). The inputs of the circuit are shared by the parties holding them. The operations in the circuit are addition and multiplication in the ring $\mathbb{A}$. The parties execute a protocol for each operation in the circuit, eventually obtaining the shares of the output value, which they all learn by running the $\mathsf{Combine}$-algorithm.

Given a value $v \in \mathbb{A}$ that is held in secret-shared form as part of a MPC protocol, we denote the sharing by $[\![v]\!]$, and the individual share of the i-th party by $[\![v]\!]_i$. If $\mathcal{J} \subseteq [n]$, then we let $[\![v]\!]_{\mathcal{J}}$ denote the tuple $([\![v]\!]_i)_{i \in \mathcal{J}}$. The write-up $[\![\boldsymbol{v}]\!]$ denotes a vector, each element of which is secret-shared. The write-up $[\![w]\!] \leftarrow [\![u]\!] + [\![v]\!]$ denotes the execution of the protocol for addition by all the parties, where the inputs are the shares of u and v, and the output shares define the value of w. Similar write-up is used for other operations with secret-shared data. Single-instruction-multiple-data operations are denoted by applying the operations to vectors of values.

A secret sharing scheme over a ring $\mathbb{A}$ is *linear* if the Combine operation from $\mathbb{A}^n$ to $\mathbb{A}$ is linear [9,39]. In this case, the protocol for $[\![u]\!] + [\![v]\!]$ is just the addition of the corresponding shares of u and v by each party. Similarly, the protocol for $c \cdot [\![u]\!]$, where $c \in \mathbb{A}$ is public, requires each party to multiply its share with c. The protocol for $[\![u]\!] \cdot [\![v]\!]$ is more complex; its details depend on the details of the secret sharing scheme, and it requires communication among participants.

3.2   Honest-Verifier Zero-Knowledge Proofs

Let $R \subseteq \{0,1\}^* \times \{0,1\}^*$, which we also consider as a function $R : \{0,1\}^* \times \{0,1\}^* \to \{0,1\}$. Write $L_R = \{x \in \{0,1\}^* \mid \exists w \in \{0,1\}^* : (x,w) \in R\}$. We assume that R is a *NP-relation*, i.e. the function R is polynomial-time computable, and there exists a polynomial p, such for all $x \in L_R$, there exists $w \in \{0,1\}^*$, such that $(x,w) \in R$ and $|w| \leq p(|x|)$.

A protocol Π_R is a *Σ-protocol* for a given NP-relation R, if it is a protocol between two parties P and V with the following properties

- **Structure:** both P and V receive $x \in \{0,1\}^*$ as input. P also receives $w \in \{0,1\}^*$ as input. P sends the first message α to V. V generates a random β (does not depend on x or α), and sends it to P as the second message. P sends the third message γ to V. V runs a check on x, α, β, γ and either accepts or rejects.
- **Completeness:** if $(x,w) \in R$, then V definitely accepts.
- **Special soundness:** there exists a number s, such that if the transcripts $(x, \alpha, \beta_i, \gamma_i)$ for $i \in [s]$ with mutually different β_i-s are all accepted by V, then a w satisfying $(x,w) \in R$ can be efficiently found from these transcripts.
- **Special honest-verifier zero-knowledge:** there exists a simulator that on input $x \in L_R$ and a random β, outputs α, γ, such that the distribution of $(x, \alpha, \beta, \gamma)$ is indistinguishable from the transcripts of the real protocol.

A Σ-protocol is an instance of honest-verifier zero-knowledge (HVZK) proofs of knowledge (PoK). It can be turned into a non-interactive ZK PoK using the Fiat-Shamir heuristic [13], which is provably secure in the *Random Oracle Model* (ROM) [38]. The same heuristic is usable if the protocol has more rounds, as long as all challenges from the verifier are freshly generated random values. In this paper, we only consider honest verifiers, as the heuristic is already usable for them.

3.3   Commitments

A *commitment scheme* [7] allows one party to bind (commit) himself to a chosen value, while keeping it hidden from others, and later reveal it, without having the option to change it. The cryptographic primitive of commitment consists of the description of a set $\mathcal{M} \subseteq \{0,1\}^*$, a randomized algorithm Commit : $\mathcal{M} \to \{0,1\}^* \times \{0,1\}^*$, and a deterministic algorithm Open :

$\mathcal{M} \times \{0,1\}^* \times \{0,1\}^* \to \{0,1\}$. Here the argument of Commit is the message $m \in \mathcal{M}$ to be commited; its outputs are the commitment c and the opening information d. The algorithm Open takes the message m, commitment c, and the opening information d, and either accepts or rejects. The commitment scheme must be *hiding*—the commitment c hides the message m in a semantically secure manner—, and *binding*—it should be intractable to construct a tuple (m_1, m_2, c, d_1, d_2), such that $m_1 \neq m_2$, but Open(m_1, c, d_1) and Open(m_2, c, d_2) both accept.

Commitments can be based on the assumption of hardness of finding discrete logarithms [36]. In the random oracle model, one can commit to $x \in \{0,1\}^*$ by generating a sufficiently long random $r \in \{0,1\}^*$, and setting $c = H(x,r)$ and $d = r$, where H is a random oracle. The Open algorithm verifies that $c = H(x,r)$.

3.4   The IKOS and ZKBoo Constructions

Fix the numbers n and $k \geq 2$, as well as a set $\mathbb{A}$ and a (n,k) secret-sharing scheme for $\mathbb{A}$. For a relation $R \subseteq \{0,1\}^* \times \mathbb{A}$, $n \in \mathbb{N}$ and $x \in \{0,1\}^*$, define the function $f_R^x : \mathbb{A}^n \to \{0,1\}$ by $f_R^x(w_1, \ldots, w_n) = R(x, \mathsf{Combine}(w_1, \ldots, w_n))$. Let $\Pi_{f_R^x}$ be a MPC protocol for f_R^x, passively secure against k parties.

The IKOS construction [25] turns the family of protocols $\{\Pi_{f_R^x}\}_{x \in \{0,1\}^*}$ into a Σ-protocol for the relation R. Let the Prover and the Verifier have an instance $x \in \{0,1\}^*$, and the Prover also have $w \in \mathbb{A}$, such that $(x,w) \in R$. In the IKOS construction, the prover first constructs a secret sharing of w by $(w_1, \ldots, w_n) \leftarrow \mathsf{Share}(w)$. He then executes the protocol $\Pi_{f_R^x}$ with inputs $w_1, \ldots, w_n$ "in his head", i.e. he performs the computations of all n *virtual* parties by himself. Through this computation, the Prover obtains the views of all n virtual parties. The Prover commits to the views of each virtual party, and sends the commitments to the Verifier. The latter randomly picks a set of indices $\{i_1, \ldots, i_k\}$. The Prover opens the views of the i_1-th, i_2-th, $\ldots$, i_k-th virtual party to the Verifier, who checks that the obtained output is 1 for all virtual parties whose views were opened, and that these views are consistent with each other.

A MPC protocol consists of two kinds of steps. In the first kind, a party performs local computations. The second kind of steps is the sending of a message from one party to another, the latter receiving the same message. We can express the message send and receive as a two-party functionality of the form $(x, \bot) \mapsto (\bot, x)$, stating how the inputs of the parties are transformed into outputs.

In the IKOS construction, the Verifier checks the correctness of both kinds of steps for all virtual parties whose views have been opened. The steps of first kind are checked by the Verifier repeating the computations of the virtual parties. The steps of second kind can be checked only if both the sender and the receiver of the message are among the virtual parties whose views have been opened. In this case, the Verifier recomputes sender's message and checks that it appears in receiver's view.

For verifying the steps of the second kind, the actual two-party functionality being executed makes no difference; it may be more complex than sending and receiving a message. Indeed, for any two-party functionality $(x, y) \mapsto (g_1(x,y), g_2(x,y))$, where g_1 and g_2 are deterministic functions, the Verifier can recompute x in the first virtual party's view, y in the second virtual party's view, and then check that $g_1(x,y)$ and $g_2(x,y)$ appear in their views. In the following, we call MPC protocols, which additionally make use of such more general two-party functionalities, *MPC-in-the-head protocols*.

A n-party MPC-in-the-head protocol for evaluating arithmetic circuits over a finite ring $\mathbb{A}$ with passive security against $(n-1)$ parties was introduced and used in the ZKBoo [18] ZK proof system. The two-party functionality used by their protocol is *oblivious linear evaluation* (OLE), where the first party ("sender") inputs a pair of values $(x, r) \in \mathbb{A}^2$, the second party ("receiver") inputs a value $y \in \mathbb{A}$, the sender obtains nothing, and the receiver obtains $xy - r$.

In the ZKBoo MPC-in-the-head protocol, private values are additively shared, i.e. $v \in \mathbb{A}$ is represented as $[\![v]\!]$, where each $[\![v]\!]_i$ is a random element of $\mathbb{A}$, subject to the condition $\sum_{i=1}^{n} [\![v]\!]_i = v$. Hence the algorithm $\mathsf{Share}(v)$ generates random $[\![v]\!]_1, \ldots, [\![v]\!]_{n-1} \leftarrow \mathbb{A}$, and computes $[\![v]\!]_n = v - \sum_{i=1}^{n-1} [\![v]\!]_i$. The algorithm $\mathsf{Combine}([\![v]\!]_1, \ldots, [\![v]\!]_n)$ adds up all its arguments, none of which may be $\bot$. In order to add two private values in the underlying MPC protocol, or to multiply a private value with a constant, each party performs that same operation with his shares. For multiplying private values $[\![u]\!]$ and $[\![v]\!]$, the parties execute the protocol in Algorithm 1. We see that each pair of parties (P_i, P_j) runs an instance of OLE in order to share between themselves the product $[\![u]\!]_i \cdot [\![v]\!]_j$.

Data: private values $[\![u]\!]$, $[\![v]\!]$
Data: private value $[\![w]\!]$, such that $w = uv$
foreach $i, j \in [n]$, $i \neq j$ **do**

> P_i picks a random $r_{ij}^{(i)} \xleftarrow{\$} \mathbb{A}$
> P_i and P_j run the following two-party functionality:
>
> > P_i inputs $([\![u]\!]_i, r_{ij}^{(i)})$
> > P_j inputs $[\![v]\!]_j$
> > P_i obtains nothing
> > P_j obtains $r_{ij}^{(j)} \leftarrow [\![u]\!]_i \cdot [\![v]\!]_j - r_{ij}^{(i)}$

foreach $i \in [n]$ **do**

> P_i computes $[\![w]\!]_i \leftarrow [\![u]\!]_i \cdot [\![v]\!]_i + \sum_{\substack{1 \leq j \leq n \\ j \neq i}} (r_{ij}^{(i)} + r_{ji}^{(i)})$

Return $[\![w]\!]$

Algorithm 1: Multiplying two private values in ZKBoo

In Algorithm 1, we have introduced the notation for two-party functionalities, generalizing the notation "$P_i \rightarrow P_j : M$" of one party sending a message to another party. In our notation, we specify the inputs each party gives to the functionality, and the outputs they get, together with the computations of the outputs from the inputs. Note that the two-party functionality will add only the output of each party to the view of that party, and nothing else.

The protocol in Algorithm 1, together with the protocols for adding private values and multiplying them with public constants, as well as protocols for secret-sharing an input value (the party doing the sharing generates a random element of $\mathbb{A}$ as the share of each party, subject to their sum being equal to the value to be shared), and recovering an output of the computation (all parties send their shares to all other parties; each party adds up the shares), is a n-party protocol passively secure against $(n-1)$ parties. Indeed, all messages a party receives, either during the sharing an input value, or as the receiver in an OLE functionality, or during the recovery of outputs, are uniformly random elements of $\mathbb{A}$ (in case of output recovery, subject to their sum being equal to the actual output, which is given to the simulator), hence can be simulated as such. These values remain uniformly random if we combine the views of up to $(n-1)$ parties.

The ZKBoo protocol considers the case $n = 3$ in particular, because this leads to the shortest proofs, due to the MPC-in-the-head protocol being *(2,3)-decomposable*. The latter condition basically means that the view of a virtual party P_i must be constructible from the random seed of this party, from his shares of private inputs, and from the view of $P_{(i+1) \bmod 3}$. In particular, there can be no information flow from $P_{(i-1) \bmod 3}$ to P_i. In Algorithm 1, this necessitates the reversal of the flow in the OLE, whenever $i + 1 \equiv j \pmod 3$. Namely, instead of P_i generating a random $r_{ij}^{(i)}$ before the start of OLE, we let P_j randomly generate $r_{ij}^{(j)}$ instead. The parties will then execute OLE with reversed roles, with P_i inputting only $[\![u]\!]_i$, P_j inputting both $[\![v]\!]_j$ and $r_{ij}^{(j)}$, P_i learning $r_{ij}^{(i)} = [\![u]\!]_i \cdot [\![v]\!]_j - r_{ij}^{(j)}$, and P_j learning nothing.

3.5   Motivation: Simulating Computations

Existing MPC protocols, and ZK proof protocols built on top of them, are suitable if the computed function f or the relation R is represented as an arithmetic circuit. In practice, such f and R are usually represented differently. They are usually given in a format executable by a computer, i.e. as programs in an imperative language, i.c. as programs for a *Random Access Machine (RAM)*. These programs can invoke storing and loading operations against memory, the cells of which are addressable with the elements of $\mathbb{A}$. These operations, and the memory structure are not easily converted into an arithmetic circuit. Examples of such R include the evaluation of a particular program, showing that certain inputs lead to certain (faulty) outputs. Another example is showing the upper or lower bounds of the length of a shortest path between two vertices in a graph, where the structure of the graph and/or the lengths of edges must remain private.

For verifying that $R(x, w) = 1$, where R is given as a RAM program, one commonly splits the execution of R on the RAM into two parts, proves the correctness of execution separately, and then shows that the two parts are connected in the right manner [2]. The first part of execution is the *processing unit*; the proof shows that at each execution step, the instruction was decoded correctly, and the result of the instruction was correctly computed from its inputs. The second part of the execution is the *memory*; the proof shows that for each memory cell, the value read from it is the same that was written to it previously. The two parts have to be connected—the sequence of load- and store-operations has to be the same at both sides. The ZK proof must check that the same sequence appears at both parts.

At processor side, it is natural to order the sequence of load- and store-operations by timestamps. When verifying the correctness of the steps made by the processor, at each execution step we need to know what value was loaded from the memory, or what value was stored there (if any). At memory side, it is natural to order this sequence first by memory address, and then by timestamps. In this manner, it is easy to verify that for each memory cell, the value loaded from there was the same that was either stored there, or loaded from there the previous time the same cell was accessed. Hence we need to show that two sequences are permutations of each other. For added flexibility, we want to have the permutation as a separate object, because we may need to show that several sequences are related to each other through the same permutation.

4 Our Construction

4.1 The Protocol

We will now present our permutation protocol, which can be used for the permutation functionality in a MPC-in-the-head protocol set that represents private values through additive sharing. Let S_m denote the group of permutations of m elements. Given a private representation of a permutation $\sigma \in S_m$, and a vector of shared values $[\![v]\!] = ([\![v_1]\!], \ldots, [\![v_m]\!])$, where $v_i \in \mathbb{A}$, we want to have a protocol for obtaining $[\![\sigma(v)]\!] = ([\![v_{\sigma(1)}]\!], \ldots, [\![v_{\sigma(m)}]\!])$. If the protocol is executed by $n \geq 3$ parties, then we want it to be passively secure against a coalition of $(n-1)$ parties.

The permutation σ originates as a part of the witness, as we do not have any operations implemented by the MPC protocol set that result in a private permutation. In order to apply the IKOS construction to our permutation protocol, σ has to be secret-shared among the n parties using a $(n, n-1)$ secret-sharing scheme. We use the following scheme: the private representation of σ is $[\![\sigma]\!] = ([\![\sigma]\!]_1, \ldots, [\![\sigma]\!]_n)$, where $[\![\sigma]\!]_i \in S_m$ is a *random* permutation of m elements, subject to the constraint $\sigma = [\![\sigma]\!]_n \circ \cdots \circ [\![\sigma]\!]_1$. Hence the sharing algorithm $\mathsf{Share}(\sigma)$ uniformly randomly picks the permutations $[\![\sigma]\!]_1, \ldots, [\![\sigma]\!]_{n-1} \in S_m$ and computes $[\![\sigma]\!]_n = \sigma \circ [\![\sigma]\!]_1^{-1} \circ \cdots \circ [\![\sigma]\!]_{n-1}^{-1}$. The algorithm $\mathsf{Combine}([\![\sigma]\!]_1, \ldots, [\![\sigma]\!]_n)$ computes $[\![\sigma]\!]_n \circ \cdots \circ [\![\sigma]\!]_1$, requiring that none of the arguments is $\bot$. The i-th computing party will hold $[\![\sigma]\!]_i$. We are not going to specify how $[\![\sigma]\!]_i$ is represented as a bit-string. If the representation allows to express also values that are not elements of S_m, then the i-th computing party must check that $[\![\sigma]\!]_i \in S_m$. Note that through the IKOS construction, this checking requirement carries over to the Verifier in the ZKP protocol, if he selects the view of the i-th computing party for opening.

The protocol for obtaining $[\![\sigma(v)]\!]$ from $[\![\sigma]\!]$ and $[\![v]\!]$ is given in Algorithm 2. Its structure is rather similar to the multiplication protocol in Algorithm 1. It uses a two-party functionality that is similar to oblivious linear evaluation; this similarity shows when thinking of the permutations as the action of the group S_m on the Abelian group $\mathbb{A}^m$. The algebraic identity—$\sigma(u+v) = \sigma(u)+\sigma(v)$— is used in the design of the protocol. Compared to the multiplication in rings, the group action lacks the other distributive law; hence there is less parallelism in Algorithm 2 than in Algorithm 1. For $n = 3$, the protocol can be made (2,3)-decomposable similarly to Algorithm 1, and it can be composed with the rest of the ZKBoo protocol set in order to express computations that consist of arithmetic operations and permutations.

Data: private vector $[\![v]\!]$, private permutation $[\![\sigma]\!]$
Result: private vector $[\![w]\!]$, where $w_i = v_{\sigma(i)}$
$[\![w^{(0)}]\!] \leftarrow [\![v]\!]$
for $i = 1$ **to** n **do**
    foreach $j \in [n]\setminus\{i\}$ **do**
        P_i generates random $r_{ij}^{(i)} \in \mathbb{A}^m$
        Parties P_i and P_j run the following two-party functionality:
            P_i inputs $[\![\sigma]\!]_i$ and $r_{ij}^{(i)}$
            P_j inputs $[\![w^{(i-1)}]\!]_j$
            P_i obtains nothing
            P_j obtains $r_{ij}^{(j)} \leftarrow [\![\sigma]\!]_i([\![w^{(i-1)}]\!]_j) - r_{ij}^{(i)}$
                        `/* Elementwise subtraction of vectors */`
        P_j defines $[\![w^{(i)}]\!]_j \leftarrow r_{ij}^{(j)}$
    P_i defines $[\![w^{(i)}]\!]_i \leftarrow [\![\sigma]\!]_i([\![w^{(i-1)}]\!]_i) + \sum_{\substack{1 \le j \le n \\ j \ne i}} r_{ij}^{(i)}$
Return $[\![w^{(n)}]\!]$

Algorithm 2: Private permutation PrivPerm

Theorem 1. *Algorithm 2 computes $[\![\sigma(v)]\!]$.*

Proof. This is established by the following loop invariant:

$$w^{(i)} = [\![\sigma]\!]_i([\![\sigma]\!]_{i-1}(\cdots[\![\sigma]\!]_1(v)\cdots)) \ . \tag{1}$$

Indeed, the vector $w^{(0)}$ is initialized as v. During the main loop, $[\![w^{(i)}]\!]$ is constructed by permuting the additive shares of the private vector $[\![w^{(i-1)}]\!]$ with the permutation $[\![\sigma]\!]_i$. The permutation of the i-th share will be learned by the i-th party, while the permutation of the j-th share ($j \ne i$) will be additively shared between the i-th and j-th parties. Due to the definition of $[\![\sigma]\!]$, we have $w^{(n)} = \sigma(v)$. This vector is then returned in secret-shared manner.   □

4.2 Security

Theorem 2. *Algorithm 2 is secure against a passive adversary corrupting at most $(n-1)$ parties.*

Proof. Let $\mathcal{J} = \{j_1, \ldots, j_k\} \subset [n]$, where $k \leq (n-1)$. Consider the joint view of a set of parties $P_{j_1}, \ldots, P_{j_k}$. Their view at the start of the protocol consists of their shares of $[\![v]\!]$ and $[\![\sigma]\!]$. Consider the i-th iteration of the protocol. If $i \in \mathcal{J}$, then no new values are added to their joint view while P_i runs the two-party functionality with all other parties; the only values added into the view are the random vectors generated by P_i. If $i \notin \mathcal{J}$, then the vectors $r_{ij_1}^{(j_1)}, \ldots, r_{ij_k}^{(j_k)}$ are added to the joint view. These are vectors of random values, perfectly masked with the random vectors $r_{ij_1}^{(i)}, \ldots, r_{ij_k}^{(i)}$. We see that for each vector $[\![w^{(i)}]\!]_j$, where $i \in [n]$ and $j \in \mathcal{J}$, there is at least one newly generated random vector contributing to its value. We also see that newly generated random vectors mask the expressions containing either $[\![\sigma]\!]_j$ or $[\![w^{(i)}]\!]_j$ for $j \notin \mathcal{J}$.

Hence we can simulate the joint view of $P_{j_1}, \ldots, P_{j_k}$ as shown in Algorithm 3. The simulator first generates the shares of the vectors $w^{(i)}$, which are random, as explained above. It will then fill out the values of the vectors $r_{ij}^{(i)}$ and $r_{ij}^{(j)}$, iff these vectors are visible to some of the parties $P_{j_1}, \ldots, P_{j_k}$. It is straightforward to verify that all these vectors are random, subject only to the equalities between them that are prescribed in Algorithm 2.

4.3   Complexity

When discussing the complexity of MPC protocols, we typically care about three quantities—the number of bits exchanged by the communication parties, the number of necessary round-trips of communication, and the computational complexity of the local computations. If the IKOS transformation is applied to the protocol, then its round complexity becomes moot—the protocol will be executed in the head of the Prover without any latency. In this transformation, the Prover has to perform the computations of all parties, hence the complexity of these is relevant. However, for information-theoretically secure MPC protocols, which Algorithm 1 and Algorithm 2 are examples of, the computational complexity tends to be small, consisting of simple arithmetic operations, and randomness generation (which is usually implemented by calls to a pseudorandom function). Hence the computation complexity is considered to be subsumed by the communication complexity, and has not received significant attention in the literature.

The same three complexity categories matter for ZKP protocols. There is also the fourth category—the soundness error. This shows the probability of the verifier accepting an invalid proof in a single session of the protocol; repetition is used to lower it.

The round complexity of the IKOS transformation is small—the generic construction is a Σ-protocol. The soundness error is $1/n$, where n is the number of the parties and the underlying MPC protocol must be secure against $(n-1)$ parties. The soundness error cannot be influenced by the design of the MPC protocol. The computation complexity of the resulting ZKP protocol is similar to the underlying MPC protocol. The communication complexity depends on that

Data: Shares $[\![v]\!]_{\mathcal{J}}$, $[\![\sigma]\!]_{\mathcal{J}}$, $[\![w]\!]_{\mathcal{J}}$
Result: Views of the parties $\{P_i\}_{i \in \mathcal{J}}$ in Alg. 2
Let i_* be an element of $[n] \backslash \mathcal{J}$
foreach $j \in \mathcal{J}$ **do**
$\quad \mid \quad [\![w^{(0)}]\!]_j \leftarrow [\![v]\!]_j$
$\quad \mid \quad [\![w^{(n)}]\!]_j \leftarrow [\![w]\!]_j$
foreach $j \in \mathcal{J}$, $i \in [n-1]$ **do**
$\quad \mid \quad$ Randomly generate $[\![w^{(i)}]\!]_j \in \mathbb{A}^m$
foreach $i \in [n]$ **do**
$\quad$ **if** $i \in \mathcal{J}$ **then**
$\quad \quad \mid \quad$ **foreach** $j \in \mathcal{J} \backslash \{i\}$ **do**
$\quad \quad \quad \mid \quad r_{ij}^{(j)} \leftarrow [\![w^{(i)}]\!]_j$
$\quad \quad \quad \mid \quad r_{ij}^{(i)} \leftarrow [\![\sigma]\!]_i([\![w^{(i-1)}]\!]_j) - r_{ij}^{(j)}$
$\quad \quad \mid \quad$ **foreach** $j \in [n] \backslash (\mathcal{J} \cup \{i_*\})$ **do**
$\quad \quad \quad \mid \quad$ Randomly generate $r_{ij}^{(i)} \in \mathbb{A}^m$
$\quad \quad \mid \quad r_{ii_*}^{(i)} \leftarrow [\![w^{(i)}]\!]_i - [\![\sigma]\!]_i([\![w^{(i-1)}]\!]_i) - \sum_{\substack{1 \le j \le n \\ j \notin \{i, i_*\}}} r_{ij}^{(i)}$
$\quad$ **else**
$\quad \quad \mid \quad$ **foreach** $j \in \mathcal{J}$ **do**
$\quad \quad \quad \mid \quad r_{ij}^{(j)} \leftarrow [\![w^{(i)}]\!]_j$
Return all values $[\![w^{(i)}]\!]_j$, $r_{ij}^{(i)}$, $r_{ij}^{(j)}$

Algorithm 3: Simulator for the view of the set of parties $\{P_i\}_{i \in \mathcal{J}}$, where $|\mathcal{J}| \le (n-1)$

of the MPC protocol, but the dependence is not very straightforward—while the size of the views of virtual parties is basically the same as the communication complexity of the MPC protocol, the verifier is able to regenerate some of it based on the views of other parties that were opened to him. A rule of thumb is, that when the general IKOS transformation is used, then the communication complexity of the resulting ZKP protocol is similar to the amount of communication from parties with unopened view to parties with opened view [8,18]. If the views of all but one party are opened, then this amounts to the size of communication originated from the last party. In case of more general two-party functionalities, the "communication" are the outputs to parties.

We see that in Algorithm 2, the communication originating from each party is $(n-1)m$ elements of $\mathbb{A}^m$. This can be seen as the contribution of our permutation protocol to the total communication complexity of the resulting ZKP protocol. This amount of communication is equal to m invocations of the multiplication protocol in Algorithm 1. The concrete communication complexity for circuits containing addition and multiplication gates has been reported to be $274 \log_2 |\mathbb{A}|$ bits per multiplication gate in ZKBoo [18] for the soundness error 2^{-80}; this complexity is halved for ZKB++ [8]. The permutation operation will contribute to the length of the proof in the same manner.

Benchmarking. We have implemented the prover and verifier for a ZK proof system similar to ZKB++, making use of the MPC-in-the-head protocols for addition and multiplication (Algorithm 1) of both shared values and constants, as well as the permutation protocol in Algorithm 2. The system uses $n = 3$ virtual parties with $(2,3)$-decomposable protocols; it is made non-interactive using the Fiat-Shamir transform. It is implemented in Haskell, using the HsOpenSSL bindings for cryptographic operations—AES-128 in CBC mode is used for expanding the random seed, and SHA-256 is used as the hash function. The system has not been optimized for execution speed and memory usage, and the running times we report are expected to be much improved; however, the length of the produced proof is the same as would be produced by an optimized system.

We have benchmarked our implementation on a program that first inputs m 32-bit values and a permutation for m elements as part of the witness, and then applies the permutation to the values; we have varied m between 2^5 and 2^{15}. The fragment of inputting a permutation and applying it to a vector of private values will appear in the encodings of relations R represented in the RAM model—the private values are the memory addresses and values in the load- and store-operations the program representing R has performed. The permutation sorts this vector by the memory addresses. Hence it makes sense to benchmark this fragment, as it precisely characterizes the cost of a crucial step of encoding R as a ZKP.

The soundness error of a single run of ZKB++ is $2/3$ [8]. In our benchmarks, we have executed the protocol 218 times in parallel, bringing the soundness error below 2^{-128}. After generating the views of the virtual parties in all 218 runs, we use the hash function according to the Fiat-Shamir transform to obtain the challenges for all runs; the challenge determines, the views of which parties in which runs have to be made available to the Verifier as the main part of the proof. In Fig. 1 we show the running times of our prover and verifier, as well as the length of the transmitted proof. We see the running times growing slightly more than linearly, and the proof size is linear in the length of the vector.

5   Comparison Against Alternatives

Let us compare the efficiency of our protocol against possible alternative implementations of a permuting a private vector in an MPC protocol suitable for the IKOS transformation, for n parties, with passive security against $(n - 1)$ parties, based on additive secret sharing, and with the values being elements of a ring (secret sharing is over the same ring). Obviously, our greatest interest is towards the case, where the values are N-bit integers for some value of N, i.e. the underlying ring is $\mathbb{Z}_{2^N}$. The following two implementation approaches are natural.

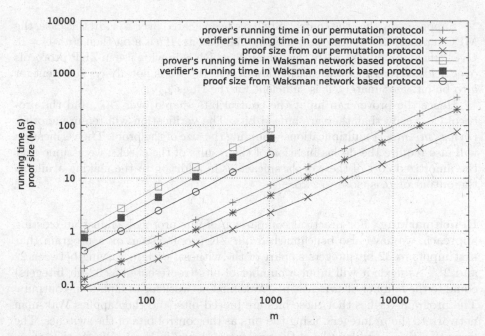

Fig. 1. Execution time and proof size for our permutation protocol, and protocol baséd on Waksman networks, for various lengths m of the permuted vector

5.1   Using a Routing Network

We can use a routing network to permute a vector of length m; this network has $O(m \log m)$ switches, each of which requires a single multiplication to process. If m is a power of two, then the number of switches in Waksman's network [42] is exactly $m \log_2 m - m + 1$. For other values of m, the size is larger. Hence the communication complexity of the permutation is at least $(m \log_2 m - m + 1)(n-1)$ elements of $\mathbb{A}$, which is greater than the complexity of Algorithm 2, as soon as $m \geq 4$.

However, this is not yet the entire complexity of the protocol based on routing networks. The control bits of the network, representing the permutation, are part of the witness w, secret-shared among the virtual parties by the prover. The protocol must make sure that these are indeed bits. The verification that the value b, represented as $[\![b]\!]$, is a bit can happen by b being shared not over $\mathbb{Z}_{2^N}$, but over $\mathbb{Z}_2$. In the following, let $\mathbf{R}[\![v]\!]$ denote that the value v is a private value, represented by additively sharing it over the ring $\mathbf{R}$.

When we have the representations of the bits $\mathbb{Z}_2[\![b]\!]$ used to control the routing network, we have to convert them to $\mathbb{Z}_{2^N}[\![b]\!]$ in order to use them in the multiplication protocol over $\mathbb{Z}_{2^N}$. Converting between different rings in MPC protocols over rings is a problem that has not received general attention. Bogdanov et al. [5] propose a conversion method for $\mathbb{Z}_2$ to larger rings for three-party computations with passive security, but this does not fit our use-case because it is secure against a single party only.

Suppose now that the control bits have been shared over $\mathbb{Z}_{2^N}$. In this case, the MPC protocol must verify that they are indeed bits. If b is a bit then $b(b-1) = 0$. Over a field, only bits satisfy this equality, which is in wide use in ZKP protocols over fields. Over rings, the satisfaction of $b(b-1) = 0$ is not always sufficient for b to be bit. Fortunately, it is sufficient for the rings $\mathbb{Z}_{2^N}$.

Hence the prover can input the control bits shared over $\mathbb{Z}_{2^N}$, and the protocol can verify that they are indeed bits. The verification will require another $(m \log_2 m - m + 1)$ multiplications, doubling the size of the proof. The verification will also require the declassification of the results of the checks; we assume that the amortized cost of these declassifications in addition to the making available the output of R is close to zero.

Benchmarking. For practical comparison of our protocol against an existing approach, we have also benchmarked our ZK proof system on a program that first inputs m 32-bit integers as part of the witness, with m varying between 2^5 and 2^{10}. As next, it will input a number of bits (represented as 32-bit integers) equal to the number of switches in a Waksman network for m inputs and outputs. The program verifies that these bits are indeed bits, and then applies Waksman network to the m integers, using the bits as the control bits of the switches. The execution times and lengths of the proofs are shown in Fig. 1. We see that these times and sizes are larger, and grow somewhat faster than for our protocol.

5.2   Verifying a Polynomial Equality

The second alternative is to use Neff's technique [35]: if two vectors u, v of length m are permutations of each other, then the polynomial $Q_{u,v}(X) = \prod_{i=1}^{m}(X - u_i) - \prod_{i=1}^{m}(X - v_i)$ is the zero polynomial. If the polynomial is over a field, then $Q_{u,v} \equiv 0$ is also sufficient for u to be a permutation of v. If the field is large, then this condition can be verified (with a small soundness error, proportional to the length m, and inversely proportional to the size of the field) by evaluating $Q_{u,v}$ at a random point, selected by the Verifier. The verification requires $2m - 2$ multiplications, which is greater than the complexity of Algorithm 2, as soon as $m \geq 3$. We see that even when working over a field, our protocol outperforms the alternatives in an IKOS-based ZKP protocol.

Moreover, Neff's check cannot be used in the ring $\mathbb{Z}_{2^N}$, because its structure is very different from a field. We could use the protocol in Algorithm 4 (taken from [31]) to convert an additive sharing over $\mathbb{Z}_{2^N}$ to an additive sharing over $\mathbb{Z}_2^N$, i.e. into a bitwise sharing. The latter can be thought of as a sharing over the finite field $GF(2^N)$, as the additive operation in both structures is the same. At this point, Neff's check can be used.

We can estimate the communication cost of Algorithm 4. The sharing done by P_i consists of P_i sending random values to every other party. These values could be generated from pairwise shared random seeds, and no actual communication would be necessary (P_i would select its own share so, that $\bigoplus_{j=1}^{n} \mathbb{Z}_2^N [u_i]_j = u_i$). The addition of two N-bit values requires $(N - 1)$ AND-operations. There are

Data: number of parties n, bit-length N, private value $\mathbb{Z}_{2^N}[\![v]\!]$
Result: private value $\mathbb{Z}_2^N[\![v]\!]$
foreach $i \in \{1, \ldots, n\}$ **do**
 | Party P_i defines $u_i \leftarrow \mathbb{Z}_{2^N}[\![v]\!]_i$, shares $\mathbb{Z}_2^N[\![u_i]\!]$
Parties privately execute the summation circuit for n N-bit values, computing
$\mathbb{Z}_2^N[\![u]\!] \leftarrow \sum_{i=1}^n \mathbb{Z}_2^N[\![u_i]\!]$
Return $\mathbb{Z}_2^N[\![u]\!]$

Algorithm 4: Bit extraction

n values to be added, hence the addition has to be repeated $(n-1)$ times. This has to be further multiplied by the length of the vector m. One addition requires $(n-1)$ bits to be communicated, which is N times less than one multiplication according to Algorithm 1. The total communication cost of converting m private values from $\mathbb{Z}_{2^N}$ to $GF(2^N)$ is equivalent to the cost of $(n-1)m(N-1)/N$ multiplications.

6 Discussion

We have proposed a passively secure MPC-in-the-head protocol for permutation. More efficient constructions of ZK proofs from MPC-in-the-head protocols are known, if the underlying protocols with several parties are *actively* secure for at least a constant fraction of the parties. Existing efficient linear secret sharing based MPC protocols [3,11] make use of homomorphic MACs, which are updated by each operation in the arithmetic circuit encoding the computation. It is unclear, what would be a suitable MAC for permutation, as it would have to have suitable homomorphic properties with respect to the application of that permutation to a vector of values.

There exist methods to turn passively secure protocols into actively secure protocols with the help of replication [10]. Most probably, these methods will not help in increasing the efficiency of the resulting ZK proof, compared to the use of the underlying passively secure protocol, because the IKOS technique would dismantle the passive-to-active construction.

Still, our construction will be useful in encoding the relations represented in the RAM model as ZK proofs built using the IKOS technique. Its efficiency can perhaps be further improved by considering a separate preprocessing step as in [27] and compressing the representations of random permutations and vectors as much as possible (e.g. as in [14]).

Acknowledgements. This research has been funded by the Defense Advanced Research Projects Agency (DARPA) under contract HR0011-20-C-0083. The views, opinions, and/or findings expressed are those of the author and should not be interpreted as representing the official views or policies of the Department of Defense or the U.S. Government. This research has also been supported by European Regional Development Fund through the Estonian Centre of Excellence in ICT Research (EXCITE), and Estonian Research Council through grant PRG920. We thank Said Daoudagh and the PC members of STM 2021 for their valuable comments.

References

1. Ames, S., Hazay, C., Ishai, Y., Venkitasubramaniam, M.: Ligero: lightweight sublinear arguments without a trusted setup. In: Thuraisingham, et al. [41], pp. 2087–2104. https://doi.org/10.1145/3133956.3134104
2. Ben-Sasson, E., Chiesa, A., Genkin, D., Tromer, E.: Fast reductions from rams to delegatable succinct constraint satisfaction problems: extended abstract. In: Kleinberg, R.D. (ed.) Innovations in Theoretical Computer Science, ITCS 2013, Berkeley, CA, USA, 9–12 January 2013, pp. 401–414. ACM (2013). https://doi.org/10.1145/2422436.2422481
3. Bendlin, R., Damgård, I., Orlandi, C., Zakarias, S.: Semi-homomorphic encryption and multiparty computation. In: Paterson, K.G. (ed.) EUROCRYPT 2011. LNCS, vol. 6632, pp. 169–188. Springer, Heidelberg (2011). https://doi.org/10.1007/978-3-642-20465-4_11
4. Beneš, V.E.: Mathematical Theory of Connecting Networks and Telephone Traffic. Academic Press, Cambridge (1965)
5. Bogdanov, D., Niitsoo, M., Toft, T., Willemson, J.: High-performance secure multiparty computation for data mining applications. Int. J. Inf. Secur. $11(6)$, 403–418 (2012). https://doi.org/10.1007/s10207-012-0177-2
6. Bootle, J., Cerulli, A., Groth, J., Jakobsen, S., Maller, M.: Arya: nearly linear-time zero-knowledge proofs for correct program execution. In: Peyrin, T., Galbraith, S. (eds.) ASIACRYPT 2018. LNCS, vol. 11272, pp. 595–626. Springer, Cham (2018). https://doi.org/10.1007/978-3-030-03326-2_20
7. Brassard, G., Chaum, D., Crépeau, C.: Minimum disclosure proofs of knowledge. J. Comput. Syst. Sci. $37(2)$, 156–189 (1988). https://doi.org/10.1016/0022-0000(88)90005-0
8. Chase, M., et al.: Post-quantum zero-knowledge and signatures from symmetric-key primitives. In: Thuraisingham, et al. [41], pp. 1825–1842. https://doi.org/10.1145/3133956.3133997
9. Cramer, R., Damgård, I., Maurer, U.: General secure multi-party computation from any linear secret-sharing scheme. In: Preneel, B. (ed.) EUROCRYPT 2000. LNCS, vol. 1807, pp. 316–334. Springer, Heidelberg (2000). https://doi.org/10.1007/3-540-45539-6_22
10. Damgård, I., Orlandi, C., Simkin, M.: Yet another compiler for active security or: efficient MPC over arbitrary rings. In: Shacham, H., Boldyreva, A. (eds.) CRYPTO 2018. LNCS, vol. 10992, pp. 799–829. Springer, Cham (2018). https://doi.org/10.1007/978-3-319-96881-0_27
11. Damgård, I., Pastro, V., Smart, N., Zakarias, S.: Multiparty computation from somewhat homomorphic encryption. In: Safavi-Naini, R., Canetti, R. (eds.) CRYPTO 2012. LNCS, vol. 7417, pp. 643–662. Springer, Heidelberg (2012). https://doi.org/10.1007/978-3-642-32009-5_38
12. Doerner, J., Shelat, A.: Scaling ORAM for secure computation. In: Thuraisingham, et al. [41], pp. 523–535. https://doi.org/10.1145/3133956.3133967
13. Fiat, A., Shamir, A.: How to prove yourself: practical solutions to identification and signature problems. In: Odlyzko, A.M. (ed.) CRYPTO 1986. LNCS, vol. 263, pp. 186–194. Springer, Heidelberg (1987). https://doi.org/10.1007/3-540-47721-7_12
14. Fleischhacker, N., Simkin, M.: On publicly-accountable zero-knowledge and small shuffle arguments. In: Garay, J.A. (ed.) PKC 2021. LNCS, vol. 12711, pp. 618–648. Springer, Cham (2021). https://doi.org/10.1007/978-3-030-75248-4_22

15. Garg, S., Lu, S., Ostrovsky, R.: Black-box garbled RAM. In: Guruswami, V. (ed.) IEEE 56th Annual Symposium on Foundations of Computer Science, FOCS 2015, Berkeley, CA, USA, 17–20 October 2015, pp. 210–229. IEEE Computer Society (2015). https://doi.org/10.1109/FOCS.2015.22

16. Gennaro, R., Rabin, M.O., Rabin, T.: Simplified VSS and fast-track multiparty computations with applications to threshold cryptography. In: Coan, B.A., Afek, Y. (eds.) Proceedings of the Seventeenth Annual ACM Symposium on Principles of Distributed Computing, PODC 1998, Puerto Vallarta, Mexico, 28 June–2 July 1998, pp. 101–111. ACM (1998). https://doi.org/10.1145/277697.277716

17. Gentry, C., Halevi, S., Lu, S., Ostrovsky, R., Raykova, M., Wichs, D.: Garbled RAM revisited. In: Nguyen, P.Q., Oswald, E. (eds.) EUROCRYPT 2014. LNCS, vol. 8441, pp. 405–422. Springer, Heidelberg (2014). https://doi.org/10.1007/978-3-642-55220-5_23

18. Giacomelli, I., Madsen, J., Orlandi, C.: ZKBoo: faster zero-knowledge for Boolean circuits. In: Holz, T., Savage, S. (eds.) 25th USENIX Security Symposium, USENIX Security 16, Austin, TX, USA, 10–12 August 2016, pp. 1069–1083. USENIX Association (2016). https://www.usenix.org/conference/usenixsecurity16

19. Goldreich, O.: The Foundations of Cryptography - Volume 2: Basic Applications. Cambridge University Press, Cambridge (2004). https://doi.org/10.1017/CBO9780511721656

20. Goldreich, O., Micali, S., Wigderson, A.: How to play any mental game or A completeness theorem for protocols with honest majority. In: Aho, A.V. (ed.) 1987 Proceedings of the 19th Annual ACM Symposium on Theory of Computing, New York, New York, USA, pp. 218–229. ACM (1987). https://doi.org/10.1145/28395.28420

21. Goldreich, O., Ostrovsky, R.: Software protection and simulation on oblivious RAMs. J. ACM **43**(3), 431–473 (1996). https://doi.org/10.1145/233551.233553

22. Goldwasser, S., Micali, S., Rackoff, C.: The knowledge complexity of interactive proof-systems (extended abstract). In: Sedgewick, R. (ed.) Proceedings of the 17th Annual ACM Symposium on Theory of Computing, Providence, Rhode Island, USA, 6–8 May 1985, pp. 291–304. ACM (1985). https://doi.org/10.1145/22145.22178

23. Groth, J.: On the size of pairing-based non-interactive arguments. In: Fischlin, M., Coron, J.-S. (eds.) EUROCRYPT 2016. LNCS, vol. 9666, pp. 305–326. Springer, Heidelberg (2016). https://doi.org/10.1007/978-3-662-49896-5_11

24. Haines, T., Müller, J.: SoK: techniques for verifiable mix nets. In: 33rd IEEE Computer Security Foundations Symposium, CSF 2020, Boston, MA, USA, 22–26 June 2020, pp. 49–64. IEEE (2020). https://doi.org/10.1109/CSF49147.2020.00012

25. Ishai, Y., Kushilevitz, E., Ostrovsky, R., Sahai, A.: Zero-knowledge from secure multiparty computation. In: Johnson, D.S., Feige, U. (eds.) Proceedings of the 39th Annual ACM Symposium on Theory of Computing, San Diego, California, USA, 11–13 June 2007, pp. 21–30. ACM (2007). https://doi.org/10.1145/1250790.1250794

26. Ishai, Y., Kushilevitz, E., Ostrovsky, R., Sahai, A.: Zero-knowledge proofs from secure multiparty computation. SIAM J. Comput. **39**(3), 1121–1152 (2009). https://doi.org/10.1137/080725398

27. Katz, J., Kolesnikov, V., Wang, X.: Improved non-interactive zero knowledge with applications to post-quantum signatures. In: Lie, D., Mannan, M., Backes, M., Wang, X. (eds.) Proceedings of the 2018 ACM SIGSAC Conference on Computer and Communications Security, CCS 2018, Toronto, ON, Canada, 15–19 October 2018, pp. 525–537. ACM (2018). https://doi.org/10.1145/3243734.3243805

28. Keller, M.: The oblivious machine. In: Lange, T., Dunkelman, O. (eds.) LATIN-CRYPT 2017. LNCS, vol. 11368, pp. 271–288. Springer, Cham (2019). https://doi.org/10.1007/978-3-030-25283-0_15

29. Keller, M., Yanai, A.: Efficient maliciously secure multiparty computation for RAM. In: Nielsen, J.B., Rijmen, V. (eds.) EUROCRYPT 2018. LNCS, vol. 10822, pp. 91–124. Springer, Cham (2018). https://doi.org/10.1007/978-3-319-78372-7_4

30. Laud, P.: Parallel oblivious array access for secure multiparty computation and privacy-preserving minimum spanning trees. Proc. Priv. Enhancing Technol. **2015**(2), 188–205 (2015). https://doi.org/10.1515/popets-2015-0011

31. Laud, P., Randmets, J.: A domain-specific language for low-level secure multiparty computation protocols. In: Ray, I., Li, N., Kruegel, C. (eds.) Proceedings of the 22nd ACM SIGSAC Conference on Computer and Communications Security, Denver, CO, USA, 12–16 October 2015, pp. 1492–1503. ACM (2015). https://doi.org/10.1145/2810103.2813664

32. Laur, S., Willemson, J., Zhang, B.: Round-efficient oblivious database manipulation. In: Lai, X., Zhou, J., Li, H. (eds.) ISC 2011. LNCS, vol. 7001, pp. 262–277. Springer, Heidelberg (2011). https://doi.org/10.1007/978-3-642-24861-0_18

33. Liu, C., Wang, X.S., Nayak, K., Huang, Y., Shi, E.: ObliVM: a programming framework for secure computation. In: 2015 IEEE Symposium on Security and Privacy, SP 2015, San Jose, CA, USA, 17–21 May 2015, pp. 359–376. IEEE Computer Society (2015). https://doi.org/10.1109/SP.2015.29

34. Lu, S., Ostrovsky, R.: How to garble RAM programs? In: Johansson, T., Nguyen, P.Q. (eds.) EUROCRYPT 2013. LNCS, vol. 7881, pp. 719–734. Springer, Heidelberg (2013). https://doi.org/10.1007/978-3-642-38348-9_42

35. Neff, C.A.: A verifiable secret shuffle and its application to e-voting. In: Reiter, M.K., Samarati, P. (eds.) CCS 2001, Proceedings of the 8th ACM Conference on Computer and Communications Security, Philadelphia, Pennsylvania, USA, 6–8 November 2001, pp. 116–125. ACM (2001). https://doi.org/10.1145/501983.502000

36. Pedersen, T.P.: Non-interactive and information-theoretic secure verifiable secret sharing. In: Feigenbaum, J. (ed.) CRYPTO 1991. LNCS, vol. 576, pp. 129–140. Springer, Heidelberg (1992). https://doi.org/10.1007/3-540-46766-1_9

37. Pippenger, N., Fischer, M.J.: Relations among complexity measures. J. ACM **26**(2), 361–381 (1979). https://doi.org/10.1145/322123.322138

38. Pointcheval, D., Stern, J.: Security proofs for signature schemes. In: Maurer, U. (ed.) EUROCRYPT 1996. LNCS, vol. 1070, pp. 387–398. Springer, Heidelberg (1996). https://doi.org/10.1007/3-540-68339-9_33

39. Shamir, A.: How to share a secret. Commun. ACM **22**(11), 612–613 (1979). https://doi.org/10.1145/359168.359176

40. Thaler, J.: Proofs, Arguments, and Zero-Knowledge (2021). Course notes. http://people.cs.georgetown.edu/jthaler/ProofsArgsAndZK.html

41. Thuraisingham, B.M., Evans, D., Malkin, T., Xu, D. (eds.): Proceedings of the 2017 ACM SIGSAC Conference on Computer and Communications Security, CCS 2017, Dallas, TX, USA, 30 October–03 November 2017. ACM (2017). https://doi.org/10.1145/3133956

42. Waksman, A.: A permutation network. J. ACM **15**(1), 159–163 (1968). https://doi.org/10.1145/321439.321449

43. Zahur, S., Evans, D.: Circuit structures for improving efficiency of security and privacy tools. In: 2013 IEEE Symposium on Security and Privacy, SP 2013, Berkeley, CA, USA, 19–22 May 2013, pp. 493–507. IEEE Computer Society (2013). https://doi.org/10.1109/SP.2013.40

Efficient Scalable Multi-party Private Set Intersection Using Oblivious PRF

Alireza Kavousi[1](✉), Javad Mohajeri[2], and Mahmoud Salmasizadeh[2]

[1] Department of Electrical Engineering, Sharif University of Technology, Tehran, Iran
kavousi.alireza@ee.sharif.edu
[2] Electronics Research Institute, Sharif University of Technology, Tehran, Iran
{mohajer,salmasi}@shairf.edu

Abstract. In this paper, we present a concretely efficient protocol for private set intersection (PSI) in the multi-party setting using oblivious pseudorandom function (OPRF). In fact, we generalize the approach used in the work of Chase and Miao [CRYPTO 2020] towards deploying a lightweight multi-point OPRF construction for two-party PSI. Our protocol only includes oblivious transfer (OT) extension and garbled Bloom filter as its main ingredients and avoids computationally expensive operations. From a communication pattern perspective, the protocol consists of two types of interactions. The first type is performed over a star-like communication graph in which one designated party interacts with all other parties via performing OTs as the sender. Besides, parties communicate through a path-like communication graph that involves sending a garbled Bloom filter from the first party to its neighboring party following the last one. This design makes our protocol to be highly scalable due to the independence of each party's complexity from the number of participating parties and thus causes a communication and computation complexities of $O(n\lambda k)$, where n is the set size, k is the number of hash functions, and λ is the security parameter. Moreover, the asymptotic complexity of the designated party is $O(tn\lambda)$ which linearly scales with the number of parties t. We prove security of the proposed protocol against semi-honest adversaries.

Keywords: Secure multi-party computation · Private set intersection · Oblivious pseudorandom function · Concrete efficiency

1 Introduction

Secure multi-party computation (MPC) has been the focus of an extensive amount of scientific works over the last few decades. It deals with the general problem of enabling a group of distrustful parties to jointly compute a function of their private inputs without revealing anything but the result. Due to the considerable progress in making the MPC protocols more and more efficient, they have become truly practical and therefore found much more applications in recent years.

© Springer Nature Switzerland AG 2021
R. Roman and J. Zhou (Eds.): STM 2021, LNCS 13075, pp. 81–99, 2021.
https://doi.org/10.1007/978-3-030-91859-0_5

Private set intersection (PSI) is one of the important and well-studied MPC protocols which allows a set of parties, each holding an input set, to compute their intersection without leaking any other information beyond their intersection. There exist many privacy-preserving potential applications for PSI such as advertising conversion [Mia+20], private contact discovery [Kal+19, Dem+18], and more. Recently and due to the spread of the COVID-19 pandemic, there has been an interdisciplinary quest to develop private contact tracing systems to contain the outbreak. In this case, PSI also plays a crucial role in building privacy-preserving solutions [DPT20, Dit+20].

During the last decade or so, many research-oriented works have been dedicated to proposing efficient constructions for the PSI functionality. In general, there are two main approaches to the design of these constructions. The first is using *generic circuit-based* protocols that deal with the computation of logical or arithmetic circuits by parties [HEK12, Pin+18, Pin+19b]. Although circuit-based protocols often yield computationally efficient constructions and are flexible to be adapted for different variants of PSI functionality, having high communication complexity for the PSI problem which requires the evaluation of large circuits is a big hurdle in making them to be practically useful. It should be remarked that it is now widely believed that communication and not computation, is the principal bottleneck in MPC protocols like PSI [Ash+13, Hal18]. Another approach is related to *special purpose* protocols that mainly rely on cryptographic primitives and various assumptions. Since this type of PSI protocols can achieve better performance compared to the previous one, it has gained significant attention among researchers.

Loosely speaking, existing special purpose PSI protocols can be categorized in the following way. PSI protocols built from oblivious polynomial evaluation [FNP04, HV17, Haz18, GS19], hard cryptographic assumptions [DT10, DT12], and oblivious transfer (OT) and hashing structures [Kol+16, Pin+20, CM20]. There has also been a branch of works on server-aided setting [KMS20, ATD20]. Since the OT-based PSI protocols achieve a good balance between communication and computation costs and indeed mainly benefit from cheap cryptographic tools, are often regarded as the fastest *concretely efficient* solutions in which by this term we refer to those constructions which do not use computationally too expensive tasks like polynomial evaluation and interpolation or vast public-key operations (see [PSZ18] for an overview on different PSI settings).[1]

Notice that a large body of literature on two-party OT-based PSI uses a primitive named *oblivious pseudorandom function* (OPRF) which is often instantiated efficiently by means of symmetric-key techniques. Particularly, the recent work of Chase and Miao [CM20] aims to investigate the trade-offs between communication and computation costs and enjoy the best of both worlds. By introducing an interesting lightweight *multi-point* OPRF protocol, they propose a highly efficient semi-honest secure two-party PSI protocol that assuming random oracle

---

[1] Although to perform OT one needs to use public-key operations, in [Ish+03] a method was introduced which enables to do quite a large number of OTs utilizing only efficient symmetric-key primitives.

model its security can be enhanced to one-sided malicious security. The idea of considering a multi-point OPRF construction instead of the common single-point version results in decreasing the communication complexity of the protocol by a constant factor due to the fact that evaluation of each element in the set will be required only for once.

Multi-party PSI. While two-party setting encompasses the majority of existing works, multi-party PSI has not attracted that much attention in the literature. This might account for the fact that there is a seemingly inevitable need to have interactions among parties which incurs an extreme communication cost to the protocol and hence makes it practically infeasible. More recently, however, few works including [Kol+17, HV17, IOP18, GN19] have come up with asymptotically efficient constructions for multi-party PSI in different security models. Regardless of the tools and primitives used, the core idea underlying all these constructions is considering a *designated* party who individually interacts with all other parties throughout the protocol execution (i.e., star topology network). This attitude towards multi-party PSI protocol appears to be useful since it results in a reduction in *intermediate* exchanges between parties but has the weakness of putting a high workload on the designated party which may be very problematic in practical scenarios. Very recently, the approaches of [Kol+17, IOP18], which led to concretely efficient constructions are extended by [Efr+21] in a maliciously secure model.

Additional Related Work. The authors in [DCW13] present a two-party OT-based PSI protocol using a variant of Bloom filter called garbled Bloom filter. [RR16] follows the approach of the aforementioned protocol and presents a maliciously secure protocol employing the cut-and-choose technique. A few constructions like [Yin+20, Bud+20] concentrate on some variants of PSI in which they study the problem of performing different sets of computations on the intersection. There are also a few works on threshold PSI such as [ZC18, GS19, Bad+20, BDP20]. In [ZC18], authors introduce a protocol based on oblivious polynomial evaluation for threshold PSI. The exciting work of [GS19] demonstrates a lower bound on the communication complexity of two-party threshold PSI. The most recent work of [Bad+20] takes this a stage further and extends the results to the multi-party setting.

1.1 Our Contribution

We study the problem of PSI in the case that there are more than two parties involved in the execution of the protocol, namely *multi-party* PSI. When practicality comes into play, most of the current protocols on multi-party PSI fail to meet the need because of suffering from either high communication or computational overhead for the considerable number of participating parties or the large set sizes. In this work, we aim to present a concretely efficient multi-party PSI protocol following the idea of [CM20] in employing an efficient multi-point OPRF construction that through leading to a better balance between communication and computation costs causes [CM20] to be the fastest two-party PSI in moderate bandwidth compared to the state-of-the-art protocols.

Our protocol leverages a combination of so-called *star* and *path* communication graphs which in the former, a designated party as the sender runs OTs with all other parties, and in the latter, each party only sends a garbled Bloom filter to his adjacent party in the direction of the last party. In light of this design, the construction can be very scalable since the communication and computation complexities of each party (except the designated party) only depend on his own input set size and not on the number of parties involved in the protocol. So, while the designated party has the asymptotic complexity of $O(tn\lambda)$ which linearly scales with the number of parties t, the complexity of each other party is $O(n\lambda k)$ where n is the party's set size, k is the number of hash functions (used in garbled Bloom filter), and λ is the security parameter. Also, thanks to this fusion of star and path communication graphs, instead of having a designated party with significantly high communication overhead compared to others, the distribution of cost is rather fair with respect to the number of parties t and the number of hash functions k and therefore this prevents the designated party from taking a lot of bandwidth. We consider semi-honest security and prove the security of our protocol in this model.

2   Preliminaries

2.1   Notation

Throughout this paper, we consider t parties $P_1, \ldots, P_t$ who each owns an input set $X_1, \ldots, X_t$, respectively. We may refer to P_t as the leader and all the other parties as clients. λ and σ are used to denote the computational and statistical security parameters which the former deals with the hardness of problems in the face of computationally bounded adversaries and the latter is concerned with the attacks that may occur during protocol interactions. $[n]$ concisely shows a set of n items $\{1, \ldots, n\}$. By $v[i]$, we refer to the i-th element of the vector v. In an $n \times m$ matrix M, the i-th column is denoted as M_i where $i \in [m]$. $\|x\|$ denotes the hamming weight of a string x. We consider $\text{negl}(\lambda)$ as a negligible function that proceeds asymptotically towards zero faster than any inverse polynomial for appropriately large inputs. Finally, we use $s \xleftarrow{R} S$ to show that s is sampled uniformly at random from S.

2.2   Secret Sharing Scheme

Secret sharing [Sha79] is one of the pivotal tools in cryptography which has numerous applications in constructing secure computation protocols. In an (t, n) secret sharing scheme, a secret s is distributed among n parties in a way that by having up to $t - 1$ shares no information about the secret is revealed. The simplest form of an (n, n) secret sharing scheme can be achieved by means of bitwise-XOR operation. In fact, one chooses $n-1$ random strings $(v_1, \ldots, v_n-1)$, and then selects the last share by computing $v_n = s \oplus v_1 \oplus \ldots \oplus v_n - 1$. This scheme has perfect security and for reconstructing the secret s having all shares are required.

2.3 Bloom Filter

Bloom filter (BF) [Blo70] is a probabilistic compact data structure which is used as a tool for efficient set membership checking. It randomly maps a set X containing n items to a binary array of size M, where every single element is mapped to a different subset of indices in the array. Bloom filter includes k independent uniform hash functions $H = \{h_1, \ldots, h_k\}$ that $h_i : \{0, 1\}^* \to [M]$. At first, all bits in the array are set to zero. To insert each element $x \in X$, one sets $BF[h_i(x)] = 1$ for all $i \in [k]$. To see whether the set X consists of an element x', one simply needs to check all the $BF[h_i(x')]$ are equal to one. Even if one of the corresponding bits in the array be equal to zero, then it can be concluded that the element x' is not in the set. On the other hand, if all of the corresponding bits in the array are equal to one, then x' is in the set but for a determined false-positive probability ϵ. The computed upper bound on ϵ is given by $p^k(1 + O(\frac{k}{p}\sqrt{\frac{\ln M - k \ln p}{M}}))$ where $p = 1 - (1 - \frac{1}{M})^{nk}$. It is shown in [DCW13] that the optimal values to accomplish the best performance are $k = \frac{M}{n} \ln 2$ and $M \geq n \log_2(e) . \log_2(\frac{1}{\epsilon})$.

Garbled Bloom Filter. A different version of BF was introduced in [DCW13] which is called garbled Bloom Filter (GBF). To give a concise description of GBF, we can refer to it as an extended Bloom filter that instead of having an array consisting of single bits, it is an array consisting of bit strings where the length of the bit string is determined by security parameter. Like BF, insertion is done in GBF by computing the hash functions for each input element x with regard to a set of uniform hash functions $H = \{h_1, \ldots, h_k\}$, but instead of dealing with just single bits, some randomly chosen shares of x are placed in those indices corresponded to x subject to the constraint that $\bigoplus_{i=1}^{k} GBF[h_i(x)] = x$. Garbled property of GBF makes it computationally impossible to know whether a given element x is in the set, unless one queries GBF on all the indices related to x. In this manner, the false-positive probability in GBF is equal to $2^{-\lambda}$.

2.4 Oblivious Transfer

A foundational cryptographic primitive used as a building block in many secure computation protocols is oblivious transfer (OT) [Rab05] whose functionality is presented in Fig. 1. In an 1-out-of-2 OT, there exist a sender and a receiver, where the sender has two strings (x_0, x_1) and the receiver has a choice bit c as their inputs, respectively. After the execution of OT, the sender learns nothing and the receiver learns x_c without obtaining any information about x_{1-c}. As shown in [IR89], it cannot be possible to do OT without relying on public-key

> **Input:** The sender inputs two strings (x_0, x_1) and the receiver inputs a choice bit $c \in \{0, 1\}$.
> **Output:** The functionality returns x_c to the receiver and returns nothing to the sender.

Fig. 1. The functionality of oblivious transfer ($\mathcal{F}_{OT}$)

operations. Thus, this was considered as the main constraint when it comes to doing a great number of OTs which is a typical task in PSI protocols. However, [Ish+03] proposed a method called OT extension which makes it possible to do an extensive number of OTs while using only a limited number of public-key operations for initial OTs (known as base-OTs). Also, some variants of OT are available. Random OT (ROT) refers to a setting in which the sender and receiver do not choose their inputs and they are chosen by the functionality itself. By using ROT, the protocol can be performed with much less communication overhead compared to OT.

2.5 Security Model

Definition 1. (Computational Indistinguishably) *Let* $X = \{X(\lambda)\}_{\lambda \in N}$ *and* $Y = \{Y(\lambda)\}_{\lambda \in N}$ *be two probability distribution ensembles, we say that* X *and* Y *are computationally indistinguishable, denoted as* $X \approx Y$, *if for every probabilistic polynomial time (PPT) algorithm* D, *there exists a negligible function* $negl(\lambda)$ *such that for all sufficiently large* λ

$$|Pr[D(\lambda, X(\lambda))] - Pr[D(\lambda, Y(\lambda))]| \leq negl(\lambda).$$

Our protocol is secure against semi-honest adversaries who follow the protocol as specified but try to obtain more information than what is allowed. Note that we assume the leader does not collude with any client. This assumption is widely used in the literature [Aba+17, Zha+19]. Having this in mind, our protocol can tolerate up to $t - 1$ corruptions.

The security of an MPC protocol is typically proven respecting real/ideal simulation paradigm. That is, a protocol is considered to be secure if the real execution of the protocol Π computationally looks like the ideal execution of the protocol $\mathcal{F}$. To put in another way, imagine an ideal world where there exists a fully trusted entity that parties can privately send their inputs to and then it computes the result and returns it back to the parties. Surely, this ideal world execution captures all the required security we want. So, if we somehow show that for any real world adversary, the real and ideal execution of the protocol are computationally indistinguishable, then we can deduce the protocol Π is secure. Here, we give the formal definition of real/ideal simulation paradigm for two-party protocol introduced in [Gol04].

Definition 2. (Semi-Honest Security) *Let denote* P_i's *view in the real execution of the protocol* Π *as* $view_i^{\Pi}(X_1, X_2)$ *for* $i \in [2]$. $\mathcal{F}_i(X_1, X_2)$ *denotes the output of* *ideal functionality for P_i. The protocol Π securely realizes the ideal functionality $\mathcal{F}$ in the presence of static semi-honest adversaries if there exist PPT simulators $\mathcal{S}_1$ and $\mathcal{S}_2$ for all inputs such that*

$$\{\mathcal{S}_1(\lambda, X_1, \mathcal{F}_1(X_1, X_2))\} \approx \{view_1^{\Pi}(X_1, X_2))\},$$
$$\{\mathcal{S}_2(\lambda, X_2, \mathcal{F}_2(X_1, X_2))\} \approx \{view_2^{\Pi}(X_1, X_2))\}.$$

2.6   Hamming Correlation Robustness

The security of some protocols can be proven using a weaker assumption than random oracle model which is called *correlation robustness* [KK13, Pin+19a, CM20]. In this paper we use the definition presented in [Pin+19a, CM20] to prove the security of our protocol.

Definition 3. (Hamming Correlation Robustness) *Let H be a hash function with the input length n. Then H is d-Hamming correlation robust if, for any $a_1, \ldots, a_m, b_1, \ldots, b_m \in \{0,1\}^n$ with $\|b_i\| \geq d = \lambda$ for each $i \in [m]$, the following distribution, induced by random sampling of $s \xleftarrow{R} \{0,1\}^n$, is pseudorandom.*

$$H(a_1 \oplus [b_1 \cdot s]), \ldots, H(a_m \oplus [b_m \cdot s]),$$

where $\cdot$ denotes bitwise-AND.

2.7   PSI from OPRF

An oblivious pseudorandom function (OPRF) is a secure two-party computation protocol which was introduced in [Fre+05]. In an OPRF protocol, the sender inputs a random PRF key K and the receiver inputs a single input x. By the end of the protocol, the sender learns nothing and the receiver learns the evaluation of the OPRF functionality on his input.

There are several works on two-party PSI protocol which use single-point OPRF construction [Pin+15, Kol+16]. At a high level, the general structure of these protocols is as follows. Firstly, the sender (P_1) and the receiver (P_2) run the OPRF protocol that at the end P_1 obtains a random key K and P_2 obtains the outcome of the functionality on his input $\mathrm{OPRF}_K(x_1^2)$. They run the protocol for all items in the receiver's set $x_1^2, \ldots, x_{n_2}^2 \in X_2$. As a result, the sender learns a set of random keys and the receiver learns a set of OPRF values. Then, P_1 evaluates OPRF functionality on his set of inputs $x_1^1, \ldots, x_{n_1}^1 \in X_1$ and sends the resulting values to P_2. We should note that in these protocols parties often use a Cuckoo hashing construction [PR04] to map every single of their elements to a separate bin and it is also assumed parties' sets have the same size $n_1 = n_2 = n$. Finally and by comparing the received values and his OPRFs, P_2 can determine the intersection.

From Single-Point to Multi-point OPRF. In [Kol+16], a hash function (which is modeled as a random oracle) is considered an OPRF whose keys are in fact parts of its input argument. Pinkas et al. in [Pin+19a] proposed a PSI protocol based on multi-point OPRF construction in which it enables parties to instead of having to evaluate n instances of OPRF protocol, do it in a way that computing OPRF values requires far less communication cost, i.e., they no longer need to use Cuckoo hashing and perform several OPRFs for every single hash bin, so each element is only evaluated once. But, multi-point OPRF of [Pin+19a] incurs a high computational overhead compared to the single-point version of [Kol+16], since it needs to evaluate and interpolate a high-degree polynomial over a large field which obviously causes much more cost than just using symmetric primitives and bitwise operations as in [Kol+16].

Efficient Multi-point OPRF. To provide a more reasonable balance between communication and computation costs, Chase and Miao [CM20] introduced a two-party PSI protocol using a lightweight multi-point OPRF where oblivious transfer protocol is the only heavy cryptographic operation needed that also itself can be performed efficiently using OT extension. To perform the multi-point OPRF, a random seed of length w is picked by the sender, $s \xleftarrow{R} \{0,1\}^w$, and the receiver constructs two $m \times w$ matrices of A and B where the entries of the former are selected randomly from $\{0,1\}$ and those of the latter are determined by evaluating a pseudorandom function with the output length of $w \cdot \log m$ on each element of the receiver's set, $v = F_K(x_i^2)$. The matrix B is formed such that for every $x_i^2 \in X_2$, the corresponding bits in two matrices are the same while other bits differ. After running w OTs between parties, the sender who acts as a receiver obtains an $m \times w$ matrix C that each of its columns is either A_i or B_i for all $i \in [w]$ depending on the chosen seed s. Then, the sender evaluates the PRF on each of his input elements $x_i^1 \in X_1$ as $v = F_K(x_i^1)$ and computes the OPRF value $\psi = H(C_1[v[1]] \parallel \ldots \parallel C_w[v[w]])$ and sends all the resulting OPRFs to the receiver. Ultimately, the receiver computes the OPRF values of his input elements and finds the intersection of the two sets. Notice that if a sender's element be in the intersection, $x_i^1 \in X_2$, its corresponding input to the OPRF is equal to one of the receiver's element input to the OPRF, otherwise the inputs to OPRF are different with overwhelming probability.

3   Our Multi-party PSI Protocol

3.1   An Overview

In this section we introduce our proposed multi-party PSI protocol. As mentioned earlier, there is a group of parties $P_1, \ldots, P_t$ with their private input sets $X_1, \ldots, X_t$, respectively, who want to jointly compute their set intersection $X_1 \cap \ldots \cap X_t$ without leaking any other private information relating to either individual or a proper subset of parties. As in many other multi-party protocols, we consider P_t as the party who learns the intersection at the end of the protocol. The functionality of multi-party PSI is defined in Fig. 2. We use the lightweight multi-point OPRF construction introduced in [CM20] to build an efficient and scalable multi-party PSI. The full description of our protocol which constitutes several steps is presented in Fig. 3.

There are t parties $P_1, \ldots, P_t$.

Input: Each party P_j has an input set $X_j = \{x_1^j, \ldots, x_{n_j}^j\}$ where every $x^j \in \{0,1\}^*$.

Output: Party P_t receives the intersection $I = X_1 \cap \ldots \cap X_t$ and other parties receive nothing.

Fig. 2. The functionality of multi-party private set intersection ($\mathcal{F}_{\text{MPSI}}$)

Generally speaking, the protocol works as follows. At first, P_t constructs a random $m \times w$ matrix A. In fact, to generate the i-th column of matrix A, P_t chooses $t - 1$ strings of length m uniformly at random and sets $A_i = A_i^1 \oplus \ldots \oplus A_i^{t-1}$. In addition, for each $j \in [t-1]$, party P_t generates the matrix B^j from the matrix A^j by computing a pseudorandom function $F_K(\cdot)$ on all of his input elements and sets $B = B^1 \oplus \ldots \oplus B^{t-1}$. After running w OTs between P_t as the sender and each $\{P_j\}_{j \in [t-1]}$ as the receiver, every P_j ends up with a matrix C^j which its column vectors are just m-bit random strings. Then, each party locally constructs a garbled Bloom filter of his input set GBF_j using the entries of the received matrix. Afterwards, P_1 sends GBF_1 to P_2 that upon getting it, he XORs GBF_1 with GBF_2 and sends the resulting GBF to the next party. This process continues until P_{t-1} computes the cumulative GBF and also OPRF values and then sends the OPRFs to the P_t to allow him to find the intersection.

Remark 1. We can consider an upper bound N on each party's input set size. Meaning, parties $P_1, \ldots, P_t$ can have different input set sizes up to N. In this way, parties' exact set sizes would not be revealed during the execution of the protocol.

Remark 2. We assume that clients are connected by secure channels, i.e., party P_t is not able to learn useful information by observing communication between $P_1, \ldots, P_{t-1}$. We stress that deploying such point-to-point channels is cheap and does not impose that much cost.

3.2 Protocol Correctness

Regarding the particular form of matrices A^j and B^j constructed by P_t, for each $x^t \in X_t$, let $v = F_K(H_1(x^t))$, it holds that $A_i^j[v[i]] = B_i^j[v[i]]$ for all $i \in [w]$. Let x be an element which is in the intersection, i.e., it exists in all the parties' input sets. Since P_t inputs uniformly random shares of each column of matrix A (using XOR secret sharing scheme) while performing OTs with clients, for each $x \in I$ it holds that $A_i[v[i]] = \bigoplus_{j=1}^{t-1} C_i^j[v[i]]$, for all $i \in [w]$. Therefore, regardless of what random string s_j is chosen by the client P_j, XORing the strings at all coordinates corresponded to x in GBF^* by P_{t-1} (Step 8) results in a string which is the same as one of the P_t's elements input to the hash function H_2. The correctness of the protocol is satisfied with all but negligible probability of a false-positive occurring.

Parameters: Parties $P_1, \ldots, P_t$ agree on security parameters λ and σ, two hash functions $H_1 : \{0,1\}^* \rightarrow \{0,1\}^{l_1}$ and $H_2 : \{0,1\}^w \rightarrow \{0,1\}^{l_2}$, and a pseudorandom function $F : \{0,1\}^\lambda \times \{0,1\}^{l_1} \rightarrow \{m\}^w$. They also agree on a garbled Bloom filter specification which includes a set of independent random hash functions $H = \{h_1, \ldots, h_k\}$ that $h_i : \{0,1\}^* \rightarrow [M]$ for $i \in [k]$, and entries string length of w.

Initial Computation:

1. Each party P_j picks a random string $s_j \xleftarrow{R} \{0,1\}^w$ for $j \in [t-1]$.
2. P_t generates an $m \times w$ matrix A in which its entries are selected randomly from $\{0,1\}$. For all $i \in [w]$, party P_t chooses $t - 1$ shares uniformly at random under the constraint that $A_i = A_i^1 \oplus \ldots \oplus A_i^{t-1}$. He also samples a uniform PRF key $K \xleftarrow{R} \{0,1\}^\lambda$.

Performing Oblivious Transfer:

3. To construct an $m \times w$ matrix B^j, party P_t computes $v = F_K(H_1(x^t))$ for all $x^t \in X_t$, and copies those bits from the corresponding positions in matrix A^j to the matrix B^j. He also flips the bits from A^j to B^j for the remaining empty positions.
4. At this stage, P_t as the sender with inputs $\{A_i^j, B_i^j\}$ independently runs w OTs with each party P_j as the receiver with inputs $s_j[i]$ for all $i \in [w]$ and $j \in [t-1]$. Eventually, for all $j \in [t-1]$ each party P_j forms an $m \times w$ matrix C^j which its columns are those strings he receives after doing OTs.
5. P_t sends the PRF key K to P_j for all $j \in [t-1]$.

Concluding the Intersection:

6. Each party $\{P_j\}_{j \in [t-1]}$ constructs a garbled Bloom filter of his input set GBF_j such that for every $x^j \in X_j$ it holds that $\bigoplus_{i=1}^k GBF_j[h_i(x^j)]$ equals concatenation of all the bits in positions $C_i^j[v[i]]$ where $v = F_K(H_1(x^j))$.
7. P_1 sends GBF_1 to P_2 that upon receiving it, he XORs GBF_1 and GBF_2 and sends the resulting GBF to the next party. This process continues until P_{t-1} computes the cumulative garbled Bloom filter $GBF^* = GBF_1 \oplus \ldots \oplus GBF_{t-1}$.
8. For each $x^{t-1} \in X_{t-1}$, P_{t-1} computes $u = \bigoplus_{i=1}^k GBF^*[h_i(x^{t-1})]$ and its OPRF value $\psi = H_2(u)$ and sends it to P_t. Let Ψ denote the set of all OPRFs.
9. After receiving the OPRFs, P_t computes his corresponding OPRF values as $\psi = H_2(A_1[v[1]] \| \ldots \| A_w[v[w]])$ for all $x^t \in X_t$, where $v = F_K(H_1(x^t))$. P_t considers x^t in the intersection iff $\psi \in \Psi$.

Fig. 3. Our multi-party private set intersection protocol (Π_{MPSI})

3.3 Protocol Security

Security Analysis. In the protocol, P_t runs OTs independently with each client using randomly chosen shares of columns of the matrix A that itself is a random matrix sampled by P_t. So, each matrix C^j formed by the P_j contains independent uniform strings as its columns. As a result, concerning the way each party computes his garbled Bloom filter (Step 7), receiving the GBF of P_i by P_j for any $i, j \in [t-1]$ leaks no useful information about P_i's input set. Also, by suitable choice of the parameters m, w (as will be discussed later) and indeed security properties of GBF, for any item in the P_{t-1}'s input set which is not in the intersection I, the corresponding OPRF value is pseudorandom to P_t. Thus, P_t is only able to obtain intersection over all parties' input sets and learns nothing about partial set intersection (i.e., elements which exist in some but not all parties' input sets).

The Parameters m, w. Choosing m and w plays an important role in providing the security of the protocol. The mentioned parameters should be selected in a way that for any common element in clients' sets which is not in the intersection (i.e., $x \in I\backslash X_t$), its OPRF value must be pseudorandom to P_t. In view of this, we need to make sure that if F is a random function and H_1 is a collision resistant hash function then for all $i \in [w]$, there exist at least λ flipped bits in the positions $B_i[v[i]]$, where $v = F_K(H_1(x))$. This is essentially because of fulfilling the correlation robustness property of H_2, and consequently preventing brute force searches by P_t. It should also be noted that for any P_{t-1}'s element which is not in client's intersection, its OPRF value is pseudorandom to P_t due to the obliviousness property of garbled Bloom filter.

Since the input to $F_K(\cdot)$ is different for every $x^t \in X_t$, the probability that any bit in each column of matrix B is flipped equals $p = (1 - \frac{1}{m})^{n_t}$. Thus, for any $x \in I\backslash X_t$, the number of flipped bits in $B_1[v[1]], \ldots, B_w[v[w]]$ has a binomial distribution, which the probability of having d flips is equal to

$$\binom{w}{d} p^d (1-p)^{w-d}.$$

So, by fixing m we can determine the proper value for w using the union bound as follows

$$N \cdot \sum_{d=0}^{\lambda-1} \binom{w}{d} p^d (1-p)^{w-d} \leq negl(\sigma).$$

It is also worth mentioning that the parameter l_2 which is the output length of H_2 needs to be chosen such that the probability of having collision in PSI protocol (Step 9) be negligible. In a similar way to [Pin+19a, CM20], it can be calculated as $l_2 = \sigma + 2\log(N)$ for the semi-honest model.

Security Proof. In this part, we formally prove the security of our proposed multi-party protocol based on the notion of real/ideal simulation paradigm in the semi-honest model. Note that we consider two cases for corruption, in one case adversary corrupts a subset of clients and in the other case only leader is corrupted.

Theorem 1. *Assume that F is a pseudorandom function, H_1 is a collision resistant hash function, and H_2 is a d-Hamming robust hash function, then protocol Π_{MPSI} (Fig. 3) securely realizes the functionality $\mathcal{F}_{\text{MPSI}}$ (Fig. 2) in the presence of semi-honest adversaries for proper choice of parameters as discussed.*

Proof. (P_t is not corrupted) We show that there exists a PPT simulator $\mathcal{S}_Z$ that given corrupted parties' inputs can generate simulated views which are computationally indistinguishable from joint distribution of corrupted parties' views in the real execution of the protocol. Let us consider a subset $\mathcal{Z}$ of parties $P_1, \ldots, P_{t-1}$ is corrupted by the adversary. Given $\{X_j\}_{j \in Z}$, the simulator $\mathcal{S}_Z$ honestly chooses random strings $\{s_j\}_{j \in Z}$ and random matrices $\{C^j\}_{j \in Z} \in \{0,1\}^{m \times w}$. Then, $\mathcal{S}_Z$ runs OT simulator in order to simulate the view of each corrupted party $P_j \in Z$ as the receiver with respect to the inputs $s_j[1], \ldots, s_j[w]$ and outputs $C_1^j, \ldots, C_w^j$. Moreover, $\mathcal{S}_Z$ sends a randomly picked PRF key to the corrupted parties. Knowing the description of garbled Bloom filter, the simulator also constructs random garbled Bloom filters on behalf of the honest parties from its randomness.

We now argue that $\mathcal{S}_Z(\lambda, \{X_j\}_{j \in Z}, \bot) \approx view_Z^\Pi(\lambda, X_1, \ldots, X_t)$. To do so, we use a sequence of hybrid distributions in which each two adjacent distributions are computationally indistinguishable and thanks to the transitive property, it can be concluded that the two desired distributions are also computationally indistinguishable.

Hybrid$_0$: The view of corrupted parties $\{P_j\}_{j \in Z}$ in the real execution of the protocol.

Hybrid$_1$: The same as **Hybrid$_0$**, except, $\mathcal{S}_Z$ instead of P_t does the following for every corrupt P_j. That is, if $s_j[i] = 0$, it randomly chooses an m-bit string A_i^j and does the same as in Step 3 to construct each corresponding column of matrix B^j; on the other hand, if $s_j[i] = 1$, it randomly picks an m-bit string B_i^j and computes A_i^j by flipping corresponding bits as mentioned in Step 3. So, this argument is essentially identical to **Hybrid$_0$**.

Hybrid$_2$: The same as previous hybrid, except, $\mathcal{S}_Z$ computes a garbled Bloom filter on behalf of each honest client (i.e., party $P_j \notin Z$) using its own randomness. Note that the indistinguishably of this hybrid and **Hybrid$_1$** stems from using XOR secret sharing scheme by P_t for his inputs to the OTs and also the special way the garbled Bloom filters are constructed.

Hybrid$_3$: The simulated view of $\mathcal{S}_Z$. Due to the security properties of OT protocol and garbled Bloom filter, this hybrid is computationally indistinguishable from **Hybrid$_2$**.

Proof. (P_t is corrupted) We show that there exists a PPT simulator $\mathcal{S}_t$ that given P_t's input and output can generate a simulated view which is computationally indistinguishable from P_t's view in the real execution of the protocol. The simulator can be considered as follows. $\mathcal{S}_t$ first receives P_t's input set X_t, P_{t-1}'s set size n_{t-1}, and the intersection I. Running the OT simulator, $\mathcal{S}_t$ simulates P_t's view as the sender by honestly constructing matrices A^j and B^j for all $i \in [t-1]$. Moreover, for any $x \in I$, it computes $\psi = H_2(A_1[v[1]] \parallel \ldots \parallel A_w[v[w]])$, where $v = F_K(H_1(x))$. Let $\Psi_\mathcal{I}$ denote this set of OPRF values. It also picks a set of size $n_{t-1} - |I|$ containing l_2-bit random strings. Let us denote this set by $\Psi_\mathcal{R}$. Then, simulator sends $\Psi_\mathcal{I} \cup \Psi_\mathcal{R}$ to P_t. Eventually, $\mathcal{S}_t$ outputs P_t' simulated view as $\mathcal{S}_t(\lambda, X_t, n_{t-1}, I)$.

We now argue that $\mathcal{S}_t(\lambda, X_t, n_{t-1}, I) \approx view_t^{\Pi}(\lambda, X_1, \ldots, X_t)$ by using a multi-step hybrid argument.

Hybrid$_0$: The view of P_t in the real execution of the protocol.

Hybrid$_1$: The same as **Hybrid$_0$**, except, the protocol terminates if there is any $x^i, x^j \in X_1 \cup X_2 \cup \ldots \cup X_t$, $x^i \neq x^j$ that $H_1(x^i) = H_1(x^j)$. The probability of termination is negligible by collision resistance property of H_1.

Hybrid$_2$: The same as **Hybrid$_1$**, except, the protocol also terminates if there is any $x \in I\,X_t$ that for all $i \in [w]$ the number of flipped bits in $B_i[v[i]]$, where $v = F_K(H_1(x))$, be fewer than the security parameter λ. As discussed earlier, the parameters m and w must be chosen such that the probability of termination be negligible.

Hybrid$_3$: The same as **Hybrid$_2$**, except, $\mathcal{S}_t$ runs the OT simulator with honestly selected inputs $\{A_i^j, B_i^j\}$ to simulate the view of P_t as the sender. On account of the security properties of OT protocol, this hybrid is computationally indistinguishable from **Hybrid$_2$**.

Hybrid$_4$: The same as **Hybrid$_3$**, except, the OPRF values sent from P_{t-1} are replaced with l_2-bit random strings for all $x \in I \backslash X_t$. Regarding correlation robustness property of the hash function H_2, it can be shown that this hybrid is computationally indistinguishable from the previous one. More specifically, for all $i \in [w]$, let a_i equals the concatenation of bits $A_i[v[i]]$ and also b_i equals the concatenation of bits $B_i[v[i]]$, where $v = F_K(H_1(x))$. In Step 8, the hash function H_2 takes the concatenation of bits $\bigoplus_{j=1}^{t-1} C_i^j[v[i]]$ as its input which is equivalent to $a_i \oplus [(a_i \oplus b_i) \cdot s]$. Since we know that $\|a_i \oplus b_i\| \geq \lambda$ and also s is a random string unknown to P_t, thanks to the correlation robustness property of H_2, the OPRF value sent to P_2 is pseudorandom.

Hybrid$_5$: The same as **Hybrid$_4$**, except, the protocol does not terminate. This hybrid is P_t's view simulated by $\mathcal{S}_t$. Indeed, what described above simply implies indistinguishably of this hybrid and **Hybrid$_4$**.

Remark 1. It is important to mention that the two-party PSI protocol of [CM20] guarantees one-sided malicious security (i.e., against a malicious sender) in the random oracle model. We believe using the same assumption our protocol can also provide security against malicious clients.

4 Complexity Analysis

4.1 Asymptotic Complexity

Now, we analyze the asymptotic complexity of our multi-party PSI protocol. We should highlight the fact that the protocol is concretely efficient since it only relies on cheap tools including oblivious transfer extension, hashing, and bitwise operations. Without loss of generality, we consider n as the set size for

Table 1. Bits sent for leader and clients. Note that we do not consider the initial base-OTs which can be done ahead of time. Also, optimal parameters are considered for garbled Bloom filter.

Communication Pattern	$P_t \to P_j$	$P_j \to P_t$	$P_j \to P_{j+1}$	$P_{t-1} \to P_t$
Star Topology	nw	$w(\lambda - 1)$	–	–
Path Topology	–	–	$1.44nwk$	nl_2

all parties.[2] Also, as in [CM20], we set $m = n$. So, by fixing m and n in our complexity analysis w can be regarded as a value depending on λ (Sect. 3.3).

Recall that we denote party P_t as the leader who takes the main overhead of the protocol and other parties as the clients. In terms of the asymptotic complexity of our protocol, P_t first constructs specially formed matrices A^j and B^j which preparing them takes him linear complexity in n. He then as the sender independently runs w OTs with each client which leads to linear communication and computation complexities in the number of OTs. Apart from running OTs, parties just do hashing and bitwise-XOR operation which regarding the optimal parameters for garbled Bloom filter (as discussed in Sect. 2.3), they incur linear complexity in both communication and computation. As shown in [CM20] for the case of two-party, it is possible to use random OT in our multi-party PSI protocol which causes the communication overhead from the leader to the clients to be dramatically decreased. We refer the reader to [CM20] to see how random OT can be used in the protocol. Thus, taking this into account and also concerning the optimized semi-honest OT extension of [Ash+13], the total amount of bits exchanged between parties are summarized in Table 1.

Remark 1. Our protocol can be separated into two phases of offline and online which the former can be done before even parties' inputs are available and the latter is executed after learning the inputs. Therefore, a considerable part of the communication and computation costs of the protocol (which includes performing base-OTs, together with the messages sent from receiver to sender in the random OTs) can be done in the offline phase and only lightweight operations take place in the online phase.

Remark 2. Although the overall communication cost is not evenly distributed over all clients and P_{t-1} has less overhead compared to others, he needs to do more evaluation of hash functions in order to compute the OPRF values. So, we can think of it as a trade-off between the P_{t-1}'s communication and computation costs. In addition, the costs in our protocol is rather balanced which makes the protocol preferable in terms of not having a single designated party who has significantly higher overhead compared to others that may cause problem in practice.

---

[2] One can think of n as the upper bound on set sizes.

Table 2. Comparison of communication and computation complexities of multi-party PSI protocols in different security models, where t is the number of parties, n is the size of input sets, k is the number of hash functions, and λ is the security parameter.

Protocol	Communication		Computation		Security	Concretely
	Leader	Client	Leader	Client	Model	Efficient
[HV17]	$O(tn\lambda)$	$O(n\lambda)$	$O(tn\log(n))$	$O(n)$	Semi-Honest	No
[IOP18]	$O(tn\lambda k)$	$O(tn\lambda k)$	$O(tn\lambda k)$	$O(tn\lambda k)$	Semi-Honest	Yes
[IOP18]	$O(\log(t)n\lambda k)$	$O(\log(t)n\lambda k)$	$O(tn\lambda k)$	$O(tn\lambda k)$	Aug Semi-Honest	Yes
[GN19]	$O((t^2 + tn)\lambda)$	$O(n\lambda)$	$O(tn\log(n))$	$O(n\log^2(n))$	Malicious	No
Ours	$O(tn\lambda)$	$O(n\lambda k)$	$O(tn\lambda)$	$O(n\lambda k)$	Semi-Honest	Yes

Remark 3. An interesting feature of our protocol is that as the number of parties involved in the protocol increases, the communication and computation complexities of each client remain the same. This is a crucial point especially when it comes to having a large number of participants and indeed makes our protocol scale well with the number of parties.

4.2 Comparison

In Table 2, we compare the communication and computation complexities of our multi-party PSI protocol with those of [HV17, IOP18, GN19]. We should mention that having various structures and security levels makes it hard to provide a fair comparison, though, we have tried to pick some recent works with different security models. As in [HV17, GN19], the client's complexities do not depend on the number of parties. However, the two mentioned protocols are not concretely efficient. We observe that the distribution of costs is asymptotically rather fair in our protocol concerning the number of parties t and the number of hash functions k. The workload of parties in [IOP18] is also balanced. We should note that the reported complexities of the augmented semi-honest secure version of [IOP18] are with regard to some optimizations and security relaxations.[3]

5 Conclusion

In this work we proposed a multi-party PSI protocol utilizing a lightweight multipoint OPRF construction. Our protocol is concretely efficient because of involving oblivious transfer extension and garbled Bloom filter as its two core building blocks and achieves linear complexity in both computation and communication concerning each party's input set size. In our protocol, interactions among parties are performed over a combination of star and path network topologies and as a consequence of this design, the asymptotic communication and computation

---

[3] Augmented semi-honest security is a weaker notion than semi-honest security. We consider the optimized version of the protocol which tries to load balance the interactions between pairs of parties at the cost of some security relaxations.

complexities of each client only rely on his input set size and not on the number of parties, namely $O(n\lambda k)$. In general, this study has gone some way towards presenting an efficient scalable multi-party PSI protocol that can be deployed in practice. This inevitably comes at a cost of relaxation on the security model, but we do believe that future works can focus on enhancing the security of multi-party PSI based on OPRF to obtain more robust security guarantees without that much compromising efficiency.

References

[Aba+17] Abadi, A., Terzis, S., Metere, R., Dong, C.: Efficient delegated private set intersection on outsourced private datasets. IEEE Trans. Dependable Secure Comput. **16**(4), 608–624 (2017)

[Ash+13] Asharov, G., Lindell, Y., Schneider, T., Zohner, M.: More efficient oblivious transfer and extensions for faster secure computation. In: Proceedings of the 2013 ACM Conference on Computer and Communications Security, pp. 535–548 (2013)

[ATD20] Abadi, A., Terzis, S., Dong, C.: Feather: lightweight multi-party updatable delegated private set intersection. Cryptology ePrint Archive, 2020/407 (2020). https://eprint.iacr.org/2020/407

[Bad+20] Badrinarayanan, S., Miao, P., Raghuraman, S., Rindal, P.: Multi-party threshold private set intersection with sublinear communication. Cryptology ePrint Archive, 2020/600 (2020). https://eprint.iacr.org/2020/600

[BDP20] Branco, P., Döttling, N., Pu, S.: Multiparty cardinality testing for threshold private set intersection. Cryptology ePrint Archive, 2020/1307 (2020). https://eprint.iacr.org/2020/1307

[Blo70] Bloom, B.H.: Space/time trade-offs in hash coding with allowable errors. Commun. ACM **13**(7), 422–426 (1970)

[Bud+20] Buddhavarapu, P., Knox, A., Mohassel, P., Sengupta, S., Taubeneck, E., Vlaskin, V.: Private matching for compute. Cryptology ePrint Archive, 2020/599 (2020). https://eprint.iacr.org/2020/599

[CM20] Chase, M., Miao, P.: Private set intersection in the internet setting from lightweight oblivious PRF. In: Micciancio, D., Ristenpart, T. (eds.) CRYPTO 2020. LNCS, vol. 12172, pp. 34–63. Springer, Cham (2020). https://doi.org/10.1007/978-3-030-56877-1_2

[DCW13] Dong, C., Chen, L., Wen, Z.: When private set intersection meets big data: an efficient and scalable protocol. In: Proceedings of the 2013 ACM Conference on Computer and Communications Security, pp. 789–800 (2013)

[Dem+18] Demmler, D., Rindal, P., Rosulek, M., Trieu, N.: PIR-PSI: scaling private contact discovery. Proc. Priv. Enhanc. Technol. **2018**(4), 159–178 (2018)

[Dit+20] Dittmer, S., et al.: Function secret sharing for PSI-CA: with applications to private contact tracing. Cryptology ePrint Archive, 2020/1599 (2020). https://eprint.iacr.org/2020/1599

[DPT20] Duong, T., Phan, D.H., Trieu, N.: Catalic: delegated PSI cardinality with applications to contact tracing. In: Moriai, S., Wang, H. (eds.) ASIACRYPT 2020. LNCS, vol. 12493, pp. 870–899. Springer, Cham (2020). https://doi.org/10.1007/978-3-030-64840-4_29

[DT10] De Cristofaro, E., Tsudik, G.: Practical private set intersection protocols with linear complexity. In: Sion, R. (ed.) FC 2010. LNCS, vol. 6052, pp. 143–159. Springer, Heidelberg (2010). https://doi.org/10.1007/978-3-642-14577-3_13

[DT12] De Cristofaro, E., Tsudik, G.: Experimenting with fast private set intersection. In: Katzenbeisser, S., Weippl, E., Camp, L.J., Volkamer, M., Reiter, M., Zhang, X. (eds.) Trust 2012. LNCS, vol. 7344, pp. 55–73. Springer, Heidelberg (2012). https://doi.org/10.1007/978-3-642-30921-2_4

[Efr+21] Efraim, A.B., Nissenbaum, O., Omri, E., Paskin-Cherniavsky, A.: Psimple: practical multiparty maliciously-secure private set intersection. Cryptology ePrint Archive, 2021/122 (2021). https://eprint.iacr.org/2021/122

[FNP04] Freedman, M.J., Nissim, K., Pinkas, B.: Efficient private matching and set intersection. In: Cachin, C., Camenisch, J.L. (eds.) EUROCRYPT 2004. LNCS, vol. 3027, pp. 1–19. Springer, Heidelberg (2004). https://doi.org/10.1007/978-3-540-24676-3_1

[Fre+05] Freedman, M.J., Ishai, Y., Pinkas, B., Reingold, O.: Keyword search and oblivious pseudorandom functions. In: Kilian, J. (ed.) TCC 2005. LNCS, vol. 3378, pp. 303–324. Springer, Heidelberg (2005). https://doi.org/10.1007/978-3-540-30576-7_17

[GN19] Ghosh, S., Nilges, T.: An algebraic approach to maliciously secure private set intersection. In: Ishai, Y., Rijmen, V. (eds.) EUROCRYPT 2019. LNCS, vol. 11478, pp. 154–185. Springer, Cham (2019). https://doi.org/10.1007/978-3-030-17659-4_6

[Gol04] Goldreich, O.: Foundations of Cryptography: Volume 2, Basic Applications (2004)

[GS19] Ghosh, S., Simkin, M.: The communication complexity of threshold private set intersection. In: Boldyreva, A., Micciancio, D. (eds.) CRYPTO 2019. LNCS, vol. 11693, pp. 3–29. Springer, Cham (2019). https://doi.org/10.1007/978-3-030-26951-7_1

[Hal18] Halevi, S.: Advanced cryptography: promise and challenges. In: ACM Conference on Computer and Communications Security, p. 647 (2018)

[Haz18] Hazay, C.: Oblivious polynomial evaluation and secure set-intersection from algebraic PRFs. J. Cryptol. 31(2), 537–586 (2018). https://doi.org/10.1007/s00145-017-9263-y

[HEK12] Huang, Y., Evans, D., Katz, J.: Private set intersection: are garbled circuits better than custom protocols? In: NDSS (2012)

[HV17] Hazay, C., Venkitasubramaniam, M.: Scalable multi-party private set-intersection. In: Fehr, S. (ed.) PKC 2017. LNCS, vol. 10174, pp. 175–203. Springer, Heidelberg (2017). https://doi.org/10.1007/978-3-662-54365-8_8

[IOP18] Inbar, R., Omri, E., Pinkas, B.: Efficient scalable multiparty private set-intersection via garbled bloom filters. In: Catalano, D., De Prisco, R. (eds.) SCN 2018. LNCS, vol. 11035, pp. 235–252. Springer, Cham (2018). https://doi.org/10.1007/978-3-319-98113-0_13

[IR89] Impagliazzo, R., Rudich, S.: Limits on the provable consequences of one-way permutations. In: Proceedings of the Twenty-First Annual ACM Symposium on Theory of Computing, pp. 44–61 (1989)

[Ish+03] Ishai, Y., Kilian, J., Nissim, K., Petrank, E.: Extending oblivious transfers efficiently. In: Boneh, D. (ed.) CRYPTO 2003. LNCS, vol. 2729, pp. 145–161. Springer, Heidelberg (2003). https://doi.org/10.1007/978-3-540-45146-4_9

[Kal+19] Kales, D., Rechberger, C., Schneider, T., Senker, M., Weinert, C.: Mobile private contact discovery at scale. In: 28th {USENIX} Security Symposium ({USENIX} Security 2019), pp. 1447–1464 (2019)

[KK13] Kolesnikov, V., Kumaresan, R.: Improved OT extension for transferring short secrets. In: Canetti, R., Garay, J.A. (eds.) CRYPTO 2013. LNCS, vol. 8043, pp. 54–70. Springer, Heidelberg (2013). https://doi.org/10.1007/978-3-642-40084-1_4

[KMS20] Kavousi, A., Mohajeri, J., Salmasizadeh, M.: Improved secure efficient delegated private set intersection. In: 2020 28th Iranian Conference on Electrical Engineering (ICEE), pp. 1–6. IEEE (2020)

[Kol+16] Kolesnikov, V., Kumaresan, R., Rosulek, M., Trieu, N.: Efficient batched oblivious PRF with applications to private set intersection. In: Proceedings of the 2016 ACM Conference on Computer and Communications Security, pp. 818–829 (2016)

[Kol+17] Kolesnikov, V., Matania, N., Pinkas, B., Rosulek, M., Trieu, N.: Practical multi-party private set intersection from symmetric-key techniques. In: Proceedings of the 2017 ACM Conference on Computer and Communications Security, pp. 1257–1272 (2017)

[Mia+20] Miao, P., Patel, S., Raykova, M., Seth, K., Yung, M.: Two-sided malicious security for private intersection-sum with cardinality. In: Micciancio, D., Ristenpart, T. (eds.) CRYPTO 2020. LNCS, vol. 12172, pp. 3–33. Springer, Cham (2020). https://doi.org/10.1007/978-3-030-56877-1_1

[Pin+15] Pinkas, B., Schneider, T., Segev, G., Zohner, M.: Phasing: private set intersection using permutation-based hashing. In: 24th {USENIX} Security Symposium ({USENIX} Security 2015), pp. 515–530 (2015)

[Pin+18] Pinkas, B., Schneider, T., Weinert, C., Wieder, U.: Efficient circuit-based PSI via cuckoo hashing. In: Nielsen, J.B., Rijmen, V. (eds.) EUROCRYPT 2018. LNCS, vol. 10822, pp. 125–157. Springer, Cham (2018). https://doi.org/10.1007/978-3-319-78372-7_5

[Pin+19a] Pinkas, B., Rosulek, M., Trieu, N., Yanai, A.: SpOT-Light: lightweight private set intersection from sparse OT extension. In: Boldyreva, A., Micciancio, D. (eds.) CRYPTO 2019. LNCS, vol. 11694, pp. 401–431. Springer, Cham (2019). https://doi.org/10.1007/978-3-030-26954-8_13

[Pin+19b] Pinkas, B., Schneider, T., Tkachenko, O., Yanai, A.: Efficient circuit-based PSI with linear communication. In: Ishai, Y., Rijmen, V. (eds.) EUROCRYPT 2019. LNCS, vol. 11478, pp. 122–153. Springer, Cham (2019). https://doi.org/10.1007/978-3-030-17659-4_5

[Pin+20] Pinkas, B., Rosulek, M., Trieu, N., Yanai, A.: PSI from PaXoS: fast, malicious private set intersection. In: Canteaut, A., Ishai, Y. (eds.) EUROCRYPT 2020. LNCS, vol. 12106, pp. 739–767. Springer, Cham (2020). https://doi.org/10.1007/978-3-030-45724-2_25

[PR04] Pagh, R., Rodle, F.F.: Cuckoo hashing. J. Algorithms $51(2)$, 122–144 (2004)

[PSZ18] Pinkas, B., Schneider, T., Zohner, M.: Scalable private set intersection based on OT extension. ACM Trans. Priv. Secur. (TOPS) $21(2)$, 1–35 (2018)

[Rab05] Rabin, M.O.: How to exchange secrets with oblivious transfer. Cryptology ePrint Archive, 2005/187 (2005). https://eprint.iacr.org/2005/187

[RR16] Rindal, P., Rosulek, M.: Faster malicious 2-party secure computation with online/offline dual execution. In: 25th {USENIX} Security Symposium ({USENIX} Security 2016), pp. 297–314 (2016)

[Sha79] Shamir, A.: How to share a secret. Commun. ACM $22(11)$, 612–613 (1979)

[Yin+20] Ying, J.H.M., Cao, S., Poh, G.S., Xu, J., Lim, H.W.: PSI-stats: private set intersection protocols supporting secure statistical functions. Cryptology ePrint Archive, 2020/623 (2020). https://eprint.iacr.org/2020/623

[ZC18] Zhao, Y., Chow, S.S.M.: Can you find the one for me? In: Proceedings of the 2018 Workshop on Privacy in the Electronic Society, pp. 54–65 (2018)

[Zha+19] Zhang, E., Liu, F.-H., Lai, Q., Jin, G., Li, Y.: Efficient multi-party private set intersection against malicious adversaries. In: Proceedings of the 2019 ACM Conference on Cloud Computing Security Workshop, pp. 93–104 (2019)

Formal Methods for Security and Trust

Secure Implementation
of a Quantum-Future GAKE Protocol

Robert Abela[1], Christian Colombo[1]([⊠]), Peter Malo[2], Peter Sýs[3], Tomáš Fabšič[2], Ondrej Gallo[2], Viliam Hromada[2], and Mark Vella[1]

[1] Department of Computer Science, University of Malta, Msida, Malta
christian.colombo@um.edu.mt
[2] Faculty of Electrical Engineering and Information Technology,
Slovak University of Technology in Bratislava, Bratislava, Slovakia
[3] Mathematical Institute, Slovak Academy of Sciences, Bratislava, Slovakia

Abstract. Incorrect cryptographic protocol implementation and malware attacks targeting its runtime may lead to insecure execution even if the protocol design has been proven safe. This research focuses on adapting a runtime-verification-centric trusted execution environment (RV-TEE) solution to a quantum-future cryptographic protocol deployment. We aim to show that our approach is practical through an instantiation of a trusted execution environment supported by runtime verification and any hardware security module compatible with commodity hardware. In particular, we provide: (i) A group chat application case study which uses the quantum-future group key establishment protocol from González Vasco et al., (ii) An implementation of the protocol from González Vasco et al. employing a resource-constrained hardware security module, (iii) The runtime verification setup tailored for the protocol's properties, (iv) An empirical evaluation of the setup focusing on the user experience of the chat application.

Keywords: Runtime verification · Post-quantum cryptography · Trustworthy systems

1 Introduction

Group authentication key exchange (GAKE) protocols are essential for constructing secure channels of communication between multiple parties over an insecure infrastructure [25]. Collaborative applications over the Internet, covering all different kinds of video and web conferencing software, are a prime example of applications that can benefit from GAKE, allowing symmetric-key cryptography to be used for both authentication and encryption whenever it is not possible to agree on shared secrets over the same medium of communication that requires securing.

This work is supported by the NATO Science for Peace and Security Programme through project G5448 Secure Communication in the Quantum Era.

R. Roman and J. Zhou (Eds.): STM 2021, LNCS 13075, pp. 103–121, 2021.
https://doi.org/10.1007/978-3-030-91859-0_6

The need for secure collaborative web applications has been emphasised with the onset of the COVID-19 pandemic. Literally, only a few days into the ensuing lockdown that forced most employees around the world into remote working, serious weaknesses in one of the most popular web conferencing applications were immediately exposed [30]. Issues ranged from insecure key establishment to inadequate block cipher mode usage. Yet this is only the latest in a string of high-profile incidents concerning insecure cryptographic protocol implementation. Root causes span weak randomness [42], insufficient checks on protocol compliance in remote party exchanges [23], as well as memory corruption bugs in code [35]. With malware code injection techniques becoming ever more sophisticated in bypassing security controls [38], possibly even leveraging microarchitectural side-channels of commodity hardware [7,26], the secure implementation of otherwise securely proven cryptography remains a challenge.

Quantum adversaries present one further challenge for GAKE and its applications. While it is difficult to gauge the level of threat concerned, NIST's announcement of the third round finalists of the post-quantum cryptography standardisation process has set the tone for the level of preparedness expected of the level of security for sensitive scenarios. In terms of implementation, the added burden is presented by the even larger operands involved in the lattice and code-based schemes [4], for example, as compared to those based on discrete-logarithm and factoring assumptions.

In this paper, we address the problem of securely implementing a quantum-future GAKE protocol through a Trusted Execution Environment (TEE) [36], in the setting of a secure group chat application. Specifically, we focus on a proposed protocol proven to be secure in a *quantum-future* scenario [22]. In doing so, its design aims to balance post-quantum security and implementation efficiency. A quantum-safe key encapsulation mechanism (KEM), e.g., CRYSTALS-Kyber [12], is only used for protecting the confidentiality of session key material. On the other hand, authentication is still based on cheaper discrete-log primitives, with the end result being the protection of message confidentiality from delayed data attacks using eventual quantum power, but without the 'unnecessary burden' of protecting from active quantum adversaries. Finally, user authentication is password-based.

Secure implementation via a TEE is specifically provided through an instantiation of *RV-TEE* [41]. RV-TEE combines the use of two components: The first is Runtime Verification (RV), a dynamic formal verification extension to static model checking [14,28]. The second component is a Hardware Security Module (HSM) of choice to provide an isolated execution environment, possibly equipped with tamper-evident features. Options encompass high-bandwidth network PCI cards with hardware-accelerated encryption [39], down to smaller onboard micro-controllers and/or smartcards used in resource-constrained devices that connect to stock hardware over USB or NFC for example [11,20]. The remit of RV is primarily the verification of correct protocol usage by conferencing/collaborative applications, as well as the protocol implementation itself. The HSM protects the execution of code associated with secret/private keys from malware

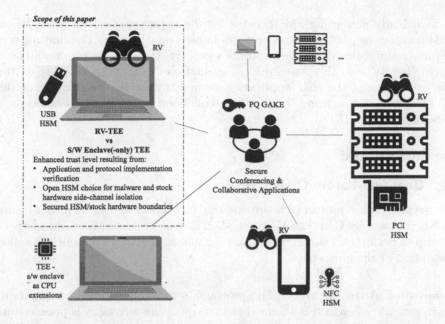

Fig. 1. The RV-TEE setup used for securing conferencing and collaborative applications based on a quantum-future GAKE.

infection while avoiding stock hardware side-channels. Furthermore, RV is also tasked with monitoring data flows between the HSM and stock hardware.

Figure 1 shows the overall setup, delineating the scope of the case study presented in this paper. Most stock hardware nowadays comes equipped with CPUs having TEE extensions based on encrypted memory to provide software enclaves [31], and which could also be a suitable choice for the HSM if deemed fit. However, by adopting the entire RV-TEE setup—i.e., including the RV component—an elevated level of trust can be achieved through:

- Application and protocol implementation verification using RV;
- Freedom in choosing the trusted HSM of choice to isolate from malware and stock hardware side-channels; and
- RV securing the HSM/stock hardware boundaries.

Despite providing direction for securely implementing conferencing/collaborative applications, RV-TEE is not prescriptive in the sense that, the RV properties for verification must be chosen carefully in terms of partial specification of the GAKE protocol, while protocol implementation must be split between the stock hardware and the HSM—with the exact delineation depending on the specific choice of the latter. This paper is about the work undertaken to bridge this gap, making the following contributions: (i) A group chat application case study based on a post-quantum protocol that is secure in a quantum-future scenario; ii) A protocol implementation using the SEcube™ [40], an inexpensive yet sufficiently powerful HSM to cater for the requirements of a lattice-based KEM used by the post-quantum protocol implementation; (iii) The runtime verification setup tailored for the protocol's properties using the automata-based LARVA [16] RV tool; (iv) An empirical evaluation of the setup focusing on the user experience of the chat application demonstrating the practicality of the RV-TEE setup for securing conferencing/collaborative applications based on a post-quantum GAKE.

2   Background

2.1   Quantum-Future GAKE Protocol

The cryptographic protocol chosen for our case study is the quantum-future GAKE protocol by González Vasco et al. [22]. The protocol allows members of a group to perform an authenticated key exchange. Below, we present a detailed description of the protocol.

Quantum-Future Security. The protocol is provably secure in a *quantum-future* scenario wherein it is assumed that no quantum-adversary is present during the execution of the protocol, and the established common secret is supposed to remain secure even if the adversary gains access to a quantum computer in the future.

Password-Based Authentication. The protocol uses password-based authentication. It employs a prime order group G in which the Decision-Diffie-Hellman assumption holds and assumes that the password dictionary $\mathcal{D}$ is a subset of G through some public and efficiently computable injection $\iota : \mathcal{D} \hookrightarrow G$.

Tools. The protocol uses the following tools:

- a *key encapsulation mechanism* (KEM)
- a *message authentication code* (MAC)
- a *deterministic randomness extractor*

Next, we describe these tools in more detail.

KEM - the protocol requires a KEM which is IND-CPA secure against fully quantum adversaries (as defined in [9]). A KEM $\mathcal{K}$ consists of the following three algorithms:

- a probabilistic *key generation* algorithm $\mathcal{K}.\mathtt{KeyGen}(1^l)$ which takes as input the security parameter l and outputs a key pair (pk, sk),
- a probabilistic *encapsulation* algorithm $\mathtt{Encaps}(pk, 1^l)$ which takes as input a public key pk and outputs a ciphertext c and a key $k \in \{0,1\}^{p(l)}$, where $p(l)$ is a polynomial function of the security parameter,
- a deterministic *decapsulation* algorithm $\mathtt{Decaps}(sk, c, 1^l)$ which takes as input a secret key sk and a ciphertext c and outputs a key k or $\perp$.

MAC - the protocol requires a MAC which is *unforgeable under chosen message and chosen verification queries attack* (UF-CMVA) (as defined in [21]). A MAC $\mathcal{M}$ consists of the following three algorithms:

- a probabilistic *key generation* algorithm $\mathcal{M}.\text{KeyGen}(1^l)$ which takes as input the security parameter l and outputs a key k,
- a probabilistic *authentication* algorithm $\text{Tag}(k, M)$ which takes as input a key k and a message M and outputs a tag t,
- a deterministic *verification* algorithm $\text{Vf}(k, M, t)$ which takes as input a key k, a message M and a tag t and outputs a decision: 1 (accept) or 0 (reject).

Deterministic Randomness Extractor - in the protocol, (uniform random) bit-strings need to be extracted from (uniform random) elements in the group G. Given a group element $g \in G$, the authors of the protocol denote by $[g]$ (statistically close to uniform random) bits extracted deterministically from g. When the authors of the protocol need to extract two independent (half-length) bit-strings from g, they divide $[g]$ into two halves denoted by $[g]_L$ and $[g]_R$ such that $[g] = [g]_L || [g]_R$.

Protocol Specification. Let $U_0, U_1, \ldots, U_n$ be the users running the protocol. It is assumed that before the protocol is started, the users share a password pw. In addition, it is assumed that every user is aware of his index and the indices of the rest of participants.

The protocol is depicted in Fig. 2. The user U_0 has a special role in the protocol - he generates a key k and transports it to the other users. The key is transported being masked by an ephemeral key generated from the key encapsulation. To ensure authentication, each pair of users establishes a Diffie-Hellman secret, with $\iota(\text{pw})$ used as a generator of the group G. The resulting Diffie-Hellman secrets are then used to derive keys for authentication tags on protocol messages. Once a user verifies all tags, the key k is accepted and is used to derive a shared session key (ssk) and a session ID (sid).

2.2 RV-TEE

RV-TEE [41] was proposed as a secure execution environment in the context of a threat model comprising adversaries that target cryptographic protocol execution at four different levels. The first three levels concern software and are labelled as high, medium, and low. At the highest level, one finds attacks exploiting logical bugs causing the protocol implementation to deviate from the (typically theoretically-verified) design. The exploitation of incorrect verification of digital certificates or authentication tags, usage of insecure groups to implement Diffie Hellman-based protocols, as well as weak sources of randomness, all fall in this category [2]. At the medium level, we find attacks that target the basic assumption of any cryptographic scheme: the secrecy of symmetric/private keys, along with the unavailability of plaintext without first breaking encryption.

Round I.

• Computation:

  – For $0 \leq i \leq n, U_i$ chooses $\beta_i \leftarrow \mathbb{Z}_q$ and computes $g_i = \iota(\mathrm{pw})^{\beta_i}$. U_0 sets $M_0 := (g_0)$.

  – For $1 \leq i \leq n, U_i$ computes $(pk_i, sk_i) \leftarrow \mathcal{K}.\mathtt{KeyGen}(1^l)$, and sets $M_i := (pk_i, g_i)$.

• Communication:

  – For $0 \leq i \leq n, U_i$ broadcasts M_i.

Round II.

• Computation:

  – Keying material:

    * U_0 chooses $k \leftarrow \{0,1\}^{p(l)}$, and for each $1 \leq j \leq n$ computes

    $$(c_j, k_j) \leftarrow \mathtt{Encaps}(pk_j, 1^l)$$

    and sets $d_j := k \oplus k_j$, $m_{0,j} := (d_j, c_j)$.

    * For $0 \leq i \leq n, U_i$ sets $g_{i,j} := g_j^{\beta_i}$ for each $j \neq i$.

  – Tags:

    * U_0 computes $t_{0,j} := \mathtt{Tag}([g_{0,j}]_L, U_0 || m_{0,j} || M_0 || ... || M_n)$ for each $1 \leq j \leq n$.

    * For $1 \leq i \leq n, U_i$ computes

    $$t_{i,j} := \begin{cases} \mathtt{Tag}([g_{i,j}]_L, U_i || M_0 || ... || M_n), & \text{for } 1 \leq i < j \leq n \\ \mathtt{Tag}([g_{i,j}]_R, U_i || M_0 || ... || M_n), & \text{for } 0 \leq j < i \leq n \end{cases}$$

• Communication:

  – U_0 sends $(m_{0,j}, t_{0,j})$ to $U_j (1 \leq j \leq n)$.

  – For $1 \leq i \leq n$,

  $$U_i \text{ sends } t_{i,j} \text{ to } U_j (0 \leq j \leq n, j \neq i)$$

• Verification and key computation:

  – All users verify all tags:

    * For $1 \leq j \leq n, U_j$ runs $\mathtt{Vf}([g_{0,j}]_L, U_0 || m_{0,j} || M_0 || ... || M_n, t_{0,j})$.

    * For $0 \leq j \leq n, U_j$ runs $\begin{cases} \mathtt{Vf}([g_{j,i}]_L, U_i || M_0 || ... || M_n, t_{i,j}), & \text{for } 1 \leq i < j \leq n \\ \mathtt{Vf}([g_{j,i}]_R, U_i || M_0 || ... || M_n, t_{i,j}), & \text{for } 0 \leq j < i \leq n \end{cases}$

  – If all checks are successful, U_0 sets:

  $$\mathtt{ssk}_0 := [k]_L, \mathtt{sid}_0 := [k]_R,$$

  – For $1 \leq i \leq n$, if all checks are successful, U_i runs $\mathtt{Decaps}(sk_i, c_i)$ to obtain k_i, computes $K_i := d_i \oplus k_i$, and sets:

  $$\mathtt{ssk}_i := [K_i]_L, \mathtt{sid}_i := [K_i]_R,$$

Fig. 2. Password-based group-key establishment protocol [22]

Adversaries at this level comprise stealthy malware that makes use of code-injection [38] or side-channels [7] to break both.

Vulnerabilities at the lowest level originate from programming bugs, resulting in the deducibility of secrets via non-constant-time operations [5], or else in memory leaks via memory corruption [35]. This level is handled differently from the other levels since information flow-based RV is used during testing, rather than post-deployment, due to the heavy information-flow analysis involved. Beneath these threat levels, there is the hardware level, which can pose a threat if the manufacturer cannot be trusted, say for fear of hardware backdoors, or due to its susceptibility to side-channel attacks. This can be particularly of concern if the hardware itself is a primitive for secure execution [44], is widely deployed and an application's implementation is specific to it. In this respect, RV-TEE is designed with HSM flexibility in mind.

Runtime Verification (RV) [14,28] in general provides two primary benefits: Firstly, monitors are typically automatically synthesised from formal notation to reduce the possibility of introducing bugs; Secondly, monitoring concerns are kept separate (at least on a logical level) from the observed system. In our case study, we make use of LARVA [16], where properties are specified using LARVA scripts that capture a textual representation of symbolic timed-automata. Listing 1.1 shows a simple example property specifying expected user lock-out scenario following 30 min of inactivity or else 3 successive unsuccessful login attempts (depicted in Fig. 3). Lines 12–16 define the states of the automaton, identifying the starting, normal and bad ones. Lines 17–23 specify the state transitions, with each transition also qualified by a guard condition and the action performed within [] and separated by \\. Lines 2–5 declare the supporting counter x and a timer t. Lines 6–10 identify the traced method calls that trigger state transitions and initialise timer objects. While LARVA natively supports the monitoring of Java code through AspectJ instrumentation, it is possible to make use of an adaptor to link it up with inline hook-based instrumentation at the binary level as well, as used in previous RV-TEE work [41].

$SEcube^{TM}$-powered hardware [40], e.g., the USEcube™ USB token[1], is our chosen HSM for the group chat case study. The chip comprises an MCU, CC EAL5+ -accredited SmartCard, and an ultra-low power FPGA, all on the same chip, with the latter components being callable through specific MCU instructions. The MCU is an STM32F4 - ARM 32-bit Cortex-M4 CPU. Its 2 MiB of Flash memory and 256 KiB of SRAM are required to host all HSM-side of the GAKE protocol's implementation, primarily the KEM. Programming the SEcube™ is facilitated by an openly available SDK[2] exposed as a 3-layered API on the host side. On the device-side, the SDK is a layer on top of an STM32Cube[3] MCU package comprising peripheral drivers and middleware. The overall setup aids in

---

[1] https://www.secube.blu5group.com/products/usecube-bundle-including-5-usecube -tokens-and-1-devkit/.

[2] https://www.secube.blu5group.com/resources/open-sources-sdk/.

[3] https://www.st.com/content/st_com/en/ecosystems/stm32cube-ecosystem.html.

```
1   GLOBAL {
2    VARIABLES {
3     int x = 0;
4     Clock t;
5    }
6    EVENTS {
7     badlogin() = {*.badlogin()}
8     timer30() = {t@30*60}
9     ...
10   }
11   PROPERTY users {
12    STATES {
13     BAD { badlogins inactive }
14     NORMAL { loggedin }
15     STARTING { loggedout }
16    }
17    TRANSITIONS {
18     loggedout -> badlogins [badlogin\x>2\]
19     loggedout -> loggedin  [goodlogin\\t.
          reset();]
20     ...
21     loggedout -> loggedout [badlogin\\x++;]
22     loggedin -> inactive [timer30\\]
23    }
24   }
25  }
```

Listing 1.1. LARVA script for: *There are no more than 3 successive bad logins and 30 minutes of inactivity when logged in* [16].

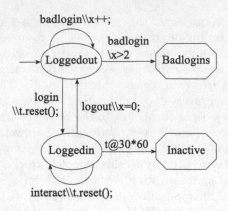

Fig. 3. Diagrammatic representation of the automaton.

developing robust firmware. For the time being, our case study focuses solely on executing all firmware on the MCU.

2.3   Related Work

Unlike model checking of cryptographic protocol design [32], literature on the verification of their software implementations is sparse. As for the available run-time verification approaches [6,33], none involve instrumentation of compiled code with the disadvantage of either dealing directly with the source code, or missing out on internal data and events. Furthermore, up to our knowledge, RV-TEE [41] is the first to attempt a comprehensive solution at securing cryptographic protocol implementations through a TEE and thereby addressing a broad threat model. Besides having been studied extensively in the setting of secure web browsing over TLS 1.3 [17], other work focused on SSH [18].

In our instantiation of RV-TEE, the LARVA RV tool, the SEcube™ HSM, and its Cortex-M4 MCU are critical enablers, and which are all proven to be of industry-grade. LARVA has been used extensively for verifying the correct operation of high-volume financial transactions systems [15]. As for SEcube™, besides its integration in various devices, several open-source projects build upon its Open SDK to demonstrate its employment in academic research [10]. Applications range from OS-agnostic file systems to securing a network's link layer, secure password wallets, and even secure IoT hubs. As for its Cortex-M4 MCU, an extensive body of work focusing on optimised cipher implementation cover both post-quantum cryptography [1,24], as well as standard symmetric encryption [37].

3   Case Study

For the purpose of this project we need a proof-of-concept application for group communication secured by quantum-safe cryptography. Therefore, we have created a library with the working title 'GKE library', and a simple text-based group chat application based on it.

The GKE library is written in C, exposing a high-level API for running the GAKE protocol[4] from [22], and AES-128 [19] en/decryption functionality in CCM mode [43] using the shared session key ssk established in the GAKE protocol. The library can be used in two different configurations: a configuration which uses both a PC and the SEcube™ chip, or using only a PC.

An example session run of the chat application follows:

```
 1  ps@Diane:~/Dokumenty/Skola/phd/NATO/gke/GKE$ ./bin/chat --repeater=localhost \\
 2  --pin --id 12
 3  Secube login with password 4:test
 4  GKE|> /help
 5  Supported commands:
 6    COMMAND          ARGUMENTS            DESCRIPTION
 7    /room new    - roomname id... - create new room
 8    /room enter  - roomname       - set active room
 9    /room list   -                - list active rooms and it users
10    /unsecure    - msg            - write unsecure message to current room
11    /msg         - ids... -- msg  - send unsecure multicast to ids
12    /sleep       - nsec           - sleep for nsec seconds
13    /get usage   -                - print cpu clock value
14    /exit        -                - exit application
15    /help        -                - print this help
16                 - msg            - send secure message to current room
17  GKE|> /room new myRoom 42 43
18  Creating room 'myRoom'
19  Room created
20  GKE|> /room enter myRoom
21  GKE|myRoom> Hello 42
22  [myRoom]12: Hello 42
23  [myRoom]42: Hello you!
24  GKE|myRoom> /exit
```

First, the user with id 12 launches the chat application, in this case connecting to a chat server running on the same machine (lines 1–2). Next, a PIN-based login to SEcube™ (line 3) is followed by a command dump (lines 5–16). Once a new chat session is requested (lines 17–18) with users 42 and 43, a full GAKE protocol run is executed, returning an instance of the shared session key ssk with the other two users. Successful completion of the GAKE protocol results in the Room created prompt. Once the user accesses the newly created session (line 20), all subsequently sent messages (lines 21–23) get routed through SEcube™

---

[4] We describe the implementation of the GAKE protocol in more detail in Sect. 4.

for encryption with the session key. Likewise, the received encrypted messages get decrypted without `ssk` ever leaving the HSM. The `/exit` command (line 24) terminates the session.

4   Implementation of the GAKE Protocol

In this section, we present some details of our implementation of the GAKE protocol from [22]. We will focus on the implementation which uses both a PC and the SEcube™ chip.

As was mentioned in Sect. 2.2, the SEcube™ chip comprises an MCU, a Smart-Card and an FPGA, supported with an openly available SDK. Our implementation uses only the MCU (STM32F4 - ARM 32-bit Cortex-M4 CPU). The reason for this is that we integrated our implementation in the available SDK and the SDK (version 1.4.1) does not provide functionality to use the FPGA or the SmartCard.

At present, our implementation does not contain protection against side-channel attacks beyond the immediate protection derived from stock hardware isolation, e.g. exploitation of non-constant time operations involving protocol secrets are still possible. We plan to address the issue of securing the implementation against side-channel attacks in future work.

4.1   Role of SEcube™

Our implementation utilizes the SEcube™ chip as follows:

- The SEcube™ chip stores the password `pw`, and the password never leaves the SEcube™. The password `pw` is a long-term password shared by members of the group. During a run of the GAKE protocol members of the group use this password for authentication.
- The SEcube™ chip generates all secret values used in the GAKE protocol, and these values never leave SEcube™.
- All computations in the GAKE protocol which involve secret data are performed by the SEcube™ chip.
- The shared session key `ssk` established in the GAKE protocol is stored on SEcube™ and never leaves it.
- We note that in this instantiation no RV component is deployed on the SEcube™. In future implementations this could be considered, bearing in mind the resource constrained nature of the HSM.

4.2   Protocol Instantiation

Our implementation targets a 128 bit security level. The protocol needs to be instantiated with proper choices of a *key encapsulation mechanism* (KEM), a Diffie-Hellman group G, a *deterministic randomness extractor*, a *message authentication code* (MAC), and a *random number generator* (RNG). Below, we describe the instantiation choices which we made in our implementation.

KEM - for KEM we chose CRYSTALS-Kyber [12], which is IND-CPA secure against fully quantum adversaries, as required by the protocol. In particular, we chose the version Kyber512 which aims at security roughly equivalent to AES-128 [19]. CRYSTALS-Kyber is one of the four KEMs selected as finalists in Round 3 of the NIST Post-Quantum Cryptography Standardization Process. It is a lattice-based cryptosystem and has favourable sizes of the key pair and the ciphertext. We use the implementation of Kyber512 from [3].

Group G - for the group G we chose the elliptic curve Curve25519 [8] which offers 128 bit security. We use the implementation of Curve25519 from [29].

Deterministic Randomness Extractor - for the deterministic randomness extractor we chose SHA-256 [34] (available within the SEcube™ API), which provides 128 bit security.

MAC - for MAC we chose HMAC-SHA-256 [27] (available within the SEcube™ API), which provides 128 bit security.

RNG - we use the RNG function provided by the SEcube™ API.

4.3   Protocol Adjustment

We made a small adjustment to the protocol to make it more amenable for resource-constrained HSM implementation (in our case, the SEcube™ chip). The adjustment is as follows.

As can be seen in Fig. 2, the protocol requires a user to compute and verify authentication tags—a computation of a tag is represented by the function Tag and verification of a tag is represented by the function Vf. Furthermore (referring once more to the figure), both these functions require $M_0|| \ldots ||M_n$ as a part of their input. Since these functions also require the secret value $g_{i,j}$ as an input, they have to be computed on the SEcube™ chip. This means that after the user receives values M_j from other users, he needs to transport these values from his PC to the SEcube™ chip. With our instantiation of the protocol, the size of M_j is 832 bytes if $j \neq 0$ and 32 bytes if $j = 0$. If the user runs the protocol with n other users, this means that the user has to transport approximately $32 + n \times 832$ bytes from a PC to SEcube™. Transporting data this large slows down the execution of the protocol. In addition, once transported, the data occupies a large amount of memory on SEcube™.

To avoid the above mentioned limitations, we adjusted the protocol as follows: instead of $M_0|| \ldots ||M_n$, the functions Tag and Vf take as part of their input the hash value of $M_0|| \ldots ||M_n$. This adjustment has no negative effect on the security of the protocol and reduces the number of transferred and stored bytes to just the 32 bytes of the hash.

Figure 4 shows our measurements of the execution time of the protocol, i.e., how long it takes a participant to run the protocol depending on: the number of participants involved in the protocol run; whether the participant is the initiator or not; and whether the protocol was implemented with our adjustment or not. Our measurements do not include the time required by participants to exchange messages (i.e. in our measurements we assumed that a participant receives messages from other participants instantly). These measurements were executed using SEcube™ and a PC with the following characteristics: Lenovo Thinkpad x220, Intel(R) Core(TM) i5-2520M CPU @ 2.50 GHz (2 Cores, 4 Threads, with AES-NI), RAM: 16 GiB (2 × 8 GiB) DDR3 Synchronous 1600 MHz (0,6 ns), OS: Linux (Linux kernel version 5.4.0–77-generic, distribution build), Ubuntu 18.04.3 LTS (Bionic Beaver) with i3wm desktop environment. We can see that for a larger number of participants our adjustment slightly improves the execution time of the protocol. What is, however, more important, our adjustment allows the protocol to run for larger sizes of the group of participants. Without the adjustment, we were not able to execute the protocol for a group of participants greater than 44. This was due to memory constraints on SEcube™. The adjustment solves this limitation.[5]

5   RV Component Implementation

In this section, we focus on the runtime verification component which checks the correct implementation of the protocol from the perspective of a chat application client. The protocol implementation and its incorporation within the chat application is organised in terms of a number of layers (Fig. 5): starting from the primitives and protocol calculations deployed on the HSM (SEcube™), which are called through the GKE library, which is in turn accessed by the chat application.

5.1   Properties

Runtime verification can be used to monitor a wide range of properties: from assertions, to temporal properties, to hyper properties [13], where each one can be considered a special case of the other: assertions as a special case of temporal properties considering one instant in time, and temporal properties being a special case of hyper properties considering only one execution of the protocol.

---

[5] Note that although the maximum number of participants in Fig. 4 is 60, this is not the limit of our implementation with the adjustment. The maximum number of participants for which we were able to successfully run our implementation was 789.

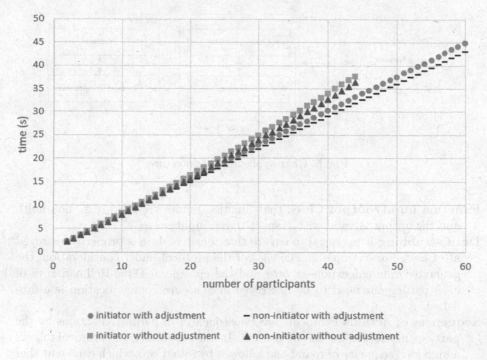

Fig. 4. Execution times of the protocol.

Table 1. Identified properties for runtime verification

Property layers	Chat app	Library	All (incl. Primitives)
Assertion	Printable decrypted chars	Sensitive data scrubbed	Non-null params, valid returns
Temporal	Chatroom lifecycle, standard sockets		Correct call sequence
Hyper		Randomness quality	

Taking each architectural layer and kind of property, we classify the properties in terms of a grid as shown in Table 1. This organisation of properties allows us to consider various aspects of the protocol systematically[6]. Other works involving the specification of properties in the case of other protocols [17,18,41] has shown a number of common properties:

---

[6] Strictly speaking, the chat app properties are not protocol properties and arguably not part of the RV-TEE. However, checking that the chat app works as expected, means that it is more likely that the underlying protocol is also being used in a correct manner.

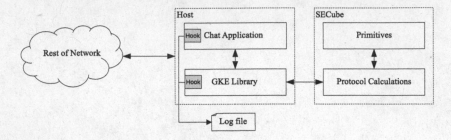

Fig. 5. Chat application architecture

Function input/output Check that function inputs are valid (e.g., non-null), and the output is valid with respect to the inputs.

Data scrubbing It is crucial to ensure that sensitive data is properly destroyed after use[7]. For example, in the case of the protocol under consideration, the generated random exponent *beta* and the ephemeral Diffie-Hellman keys of each participant need to be destroyed once secure communication is established.

Sequences of actions Protocols involve sequences of permitted actions by the participants depending on the context. In our case study, the protocol follows a high level sequence of round one followed by round two, which can be further split into sequences of actions such as loading the password, generating *beta*, and calculating the Diffie-Hellman group generator *g*, etc.

Randomness To ensure security, protocols depend on high quality random number generation, e.g., the exponent *beta* is randomly generated in our case study.

Together, this description list covers all the protocol properties in Table 1. The rest of the properties are chat application-specific properties, particularly properties dealing with the chatroom lifecycle.

5.2   RV Experimentation Setup

Frida, a dynamic instrumentation toolkit, and more specifically frida-trace[8] was used for instrumenting the chat application. This decision came with the advantages of not having to recompile the chat application and allowing for relatively simple JavaScript code to hook the required functions. During the frida-trace engine initialisation stage (before the first function handler is called), JavaScript code defines globally visible functions (e.g., helpers and logging) and a state object. This object is passed to every event handler to maintain information across function calls. Adding fields to the state objects allows for sequential

---

[7] This applies to the PC only implementation configuration. In the case of PC + HSM, the sensitive data never leaves the hardware security module.
[8] https://frida.re/docs/frida-trace/.

tracking, monitoring native pointers, keeping shadow copies of data and mapping API context to protocol run and eventually to participants.

We extended the chat application to accept scripted session runs and created two testing scenarios. In each one, the chat client with `id=1` was instrumented, while all the other clients and server were running on the same machine.

- Scenario A: 3 clients involved, with client `id=1` creating a room (following the protocol steps for an initiator participant U_0).
- Scenario B: 3 clients involved, with client `id=1` joining the room (following the protocol steps for a non-initiator participant $U_{1 \leq i \leq n}$).

The scenarios include 20 and 13 s of thread sleeps respectively to mimic a realistic chat. This will be factored in the results discussion.

5.3 Instrumentation Overhead Results

Starting by looking at the instrumentation (i.e. the introduction of frida-trace), Table 2 gives an overview of the overhead penalty, ranging from 0.41s to 1.38s (using the same setup as reported in Sect. 4.3). Given that sleeps are included in the scenarios, this overhead is substantial. We also try the same experiment when the implementation uses the HSM vs. when it doesn't: It is clear that there is a penalty for using the resource constrained HSM, but to a lesser extent than instrumentation. Overall, considering the instrumentation and the HSM, we have an increase of (34.98–33.03) 1.95s over the whole duration of the chat scenario. The number of experiments is too limited to extrapolate this result to the general case, however, the indication is that the overheads are within acceptable bounds, especially considering the case study of a chat application where a few milliseconds of delay for each command would go unnoticed.

Table 2. Instrumentation overheads measured per scenario, with/out the HSM.

Time (s)	Without SEcube™			Using SEcube™		
Scenario	A	B	All	A	B	All
Non-instrumented	20.02	13.01	33.03	20.18	13.27	33.45
Instrumented	20.44	14.39	34.83	21.30	13.68	34.98
Increase	0.44	1.38	1.70	1.12	0.41	1.53

5.4 Runtime Verification Empirical Results

Using RV, we checked six properties[9]: three classified as control flow, and three as data properties. The control flow properties checked the sequence of actions

---

[9] Our analysis leaves out assertion checks such as non-null arguments. Our reasoning is that these checks could be implemented as simple assertions in the code and thus arguably not strictly part of RV.

for the protocol and chatapp execution, while the third property kept track of sockets being written to, reporting any suspicious ones. The data flow properties involved checking data is scrubbed, assessing the quality of the generated random numbers, and finally, checking that all input characters are printable. As expected, the scenario involving U_0 required more RV effort as it plays a bigger role in the setting up of the chatroom. Looking at the property categories (control flow vs. data), there is no substantial difference. However, we note that randomness checking is rather basic—involving an entropy check, a monobits test, and a runs test. A complete state-of-the-art randomness check would certainly push the numbers substantially higher.

The properties were expressed as LARVA properties and monitored offline by parsing the log files on a MacBook Pro with 2.3 GHz Quad-Core Intel Core i5 machine with 8Gib 2133 MHz LPDDR3 RAM. Each experiment was run ten times and the results shown in Table 3 are the average (excluding log parsing time).

Table 3. RV time taken by property and scenario.

Time (μs)	Control Flow				Data				RV component[a] (ms)
Scenario	Protocol	Chatapp	Socket	All	Scrub	Random	Printable	All	
A (U_0)	191	860	892	1943	982	253	298	1532	8.8
B (U_i)	189	448	286	924	110	168	101	378	3.8

[a] The measurement of each property only captures the time inside the property logic, leaving out other generic RV logic particularly parameter bindings and monitor retrieval; this explains why the RV component takes significantly more time than the total of all properties.

5.5   Discussion

The empirical results indicate that the overheads introduced by the instrumentation and the HSM are non-negligible. However, in this work, our main aim was to show the feasibility of the approach rather than to have an optimal solution. We note several ways in which instrumentation could have been carried out more efficiently. We use frida-trace at the level of JavaScript not only for setting up in-line hooks dynamically, but also for the instrumentation code itself that records the events of interest. Alternatively, it is also possible to make use of natively-compiled code for this purpose, but this would require more extensive testing to make sure that the application's robustness is not compromised. Furthermore, through instrumentation, we gathered all events which could be useful for RV. This provided us with experimental flexibility at the expense of higher overheads. We foresee substantial immediate gains if we keep the use of JavaScript to a minimum and limit the events to those strictly needed.

Compared to the other overheads, the time required for the actual verification is small. Therefore this could just as well be done online and in sync with the chat app execution, i.e., the application waits for the monitor's go ahead at every step. However, in case heavier RV is needed (e.g., for more thorough randomness checking), one could consider splitting the properties into two categories: those which just involve a state check (*if the current monitor state is X, then A is expected to happen*), and those which involve checking data (*data is scrubbed; data is random*). The former category of properties can be monitored synchronously, while the latter can be monitored asynchronously.

6   Conclusion

Insecure execution of theoretically-proven communication protocols is still a major concern, particularly due to malware attacks ready to exploit any vulnerability at the various logical levels of the implementation. Moreover, with the advancements of quantum computers, coming up with novel quantum-safe protocols is inevitable. In this work, we have proposed an RV-TEE instantiation for the quantum-future group key establishment protocol from González Vasco et al., securing the protocol implementation from the hardware level, up till the logical level of the application utilising it. Through an empirical evaluation based on a chat application case study, we show the feasibility of the approach—involving substantial overhead, yet with minimal to no impact from a usability perspective.

Future work is to leverage RV-TEE further by hardening the execution environment by extending RV to the HSM code and implementing a taint inference-based RV monitor to fend off code-injection malware targeting the chat application's process memory on the PC.

References

1. Alkim, E., Bilgin, Y.A., Cenk, M., Gérard, F.: Cortex-M4 optimizations for {R, M} LWE schemes. IACR Trans. Cryptogr. Hardw. Embed. Syst. **2020**, 336–357 (2020)
2. Aumasson, J.P.: Serious Cryptography: A Practical Introduction to Modern Encryption. No Starch Press, San Francisco (2017)
3. Avanzi, R., et al.: Kyber - public GitHub repository (2021). https://github.com/pq-crystals/kyber. Accessed 13 July 2021
4. Barak, B.: The complexity of public-key cryptography. In: Tutorials on the Foundations of Cryptography. ISC, pp. 45–77. Springer, Cham (2017). https://doi.org/10.1007/978-3-319-57048-8_2
5. Barthe, G., Grégoire, B., Laporte, V.: Secure compilation of side-channel countermeasures: the case of cryptographic "constant-time". In: 2018 IEEE 31st Computer Security Foundations Symposium (CSF), pp. 328–343. IEEE (2018)
6. Bauer, A., Jürjens, J.: Runtime verification of cryptographic protocols. Comput. Secur. **29**(3), 315–330 (2010)
7. Bernstein, D.J.: Cache-timing attacks on AES (2005)
8. Bernstein, D.J.: Curve25519: new Diffie-Hellman speed records. In: Yung, M., Dodis, Y., Kiayias, A., Malkin, T. (eds.) PKC 2006. LNCS, vol. 3958, pp. 207–228. Springer, Heidelberg (2006). https://doi.org/10.1007/11745853_14
9. Bindel, N., Herath, U., McKague, M., Stebila, D.: Transitioning to a quantum-resistant public key infrastructure. In: Lange, T., Takagi, T. (eds.) PQCrypto 2017. LNCS, vol. 10346, pp. 384–405. Springer, Cham (2017). https://doi.org/10.1007/978-3-319-59879-6_22

10. Blu5 Labs: SEcube - open source projects (2021). https://www.secube.blu5group. com/resources/open-source-projects/. Accessed 13 July 2021
11. Blu5 Labs: SEcube - reconfigurable silicon (2021). https://www.secube.eu/site/ assets/files/1145/secube_datasheet-_r7.pdf. Accessed 16 June 2021
12. Bos, J., et al.: CRYSTALS-Kyber: a CCA-secure module-lattice-based KEM. In: 2018 IEEE European Symposium on Security and Privacy (EuroS&P), pp. 353– 367. IEEE (2018)
13. Clarkson, M.R., Schneider, F.B.: Hyperproperties. In: Proceedings of the 21st IEEE Computer Security Foundations Symposium, CSF 2008, Pittsburgh, Pennsylvania, USA, 23–25 June 2008, pp. 51–65. IEEE Computer Society (2008). https://doi.org/ 10.1109/CSF.2008.7
14. Colin, S., Mariani, L.: 18 run-time verification. In: Broy, M., Jonsson, B., Katoen, J.-P., Leucker, M., Pretschner, A. (eds.) Model-Based Testing of Reactive Systems. LNCS, vol. 3472, pp. 525–555. Springer, Heidelberg (2005). https://doi.org/10. 1007/11498490_24
15. Colombo, C., Pace, G.J.: Industrial experiences with runtime verification of financial transaction systems: lessons learnt and standing challenges. In: Bartocci, E., Falcone, Y. (eds.) Lectures on Runtime Verification. LNCS, vol. 10457, pp. 211– 232. Springer, Cham (2018). https://doi.org/10.1007/978-3-319-75632-5_7
16. Colombo, C., Pace, G.J., Schneider, G.: LARVA – safer monitoring of real-time java programs (tool paper). In: Seventh IEEE International Conference on Software Engineering and Formal Methods (SEFM), pp. 33–37. IEEE Computer Society, November 2009
17. Colombo, C., Vella, M.: Towards a comprehensive solution for secure cryptographic protocol execution based on runtime verification. In: Proceedings of the 6th International Conference on Information Systems Security and Privacy, ICISSP, pp. 765–774. SCITEPRESS (2020)
18. Curmi, A., Colombo, C., Vella, M.: Runtime verification for trustworthy secure shell deployment (2021)
19. Daemen, J., Rijmen, V.: The Design of Rijndael. Springer, Heidelberg (2002). https://doi.org/10.1007/978-3-662-04722-4
20. Das, S., Russo, G., Dingman, A.C., Dev, J., Kenny, O., Camp, L.J.: A qualitative study on usability and acceptability of Yubico security key. In: Proceedings of the 7th Workshop on Socio-Technical Aspects in Security and Trust, pp. 28–39 (2018)
21. Dodis, Y., Kiltz, E., Pietrzak, K., Wichs, D.: Message authentication, revisited. In: Pointcheval, D., Johansson, T. (eds.) EUROCRYPT 2012. LNCS, vol. 7237, pp. 355–374. Springer, Heidelberg (2012). https://doi.org/10.1007/978-3-642-29011- 4_22
22. González Vasco, M.I., Pérez del Pozo, Á.L., Steinwandt, R.: Group key establishment in a quantum-future scenario. Informatica $31(4)$, 751–768 (2020)
23. Jager, T., Schwenk, J., Somorovsky, J.: Practical invalid curve attacks on TLS- ECDH. In: Pernul, G., Ryan, P.Y.A., Weippl, E. (eds.) ESORICS 2015. LNCS, vol. 9326, pp. 407–425. Springer, Cham (2015). https://doi.org/10.1007/978-3-319- 24174-6_21
24. Kannwischer, M.J., Rijneveld, J., Schwabe, P.: Faster multiplication in $\mathbb{Z}_{2^m}[x]$ on Cortex-M4 to speed up NIST PQC candidates. In: Deng, R.H., Gauthier-Umaña, V., Ochoa, M., Yung, M. (eds.) ACNS 2019. LNCS, vol. 11464, pp. 281–301. Springer, Cham (2019). https://doi.org/10.1007/978-3-030-21568-2_14
25. Katz, J., Yung, M.: Scalable protocols for authenticated group key exchange. In: Boneh, D. (ed.) CRYPTO 2003. LNCS, vol. 2729, pp. 110–125. Springer, Heidelberg (2003). https://doi.org/10.1007/978-3-540-45146-4_7

26. Kocher, P., et al.: Spectre attacks: exploiting speculative execution. In: 2019 IEEE Symposium on Security and Privacy (SP), pp. 1–19. IEEE (2019)
27. Krawczyk, H., Bellare, M., Canetti, R.: HMAC: keyed-hashing for message authentication. IETF RFC 2104 (1997)
28. Leucker, M., Schallhart, C.: A brief account of runtime verification. J. Log. Algebraic Program. **78**(5), 293–303 (2009)
29. Libsodium (2021). https://libsodium.gitbook.io/doc/. Accessed 13 July 2021
30. Marczak, B., Scott-Railton, J.: Move fast and roll your own crypto: a quick look at the confidentiality of zoom meetings. Technical report (2020). https://citizenlab.ca/2020/04/move-fast-roll-your-own-crypto-a-quick-look-at-the-confidentiality-of-zoom-meetings/. Accessed 15 June 2021
31. McKeen, F., et al.: Intel® software guard extensions (intel® sgx) support for dynamic memory management inside an enclave. In: Proceedings of the Hardware and Architectural Support for Security and Privacy 2016, pp. 1–9 (2016)
32. Meier, S., Schmidt, B., Cremers, C., Basin, D.: The TAMARIN prover for the symbolic analysis of security protocols. In: Sharygina, N., Veith, H. (eds.) CAV 2013. LNCS, vol. 8044, pp. 696–701. Springer, Heidelberg (2013). https://doi.org/10.1007/978-3-642-39799-8_48
33. Morio, K., Jackson, D., Vassena, M., Künnemann, R.: Modular black-box runtime verification of security protocols (2020)
34. NIST: FIPS PUB 180–2, SHA256 Standard (2002)
35. Poulin, C.: What to do to protect against Heartbleed OpenSSL vulnerability (2014). https://www.yubico.com/. Accessed 13 July 2021
36. Sabt, M., Achemlal, M., Bouabdallah, A.: Trusted execution environment: what it is, and what it is not. In: 14th IEEE International Conference on Trust, Security and Privacy in Computing and Communications (2015)
37. Schwabe, P., Stoffelen, K.: All the AES you need on Cortex-M3 and M4. In: Avanzi, R., Heys, H. (eds.) SAC 2016. LNCS, vol. 10532, pp. 180–194. Springer, Cham (2017). https://doi.org/10.1007/978-3-319-69453-5_10
38. Somech, N., Kessem, L.: Breaking the ice: a deep dive into the IcedID banking trojan's new major version release (2020). https://securityintelligence.com/posts/breaking-the-ice-a-deep-dive-into-the-icedid-banking-trojans-new-major-version-release/. Accessed 15 June 2021
39. Thales: High assurance hardware security modules (2020). https://cpl.thalesgroup.com/encryption/hardware-security-modules/network-hsms. Accessed 13 July 2021
40. Varriale, A., Prinetto, P., Carelli, A., Trotta, P.: SEcube (TM): data at rest and data in motion protection. In: Proceedings of the International Conference on Security and Management (SAM), p. 138 (2016)
41. Vella, M., Colombo, C., Abela, R., Špaček, P.: RV-TEE: secure cryptographic protocol execution based on runtime verification. J. Comput. Virol. Hack. Tech. **17**(3), 229–248 (2021). https://doi.org/10.1007/s11416-021-00391-1
42. Wang, Z., Yu, H., Zhang, Z., Piao, J., Liu, J.: ECDSA weak randomness in Bitcoin. Futur. Gener. Comput. Syst. **102**, 507–513 (2020)
43. Whiting, D., Housley, R., Ferguson, N.: Counter with CBC-MAC (CCM). IETF RFC 3610 (2003)
44. Wojtczuk, R., Rutkowska, J.: Attacking intel trusted execution technology. Black Hat DC 2009 (2009)

Deciding a Fragment of (α, β)-Privacy

Laouen Fernet$^{(\boxtimes)}$ⓘ and Sebastian Mödersheimⓘ

DTU Compute, Richard Petersens Plads, Building 321,
2800 Kongens Lyngby, Denmark
{lpkf,samo}@dtu.dk

Abstract. We show how to automate fragments of the logical framework (α, β)-privacy which provides an alternative to bisimilarity-based and trace-based definitions of privacy goals for security protocols. We consider the so-called message-analysis problem, which is at the core of (α, β)-privacy: given a set of concrete messages and their structure, which models can the intruder rule out? While in general this problem is undecidable, we give a decision procedure for a standard class of algebraic theories.

Keywords: Privacy · Formal methods · Security protocols · Automated verification

1 Introduction

The problem of privacy in security protocols is relevant in many fields, such as electronic voting, digital health information, mobile payments and distributed systems in general. Privacy is a security goal of its own, it cannot be described as regular secrecy. For example, in voting it is not the values of the votes that are secret, since there is a public tally, but rather the *relation* between a voter and a vote. It is best if privacy is taken into account during the design of communication protocols. But even then, it is difficult to get enough guarantees about privacy goals. Formal methods are a successful way of addressing the issue. By studying a protocol at an abstract level, they can be used to check digital applications against possible misuse.

The symbolic modeling of protocols allows one to define various privacy goals. The standard approach uses the notion of *observational equivalence* [8,9]: it is common to consider privacy as a bisimilarity between processes in the applied π-calculus. For instance, for electronic voting protocols, a privacy goal could be that two processes differing only by a swap of votes are *indistinguishable* [5,10,16]. There are many examples of communication protocols that are not secure with regards to privacy. This is the case also for protocols which have been designed to provide some privacy goals. Indeed, recent papers show privacy issues in voting protocols (Helios [5,10]) as well as contact-tracing applications (GAEN API [7], SwissCovid [14,17]). While tools exist to provide automated verification [4,6], it can be hard to formalize a privacy goal as a bisimilarity property, so automated

R. Roman and J. Zhou (Eds.): STM 2021, LNCS 13075, pp. 122–142, 2021.
https://doi.org/10.1007/978-3-030-91859-0_7

verification is actually challenging. In such cases, it is hard to specify all desirable privacy goals using the notion of observational equivalence. Additionally, the standard approach cannot guarantee that the privacy goals verified cover all possibilities of misuse. These limits are the motivation for studying a new approach that is declarative and more intuitive.

(α, β)-privacy [13,15] is an approach based on first-order logic with Herbrand universes, which allows for a novel way of specifying privacy goals. Instead of specifying pairs of things that should be indistinguishable to the intruder, one instead positively specifies what relations about the private data the intruder is *allowed* to learn and it is then considered a violation if the intruder is actually able to find out more.

The authors of [15] mainly argue that (α, β)-privacy is a more declarative way to specify goals without emphasis on questions of automation. For instance, they describe the goal of a voting protocol as releasing to the intruder the number of votes for each candidate or option and that this can actually justify the more technical "encoding" into bisimilarity-based approaches with the vote-swap idea mentioned before.

We now argue that actually the direct automation of (α, β)-privacy fragments can have advantages over bisimilarity approaches. The reason is that (α, β)-privacy is a reachability problem [12]: there is a state-transition system where every state is characterized by two Herbrand formulae α and β, namely what payload information α is currently published as well as the technical information β like exchanged messages between honest agents and intruder and what the intruder knows about the structure of these messages. The privacy question is now whether in any *reachable* state, β allows to rule out a model of α.

Thus, the main challenge lies in checking the (α, β)-privacy property for a given state, while in bisimilarity approaches, the main challenge lies in checking for every state S that is reachable in one process if there exists a reachable state S' in the other process so that S and S' are in a certain relation. This includes that the intruder knowledge in these states is statically equivalent, i.e., the intruder cannot tell S and S' apart. Bisimilarity thus means a challenge on top of static equivalence that is hard to handle in automated methods, while in (α, β)-privacy, reachability is trivial, but verifying privacy in the reached states is in general undecidable.

In this paper we show that for the fragment of *message-analysis problems* identified in [15] (and a suitable intruder theory), the check for (α, β)-privacy in each state is akin—and typically not more complex—than a static equivalence problem of the same size. For this fragment, (α, β)-privacy thus allows us to get rid of all the troubles of bisimilarity and reduce everything to a static-equivalence-style problem.

We present our first contributions in Sect. 3 by introducing the notions of destructor theories and frames with shorthands. In Sect. 4, we present our main contribution under the form of several algorithms constituting a decision procedure. Proofs for our results are presented in Appendix A.

2   Preliminaries

2.1   Herbrand Logic

Much of the preliminaries are adapted from [15]. The approach of (α, β)-privacy is based on Herbrand logic [11], which is First-Order Logic (FOL) with Herbrand universes. A reachable state of a protocol will later be characterized by two formulae α and β in Herbrand logic.

In Herbrand logic, an alphabet $\Sigma = \Sigma_f \uplus \Sigma_i \uplus \Sigma_r$ consists of Σ_f the set of *free function symbols*, Σ_i the set of *interpreted function symbols* and Σ_r the set of *relation symbols*. The main difference to standard FOL (that has no free function symbols Σ_f) is that the universe is fixed by the set of terms that can be built using Σ_f. More precisely, let $\mathcal{V}$ be a countable set of *variable symbols*, disjoint from Σ. We denote with $\mathcal{T}_\Sigma(\mathcal{V})$ the set of all *terms* that can be built from the function symbols in Σ and the variables in $\mathcal{V}$, i.e., a term is either a variable x or a function applied to subterms $f(t_1, \ldots, t_n)$. We simply write $\mathcal{T}_\Sigma$ when $\mathcal{V} = \emptyset$, and call its elements *ground terms* (over signature Σ). Let $\approx$ be a congruence relation on $\mathcal{T}_{\Sigma_f}$.

The *Herbrand universe U (over Σ and $\mathcal{V}$)* is defined in the quotient algebra $\mathcal{A}_\approx = \mathcal{T}_{\Sigma_f/\approx}$, i.e., $U = \{[\![t]\!]_\approx \mid t \in \mathcal{T}_{\Sigma_f}\}$, where $[\![t]\!]_\approx = \{t' \in \mathcal{T}_{\Sigma_f} \mid t \approx t'\}$. The algebra interprets every n-ary function symbol $\mathsf{f} \in \Sigma_f$ as a function $\mathsf{f}^\mathcal{A} : U^n \mapsto U$ such that $\mathsf{f}^\mathcal{A}([\![t_1]\!]_\approx, \ldots, [\![t_n]\!]_\approx) = [\![\mathsf{f}(t_1, \ldots, t_n)]\!]_\approx$.

A $(\Sigma, \mathcal{V})$-*interpretation* $\mathcal{I}$ maps every interpreted function symbol $f \in \Sigma_i$ to a function $\mathcal{I}(f) : U^n \mapsto U$, every relation symbol $r \in \Sigma_r$ to a relation $\mathcal{I}(r) \subseteq U^n$, and every variable $x \in \mathcal{V}$ to an element $\mathcal{I}(x) \in U$. We extend $\mathcal{I}$ to a function on $\mathcal{T}_\Sigma(\mathcal{V})$ as expected:

$$\mathcal{I}(\mathsf{f}(t_1, \ldots, t_n)) = \mathsf{f}^\mathcal{A}(\mathcal{I}(t_1), \ldots, \mathcal{I}(t_n)) \text{ for } \mathsf{f} \in \Sigma_f$$
$$\mathcal{I}(f[t_1, \ldots, t_n]) = \mathcal{I}(f)(\mathcal{I}(t_1), \ldots, \mathcal{I}(t_n)) \text{ for } f \in \Sigma_i$$

Note that we write $f[t_1, \ldots, t_n]$ for $f \in \Sigma_i$ with square parentheses to visually distinguish interpreted functions from free functions. The rest of the syntax and semantics is like in standard FOL. We write $\mathcal{I} \models \phi$ when a formula ϕ over Σ and $\mathcal{V}$ is true in a $(\Sigma, \mathcal{V})$-interpretation $\mathcal{I}$, and we then call $\mathcal{I}$ a $(\Sigma, \mathcal{V})$-*model*. We may just say *interpretation* and *model* when Σ and $\mathcal{V}$ are clear from the context. We also say ϕ *entails* ψ and write $\phi \models \psi$, if all ϕ-models are ψ-models.

We employ the standard syntactic sugar and write, for example, $\forall x.\phi$ for $\neg \exists x.\neg \phi$ and $x \in \{t_1, \ldots, t_n\}$ for $x = t_1 \vee \cdots \vee x = t_n$. Slightly abusing notation, we will also consider a substitution $[x_1 \mapsto t_1, \ldots, x_n \mapsto t_n]$ as a formula $x_1 = t_1 \wedge \cdots \wedge x_n = t_n$. This allows us to write $\theta \models \phi$ for a substitution θ and a formula ϕ that has no symbols to interpret other than variables in the domain of θ. In particular, we can write $\sigma' \models \sigma$ when the substitution σ' is an instance of σ. We denote with ε the identity substitution.

2.2   Frames

We use frames to represent the knowledge of the intruder. The idea is that the intruder has recorded a number of messages and can refer to them using labels.

We identify a subset $\Sigma_{op} \subseteq \Sigma_f$ of free functions, that we call *cryptographic operators*. They are used to represent a black-box model of cryptography, which is defined with a set of algebraic equations.

Definition 1 (Frame). *A frame is written as* $F = \{\!| \, l_1 \mapsto t_1, \ldots, l_k \mapsto t_k \, |\!\}$, *where the* l_i *are distinguished constants and the* t_i *are terms that do not contain any* l_i. *We call* $\{l_1, \ldots, l_k\}$ *and* $\{t_1, \ldots, t_k\}$ *the domain and the image of the frame, respectively. The set* $\mathcal{R}_F = \mathcal{T}_{\Sigma_{op}}(\{l_1, \ldots, l_k\})$ *is the set of* recipes, *i.e., the least set that contains* $l_1, \ldots, l_k$ *and that is closed under all the cryptographic operators of* Σ_{op}. *We will simply write* $\mathcal{R}$ *when* F *is clear from the context.* □

A frame F can be regarded as a substitution that replaces every l_i of its domain with the corresponding t_i. For a recipe r, we thus write $F\{\!|\, r \,|\!\}$ for the term obtained by applying this substitution to r. A *generable term* is any term t for which there is a recipe r with $t \approx F\{\!|\, r \,|\!\}$. Note that by default, the intruder does not know all constants but they can be explicitly included in the frame if needed.

Two frames F_1 and F_2 with the same domain are *statically equivalent*, written $F_1 \sim F_2$, if the intruder cannot distinguish them, i.e., when for all pairs of recipes r_1 and r_2 it holds that $F_1\{\!|\, r_1 \,|\!\} \approx F_1\{\!|\, r_2 \,|\!\} \iff F_2\{\!|\, r_1 \,|\!\} \approx F_2\{\!|\, r_2 \,|\!\}$. It is possible to axiomatize in Herbrand logic the notions of frames, recipes, generable terms, and static equivalence of frames [15].

2.3 (α, β)-Privacy

The idea of (α, β)-privacy is to declare a *payload-level formula* α over an alphabet $\Sigma_0 \subset \Sigma$ at the abstract level, defining intentionally released information (for instance the number of votes cast in an election), and a *technical-level formula* β over the full Σ, including all information visible to the intruder (e.g., cryptographic messages of a voting system and information about their structure). Intuitively, we want that the intruder does not learn from β anything on the payload-level that does not already follow from α, i.e., every model of α can be extended to a model of β:

Definition 2 (Model-theoretical (α, β)-privacy). *Let* Σ *be a countable signature,* $\Sigma_0 \subset \Sigma$ *a payload alphabet,* α *a formula over* Σ_0 *and* β *a formula over* Σ *such that* $fv(\alpha) = fv(\beta)$, *both* α *and* β *are consistent and* $\beta \models \alpha$. *We say that* (α, β)-*privacy holds iff for every* $(\Sigma_0, fv(\alpha))$-*model* $\mathcal{I} \models \alpha$ *there exists a* $(\Sigma, fv(\beta))$-*model* $\mathcal{I}' \models \beta$, *such that* $\mathcal{I}$ *and* $\mathcal{I}'$ *agree on the interpretation of all interpreted function and relation symbols of* Σ_0 *and all free variables of* α. □

3 The Fragment

In the (α, β)-privacy framework, we have a state transition system where every state contains at least a pair of formulae α and β, as well as other information to represent the current state of some honest agents. Privacy is then a *reachability problem* [12], i.e., whether we can reach a state where β allows the intruder to exclude at least one model of α. We focus in this paper only on the problem for a single state, i.e., deciding (α, β)-privacy for a given pair (α, β).

Even this is undecidable due to the expressiveness of Herbrand logic. We therefore restrict ourselves in this paper to (α, β)-pairs of a particular form that is called *message-analysis problem* in [15], which consists of two restrictions. The first restriction here is that the payload alphabet Σ_0 is a finite set of free constants that are part of Σ_{op}. We say in this case that α is *combinatoric*. Thus the Herbrand universe U of Σ_0 is also finite, and every model of α is just a mapping from $fv(\alpha)$ to U. We will write θ for such a mapping in the following. For example if $\alpha \equiv x \in \{a, b, c\} \wedge y \in \{a, b\} \wedge x \neq y$, then $\theta = [x \mapsto a, y \mapsto b]$ is a model of α. We also call $fv(\alpha)$ the *privacy variables*, and say the domain of a privacy variable x are those values from Σ_0 that x can have in any model of α. We denote with Θ the set of all models of α. The second restriction is that in every reachable state of the system, the intruder knowledge can be characterized by a frame *struct* where the messages can contain variables from α, and a frame $concr = \theta(struct)$, where θ is a model of α representing the true values of the privacy variables in this state, and thus *concr* are the concrete messages that the intruder observes. The formula β then consists of α, the definition of *struct* and *concr*, and stipulates that $struct \sim concr$.

Example 1. Consider a structural frame

$$struct = \{| \, l_1 \mapsto \mathsf{scrypt}(k, x), l_2 \mapsto \mathsf{scrypt}(k, y), l_3 \mapsto \mathsf{scrypt}(k, z) \, |\}$$

and the model $\theta = [x \mapsto 0, y \mapsto 1, z \mapsto 0]$, where the variables x, y, z in *struct* represent some votes that have been symmetrically encrypted (scrypt) by a trusted authority with a key k. (We formally introduce this algebraic theory in Example 3.) Let the payload formula be $\alpha \equiv x, y, z \in \{0, 1\}$. The intruder is not able to learn the values of the votes without the key. However, they[1] can observe that $concr\{| \, l_1 \, |\} \approx concr\{| \, l_3 \, |\}$. Using static equivalence between *struct* and *concr*, the intruder deduces that $struct\{| \, l_1 \, |\} \approx struct\{| \, l_3 \, |\}$. The only way to unify the equation, with respect to $\approx$, is with $x = z$. This constitutes a breach of privacy, as it does not follow from α (some models have been excluded). There are also other relations that can be derived at this point: $x \neq y$ and $y \neq z$.

The problem we solve in this paper is thus: given an (α, β)-pair that is a message-analysis problem, check whether (α, β)-privacy holds. Note here a fundamental difference with respect to approaches based on static equivalence of frames where privacy means that the intruder cannot distinguish two frames that represent different possibilities. In (α, β)-privacy, in contrast, we have a symbolic frame *struct* and an instance *concr*, and the intruder *knows* that *concr* is the instance of *struct* that represents what really happened. Thus the intruder can exclude every model of α under which *struct* and *concr* would be distinguishable.

Interestingly, the problem of (α, β)-privacy in a message-analysis problem *is* related to static equivalence of frames. As [15] observes, in theory one could compute *all* models of the given α (there are finitely many since α is combinatoric)

---

[1] We use the pronoun "they" for gender-neutral expression.

and compute $concr_i = \theta_i(struct)$ for every model θ_i; then (α, β)-privacy holds iff the $concr_i$ are all statically equivalent. This is practically not feasible, since the number of models is in general in the order of $|\Sigma_0|^{|fv(\alpha)|}$. The algorithms we present here will typically not be more complex than standard static equivalence algorithms (in the same algebraic theory). However, in corner cases our current implementation can produce in general an exponential set of recipes. It is part of the future work to investigate whether this can be avoided with another representation that avoids the enumeration of combinations.

Reachable States. Before we go into detail about the algorithm itself, we want to briefly sketch what kinds of protocol descriptions can be considered, so that in every reachable state we have a message-analysis problem. This is only a sketch because we lack the space to make a fully-fledged definition. What we can support with message-analysis problems is basically what one would have in strand spaces: protocols where every role can be described as a linear sequence of message exchanges. This corresponds in the applied π-calculus to processes for roles that do not contain any repetition, parallelism, or branching. That is, when checking incoming messages with an `if` or `let` statement, the `else` branch has to be empty (i.e., when the conditions are not satisfied, the protocol aborts). In this case, the intruder always learns the outcome of the check, and for privacy it is sometimes interesting to consider protocols that can hide this, e.g., sending in the negative case a decoy-answer [2]. This is a generalization of the message-analysis problem, i.e., the intruder in general does no longer know the structure of a message for sure, but only that it is one of several possibilities, say $struct_1, \ldots, struct_n$, and figuring out which $struct_i$ it is may allow for breaking the privacy. This requires an extension to our algorithms that is not overly difficult, but we lack the space to present it here. However, with message-analysis problems we cover the realm of standard security protocols that could be written in Alice-and-Bob notation.

In addition to normal variables for received messages, we have the mentioned privacy variables (recall they are non-deterministically chosen from a given subset of Σ_0). The formalism for describing the state transition system should thus include a mechanism to specify the choice of such variables, and what information about them is released by augmenting α upon state transitions. Note that the intruder is active and can send a message determined by a recipe over the domain of $struct$ in that state. Since $struct$ contains privacy variables, the intruder can "experiment" by sending a message with a privacy variable to an honest agent, and thus observe if there is an answer (i.e., passing checks that the agent makes) and learn the message structure of the answer.

Example 2. Consider a door with a tag reader. Agents a, b, c can use a personal tag to open the door; their tags each have a symmetric key $k(a)$, $k(b)$ and $k(c)$, respectively (where k is a private free function). The toy protocol is that the reader sends a nonce and the tag replies with the encrypted nonce. For instance the following state is reachable in two protocol executions: the structural knowledge is $struct = \{| \, l_1 \mapsto n, l_2 \mapsto \mathsf{scrypt}(k(x_1), n), l_3 \mapsto n', l_4 \mapsto \mathsf{scrypt}(k(x_2), n') \, |\}$, where n, n' represent nonces and x_1, x_2 are variables for agent names, and the concrete instantiation is $\theta = [x_1 \mapsto \mathsf{a}, x_2 \mapsto \mathsf{a}]$, i.e., both interactions were with the same agent $x_1 = x_2 = \mathsf{a}$. The privacy goal of *unlinkability* can be expressed by a payload formula that every agent variable can be any of the agents, i.e., in the example state we have $\alpha \equiv x_1, x_2 \in \{\mathsf{a}, \mathsf{b}, \mathsf{c}\}$. Thus, the intruder should not be able to tell whether replies come from the same agent. If the intruder is just passively listening (as in the example state above), unlinkability indeed holds (since the nonces n and n' are different). However, if the intruder impersonates a reader and replays a nonce n to a tag, we would get to the state $struct = \{\!| \, \mathsf{l}_1 \mapsto n, \mathsf{l}_2 \mapsto \mathsf{scrypt}(k(x_1), n), \mathsf{l}_3 \mapsto n, \mathsf{l}_4 \mapsto \mathsf{scrypt}(k(x_2), n) \, |\!\}$. Here, they can deduce that $\mathsf{scrypt}(k(x_1), n) \approx \mathsf{scrypt}(k(x_2), n)$ and thus $x_1 = x_2$. This could be fixed by including also a nonce from the tag in the message, but note this is only a toy protocol, and one would need to also solve distance bounding.

3.1 Destructor Theories

Even with the restriction to message-analysis problems, (α, β)-privacy is still undecidable, since the *word problem* (whether $s \approx t$, given s and t) in algebraic theories is. We restrict ourselves here to theories we call *destructor theories*, a concept similar to subterm-convergent theories. The main difference is that we like to distinguish constructors like encryption and destructors like decryption and be able to verify if the application of a destructor was successful.

This verification is motivated by the fact that most modern cryptographic primitives allow one to check whether a decryption is successful or not, e.g., by including MACs or specific padding. In some protocol verification approaches, this is modeled by applying encryption again to the result of the decryption and comparing with the original term, i.e., checking $\mathsf{crypt}(\mathsf{pub}(k), \mathsf{dcrypt}(\mathsf{priv}(k), c)) \approx c$. This seems a bit absurd and would not work with randomized encryption in general. We therefore model destructors to yield an error value if it is applied to terms for which it does not work. Given that this error message does not normally occur in protocols, we can regard this as destructors having the return type `Maybe Msg` in Haskell notation, i.e., returning `Just r` if successful or `Nothing` in case of an error. This allows us to discard all "garbage terms" and makes reasoning a bit simpler.

Definition 3 (Destructor theory). *A destructor theory consists of*

- *a set $\Sigma_{pub} \subseteq \Sigma_f$ of public functions that the intruder is able to apply; it is further partitioned into constructors and destructors. Let in the following* constr *and* destr *range over constructors and destructors, respectively.*
- *a set E of algebraic equations of the form* $\mathsf{destr}(k, \mathsf{constr}(t_1, \ldots, t_n)) = t_i$, *where $i \in \{1, \ldots, n\}$, $fv(k) \subseteq fv(t_1, \ldots, t_n)$ and the symbols of E are disjoint from Σ_0. The first argument of a destructor is called a* key.[2]

---

[2] For some destructors, e.g., opening a pair, one does not need a key; for uniformity one could use here a fixed public constant as a dummy value, but slightly abusing notation, we just omit the key argument in such a case.

We also require that for any two equations $\mathsf{destr}(k, \mathsf{constr}(t_1, \ldots, t_n)) = t_i$ *and* $\mathsf{destr'}(k', \mathsf{constr'}(t'_1, \ldots, t'_m)) = t'_j$ *of* E, *it must be the case that either*
- $\mathsf{constr} \neq \mathsf{constr'}$ *or*
- $k = k'$, $n = m$, *and* $t_1 = t'_1, \ldots, t_m = t'_m$.

i.e., when we deal with the same constructor, the respective subterms and keys must be the same (but the extracted t_i *and* t'_j *may be different).*

Finally, every destructor occurs in only one equation.

Let $\approx_0$ be the least congruence relation on ground terms induced by E. We define the congruence $\approx$ of the destructor theory as the least congruence relation over ground terms that subsumes $\approx_0$ and such that for all ground terms k and m $\mathsf{destr}(k, m) \approx \mathsf{error}$ whenever $\mathsf{destr}(k, m) \not\approx_0 m'$ for all destructor-free m'. Here error is a distinguished constant in $\Sigma \setminus \Sigma_0$.

Finally, we require that in all given frames, the image contains no destructors (and the algorithms will preserve this property). $\qquad\qquad\square$

Note that the error behavior cannot directly be represented by algebraic equations because of the negative side-condition. However, observe that the underlying theory E gives rise to a term rewriting system (replacing $=$ with $\rightarrow$) that is convergent: termination is obvious and for confluence observe that there are no critical pairs (see, e.g., [3]). This gives immediately a decision procedure for the word problem in $\approx_0$ (normalize and compare syntactically) and in $\approx$ (build the $\approx_0$-normal forms, replace all remaining destructor-subterms by error; again compare syntactically).

3.2 Unification and All that

In general, we will deal with terms that contain variables, albeit only privacy variables, i.e., ranging over constants of Σ_0. Thus destructor-free symbolic terms cannot give rise to a redex and we can use the standard syntactic unification algorithm on destructor-free terms—with one exception. We need to adapt the unification of variables slightly: the unification of x with t is only possible if either t is a constant in the domain of x, or another variable y such that their domains have a non-empty intersection; their domains are then restricted to this intersection. Since a substitution $[x_1 \mapsto t_1, \ldots, x_n \mapsto t_n]$ can be expressed as a set of equations $\{x_1 = t_1, \ldots, x_n = t_n\}$, we allow to use the notation $unify(\sigma_1, \ldots, \sigma_n)$ for a most general unifier (MGU) of all equations from the σ_i.

3.3 The *ana* Function

Finally, we can repackage the destructor equations into a function *ana* that, given a term with a constructor, yields which destructors may be applicable:

Definition 4

$$ana(\mathsf{constr}(t_1, \ldots, t_n)) = (k, \{(\mathsf{destr}, t_i) \mid \mathsf{destr}(k, \mathsf{constr}(t_1, \ldots, t_n)) = t_i \in E\})$$

Intuitively, given a term that can be decrypted, ana returns the key required for decryption and all derivable terms according to the algebraic equations. $\qquad\square$

Example 3. The theory we use in examples throughout this paper is as follows (adapted from [15]). Let $\Sigma = \Sigma_f \uplus \Sigma_i \uplus \Sigma_r$ be an alphabet and $\mathcal{V}$ a set of variables. We consider the cryptographic operators defined in Table 1 and $\Sigma_{pub} = \Sigma_{op}$.

- $\mathsf{pub}(s)$ and $\mathsf{priv}(s)$ represent an asymmetric key pair from a secret seed (where the lack of destructors reflects that it is hard to find the seed from the keys);
- $\mathsf{crypt}(p, r, t)$ and $\mathsf{dcrypt}(p', t)$ formalize asymmetric encryption with randomness;
- $\mathsf{sign}(p', t)$ and $\mathsf{retrieve}(p', t)$ formalize digital signatures;
- $\mathsf{scrypt}(k, t)$ and $\mathsf{dscrypt}(k, t)$ formalize symmetric cryptography;
- pair, proj_1 and proj_2 formalize serialization;
- h is a cryptographic hash function (where the lack of destructors reflects that it is hard to find a pre-image).

Table 1. Example set Σ_{op}

Constructors	Destructors	Properties
pub, priv		
crypt	dcrypt	$\mathsf{dcrypt}(\mathsf{priv}(s), \mathsf{crypt}(\mathsf{pub}(s), r, t)) = t$
sign	retrieve	$\mathsf{retrieve}(\mathsf{pub}(s), \mathsf{sign}(\mathsf{priv}(s), t)) = t$
scrypt	dscrypt	$\mathsf{dscrypt}(k, \mathsf{scrypt}(k, t)) = t$
pair	$\mathsf{proj}_1, \mathsf{proj}_2$	$\mathsf{proj}_1(\mathsf{pair}(t_1, t_2)) = t_1$
		$\mathsf{proj}_2(\mathsf{pair}(t_1, t_2)) = t_2$
h		

In case there is no key required, the argument is omitted as written in the equations in Table 1. We introduce a "dummy" key k_0 known by the intruder covering this case for the return value of *ana*.

$$ana(t) = \begin{cases} (\mathsf{priv}(s), \{(\mathsf{dcrypt}, t')\}) & \text{if } t = \mathsf{crypt}(\mathsf{pub}(s), r, t') \\ (k, \{(\mathsf{dscrypt}, t')\}) & \text{if } t = \mathsf{scrypt}(k, t') \\ (\mathsf{pub}(s), \{(\mathsf{retrieve}, t')\}) & \text{if } t = \mathsf{sign}(\mathsf{priv}(s), t') \\ (\mathsf{k}_0, \{(\mathsf{proj}_1, t_1), (\mathsf{proj}_2, t_2)\}) & \text{if } t = \mathsf{pair}(t_1, t_2) \\ (\mathsf{k}_0, \{\}) & \text{otherwise} \end{cases}$$

3.4   Frames with Shorthands

We define an extension of the concept of frames to easily handle decryption of terms. A frame with shorthands consists in a frame with additional labels, which are actually recipes over the initial labels.

Definition 5 (Frame with shorthands). *A frame with shorthands is written as* $F' = \{\!| \, l_1 \mapsto t_1, \ldots, l_k \mapsto t_k, m_1 \mapsto s_1, \ldots, m_n \mapsto s_n \, |\!\}$, *where* $F = \{\!| \, l_1 \mapsto t_1, \ldots, l_k \mapsto t_k \, |\!\}$ *is a frame, the* m_j *are recipes over the* l_i *and* $F\{\!| \, m_j \, |\!\} \approx s_j$. *We call the mappings* $m_1 \mapsto s_1, \ldots, m_n \mapsto s_n$ *shorthands. The domain of a frame with shorthands is defined to be the domain of the underlying frame.* $\square$

We will treat these m_j like the labels l_i. As a consequence, the set $\mathcal{R}_{F'}$ is now $\mathcal{T}_{\Sigma_{op}}(\{l_1, \ldots, l_k, m_1, \ldots, m_n\})$, i.e., all the shorthands can be used. This gives the same recipes as $\mathcal{R}_F$, but the shorthands make a difference when we restrict ourselves to *constructive recipes*, i.e., recipes without destructors which we define as $\mathcal{R}_F^c = \mathcal{T}_{\Sigma_{op}^c}(\{l_1, \ldots, l_k\})$ and $\mathcal{R}_{F'}^c = \mathcal{T}_{\Sigma_{op}^c}(\{l_1, \ldots, l_k, m_1, \ldots, m_n\})$ where Σ_{op}^c are the constructors. Thus $\mathcal{R}_{F'}^c$ can use destructors from the shorthands, but otherwise only constructors, and thus in general $\mathcal{R}_{F'}^c \supsetneq \mathcal{R}_F^c$. Similarly, we say that a term t is *constructive* if it does not contain any destructor.

Recall that initially all terms in a frame's image are constructive. Our algorithms will ensure that all s_j added through shorthands are also constructive.

Example 4. Let $k \in \mathcal{T}_{\Sigma}(\mathcal{V})$ and $x \in \mathcal{V}$. Consider the frames

$$F = \{\!| \, l_1 \mapsto \mathsf{scrypt}(k, x), l_2 \mapsto k \, |\!\}$$
$$F' = \{\!| \, l_1 \mapsto \mathsf{scrypt}(k, x), l_2 \mapsto k, m_1 \mapsto x \, |\!\}$$

where $m_1 = \mathsf{dscrypt}(l_2, l_1)$. Here F' is the frame F with the shorthand $m_1 \mapsto x$. Indeed, we have that $F\{\!| \, \mathsf{dscrypt}(l_2, l_1) \, |\!\} = \mathsf{dscrypt}(k, \mathsf{scrypt}(k, x)) \approx x$.

4 Decision Procedure

We now give a decision procedure for the fragment of (α, β)-privacy that we have defined in the previous section: a message-analysis problem with respect to a destructor theory. We are thus given a triple $(\alpha, struct, \theta)$ where α expresses the privacy goal at this state and the models of α can be characterized by substitutions from the free variables of α to constants of Σ_0. The substitution θ is one of the models, namely what is the reality, i.e., the true value of the free variables of α. Finally, *struct* is a frame with privacy variables representing all the messages that the intruder received in the exchange with honest agents up to this state. This means that the intruder knows the structure of each message, because the protocol description is public and there is no branching; what the intruder might not know is the value θ of the privacy variables (as well as constants representing strong keys and nonces). The intruder also knows the concrete messages $concr = \theta(struct)$. The question our algorithm will answer is what models of α the intruder can exclude from this, i.e., the $\theta' \models \alpha$ such that $concr \not\approx \theta'(struct)$. To avoid enumerating all models (there are exponentially many in general) and to be able to easily integrate our algorithm with reasoning about other constraints, the algorithm returns a set of equations and inequations that can be derived by the intruder.

4.1   Composition

Composition in a Structural Frame. This first piece of the procedure is concerned with the intruder composing messages, i.e., using only constructive recipes. Note that the intruder can also use shorthands that represent the result of previous decryption operations. This composition task is similar in many intruder algorithms: either the goal term t is directly in the knowledge or it is of the form $f(t_1, \ldots, t_n)$ where f is a public constructor and the t_i can be composed recursively. The novelty of our algorithm here is that both the terms in *struct* and t may contain privacy variables, and composition may reveal information about these variables to the intruder. For a variable $x \in \mathcal{V}$, the intruder knows all values in the domain of x. Thus, if the variable occurs in a term to compose with only public constructors, they can compare all possibilities and see which one is correct, i.e., to what constant the variable x is mapped. Much of this evaluation must be postponed to a later stage of the algorithm. For now the composition algorithm just computes under which values of the variables the goal term t can be produced, i.e., it returns a set of pairs (r, σ) of a recipe r and a substitution σ where σ is an MGU under which r produces the goal t.

Example 5. As in Example 1, $struct = \{\!| \, l_1 \mapsto \mathsf{scrypt}(k, x), l_2 \mapsto \mathsf{scrypt}(k, y), l_3 \mapsto \mathsf{scrypt}(k, z) \, |\!\}$ and $\theta = [x \mapsto 0, y \mapsto 1, z \mapsto 0]$. The intruder has several ways to compose the term $\mathsf{scrypt}(k, x)$, depending on which model of α is true:

$$composeUnder(\theta, struct, \mathsf{scrypt}(k, x)) = \{(l_1, \varepsilon), (l_2, [x \mapsto y]), (l_3, [x \mapsto z])\}$$

The other algorithms will actually rule out $[x \mapsto y]$ since $\theta \not\models x = y$.

Algorithm 1: Composition in a structural frame

---

1 $composeUnder(\theta, struct, t) =$
2   **let** $RU = \{(l, \sigma) \mid l \mapsto t' \in struct, \sigma = unify(t = t')\}$ **in**
3   **if** $t \in \mathcal{V}$ **then**
4        $RU \cup \{(\theta(t), [t \mapsto \theta(t)])\}$
5   **else if** $t = f(t_1, \ldots, t_n)$ *and* $f \in \Sigma_{pub}$ **then**
6        $RU \cup \{(f(r_1, \ldots, r_n), \sigma) \mid (r_1, \sigma_1) \in composeUnder(\theta, struct, t_1),$
7                        $\ldots,$
8                        $(r_n, \sigma_n) \in composeUnder(\theta, struct, t_n),$
9                        $\sigma = unify(\sigma_1, \ldots, \sigma_n)\}$
10   **else**
11   RU

We argue that the algorithm is correct, in the sense that the pairs found by this algorithm really allow to compose the term in the given frame, under a unifier; the algorithm finds all constructive recipes together with an MGU.

Theorem 1 (Correctness of *composeUnder***).** *Let θ be a substitution, struct be a frame and $t \in \mathcal{T}_\Sigma(\mathcal{V})$. Then*

1. $\forall (r, \sigma) \in composeUnder(\theta, struct, t), \sigma(struct\{\!| r |\!\}) = \sigma(t)$.
2. $\forall r \in \mathcal{R}^c, \exists \tau, \tau(struct\{\!| r |\!\}) = \tau(t) \implies$
   $(\exists \sigma, (r, \sigma) \in composeUnder(\theta, struct, t)$ *and* $\tau \models \sigma)$.

Composition in a Ground Frame. At the concrete level, the terms in the frame are all *ground*, i.e., they do not contain variables. The intruder does not have to reason about possible variable instantiations but only cares about the recipes they can use. This can be seen as a special case of the previous algorithm. We will use the function *compose* which does the same as *composeUnder* but drops the unifiers attached to the recipes (they are always the identity, for a ground frame and a ground term).

4.2 Analysis

The next step in our procedure is to augment the frame with shorthands as far as possible with messages the intruder can decrypt. This follows again common lines of intruder deduction reasoning, namely performing a saturation [1], but there are several crucial differences here. While the standard approach in static equivalence of frames just looks at each frame in isolation and computes a set of subterms that are derivable, we need to look at both *concr* and *struct* side by side here, because some analysis steps may only be possible for some instances of *struct*. Roughly speaking, if a decryption step is possible in *concr* but not in all instances of *struct*, we can exclude those instances, and vice-versa, if a decryption step is possible in some instances of *struct*, but not in *concr*, we can exclude those.

The intruder analyzes *struct* and adds shorthands for terms that can be decrypted. This will make all derivable subterms available with only composition (constructive recipes).

Example 6. Let $k_1, k_2, a \in \Sigma_0$ and $x, y, z \in \mathcal{V}$. Consider the substitution $\theta = [x \mapsto k_1, y \mapsto a, z \mapsto k_1]$ and the frame $struct = \{\!| l_1 \mapsto scrypt(x, y), l_2 \mapsto z |\!\}$. Then the analysis extends the frame by adding a shorthand like so: $struct_{ana} = \{\!| l_1 \mapsto scrypt(z, y), l_2 \mapsto z, dscrypt(l_2, l_1) \mapsto y |\!\}$. Since the decryption is successful in $concr = \theta(struct)$, the intruder is able to compose the key in *struct* with the same recipe l_2. This also enables the intruder to learn that $x = z$. Note that x is changed to z in the frame because $concr\{\!| dscrypt(l_2, l_1) |\!\} \not\approx error$, so we can rule out all instances of x and z so that $struct\{\!| dscrypt(l_2, l_1) |\!\} \approx error$. However, there are more relations that could be deduced. For instance, the intruder is now able to check the pair of recipes $(l_2, dscrypt(l_2, l_1))$ with composition only (using the shorthand). The intruder can therefore learn that also $x \neq y$, but this is handled by the final algorithm *findRelations* below.

Consider the same *struct* but with $\theta = [x \mapsto k_1, y \mapsto a, z \mapsto k_2]$, so that the above analysis step is not possible. When trying to compose the key x, the algorithm *composeUnder* returns $(I_2, [x \mapsto z])$ as a possibility. This does not work in *concr*, so the intruder cannot actually obtain a new term, but conclude that $x \neq z$.

We define a recursive function *analyzeRec* that will apply one analysis step from calling *ana*, add terms if the decryption was successful, and call itself to perform the other analysis steps. To tackle the problem, we first consider that the intruder knowledge has been split into three frames. That way, we can make the distinction between the terms that have to be analyzed in the future, the terms that might be decrypted later, and the terms that have already been completely analyzed. Note that we do need to consider the terms "on hold", i.e., that might be decrypted later, because the intruder might learn at a later point how to compose the required key.

The wrapper function *analyze* simply calls *analyzeRec* with the arguments properly initialized. All terms are initially considered "new" because they have to be analyzed. There are, at the start, no elements "on hold" or "done". The intruder does not know any equations between the variables at the beginning, so we indicate the identity substitution ε as the initial value. Moreover, we also indicate an empty set as the initial value of the set *Ex* of substitutions excluding some models of the variables ("exceptions").

The result of applying *ana* gives the key required to decrypt the term, and a set *FT* of pairs (function, term) of derivable terms. If the decryption fails in *concr*, i.e., the key cannot be composed at the concrete level, then it also fails in *struct* and no new terms can be added. However, since composition of the key at the structural level might be possible even in this case, the unifiers allowing to compose the key in *struct* exclude some models. We add such substitutions to the set *Ex*. Note that in the algorithms we write I as a label even though it can actually be a recipe, because we treat the recipes from shorthands as regular labels.

If the decryption is successful in *concr*, then it is also successful in *struct* and we can define recipes for the new terms. The shorthands added at this point use the destructors paired with the new terms, and some recipe found for composing the key in *concr*. The choice of this recipe is irrelevant: we also add a shorthand in *D* for the key, if there is not one already in the frame, so that we can later check the different ways to compose it. The keyword "**pick**" in the definition below refers to this choice, it means "take any one element from the set".

We put the new mappings in a frame LT_{new} and add this to the new terms to analyze. We do not need to add terms for which the intruder already has a label or shorthand. All terms that were on hold also need to be analyzed again, as the intruder might be able to successfully decrypt them with the new knowledge. We apply the substitution σ_{new}, required to compose the key with the different recipes the intruder found in *concr* for the corresponding ground key, to all terms in the split frame so that the shorthands are correct. We update the equations that the intruder found by unifying with the previous substitution σ.

The analysis adds shorthands for any successful decryption of terms. The function *analyze* also preserves the property of static equivalence between *struct*

Algorithm 2: Analysis of a structural frame

---

1 $analyze(\theta, struct) =$
2 $\quad \lfloor \; analyzeRec(\theta, struct, \{\! | \; | \!\}, \{\! | \; | \!\}, \varepsilon, \{\})$

3 $analyzeRec(\theta, N, H, D, \sigma, Ex) =$
4 $\quad$ **if** $N = \{\! | \; | \!\}$ **then**
5 $\quad\quad \lfloor \; (H \cup D, \sigma, Ex)$

6 $\quad$ **else**
7 $\quad\quad$ **let** $\{\! | \; \mathsf{l} \mapsto t \; | \!\} \cup LT = N$
8 $\quad\quad\quad (k, FT) = ana(t)$
9 $\quad\quad\quad struct = N \cup H \cup D$
10 $\quad\quad\quad concr = \theta(struct)$
11 $\quad\quad\quad SR = composeUnder(\theta, struct, k)$
12 $\quad\quad\quad GR = compose(concr, \theta(k))$
13 $\quad\quad\quad \sigma_{new} = unify(\{\sigma \mid (r, \sigma) \in SR, r \in GR\})$
14 $\quad\quad\quad Ex_{new} = \{\sigma \mid (r, \sigma) \in SR, r \notin GR\}$ **in**
15 $\quad\quad$ **if** $GR = \{\}$ **then**
16 $\quad\quad\quad \lfloor \; analyzeRec(\theta, LT, \{\! | \; \mathsf{l} \mapsto t \; | \!\} \cup H, D, \sigma, Ex \cup Ex_{new})$

17 $\quad\quad$ **else**
18 $\quad\quad\quad$ **pick** $r \in GR$
19 $\quad\quad\quad$ **let** $LT_{new} = \{\! | \; f(r, \mathsf{l}) \mapsto t' \mid (f, t') \in FT,$
20 $\quad\quad\quad\quad\quad\quad\quad\quad\quad \forall r', r' \mapsto t' \notin struct \; | \!\}$ **in**
21 $\quad\quad\quad analyzeRec(\theta,$
22 $\quad\quad\quad\quad\quad \sigma_{new}(LT_{new} \cup LT \cup H),$
23 $\quad\quad\quad\quad\quad \{\! | \; | \!\},$
24 $\quad\quad\quad\quad\quad \sigma_{new}(\{\! | \; \mathsf{l} \mapsto t \; | \!\} \cup \{\! | \; r \mapsto k \mid \forall r', r' \mapsto k \notin struct \; | \!\} \cup D),$
25 $\quad\quad\quad\quad\quad unify(\sigma, \sigma_{new}),$
26 $\quad\quad\quad\quad\quad Ex \cup Ex_{new})$

---

and *concr*. Recall that Θ denotes the set of models of α. Our results are expressed over Θ so that they can be used to check whether some models can be excluded. The algorithm presented here does not simply return the analyzed frame, but also a unifier σ and a set of substitutions Ex. The intruder knows that the concrete instantiation of variables is an instance of σ and can exclude all substitutions in Ex. These properties are formally expressed in Theorem 2.

Theorem 2 (Correctness of *analyze***).** *Let θ be a substitution, struct be a frame and $(struct_{ana}, \sigma, Ex) = analyze(\theta, struct)$. Then*

1. $\forall r \in \mathcal{R}, struct_{ana}\{\! | \; r \; | \!\} \approx \sigma(struct\{\! | \; r \; | \!\})$.
2. $\forall r \in \mathcal{R}, \exists r' \in \mathcal{R}^c_{struct_{ana}}, struct_{ana}\{\! | \; r' \; | \!\} \approx \sigma(struct\{\! | \; r \; | \!\})$.
3. $\forall \theta' \in \Theta, \theta'(struct) \sim \theta(struct) \implies \theta' \models \sigma \wedge \bigwedge_{\sigma' \in Ex} \neg \sigma'$.
4. $\forall \theta' \in \Theta, \theta' \models \sigma \implies (\theta'(struct) \sim \theta(struct) \iff \theta'(struct_{ana}) \sim \theta(struct_{ana}))$

Theorem 3 (Termination of *analyze***).** *Let θ be a substitution and struct be a frame. Then the call $analyze(\theta, struct)$ terminates.*

4.3   Intruder Findings

The final algorithm we present generates a formula ϕ, which contains all equations and inequations between variables that the intruder is able to derive from their knowledge. We argue that, after analysis, all checks that the intruder can do to compare *struct* and *concr* are covered by only composing the terms in the frames. We show that this procedure allows automated verification of (α, β)-privacy goals.

We specify a function *findRelations* that starts by analyzing the frame before trying to find more relations. The analysis of *struct* includes the analyzed frame $struct_{ana}$ as well as a unifier and a set of substitutions, excluding some models of the variables. These relations have to be included in the formula ϕ, since it already constitutes some deduction that the intruder was able to make.

First, the intruder tries to compose the terms inside *concr* in different ways. If the intruder has several ways to compose a term, i.e., the composition algorithm returned several recipes, then pairs of recipes from these possibilities must also produce the same corresponding term in *struct*. This gives a number of equations.

Second, the intruder tries to compose the terms inside *struct* in different ways, under some unifiers. If they are able to compose a term in several ways, then we check whether the pairs of recipes produce the same corresponding term in *concr*. If it is the case, then there is nothing to deduce, as this follows from static equivalence. However, if a pair of recipes distinguishes the frames, i.e., we have found (l, r) such that $concr \{\!| \, l \, |\!\} \not\approx concr \{\!| \, r \, |\!\}$, then the intruder knows that the unifier attached to r can be excluded. They can deduce the negation of the unifier, i.e., a disjunction of inequations.

Pairs from Equivalence Classes. When we want to compare all elements of a set $R = \{r_1, \ldots, r_n\}$ for equality, it is obviously sufficient to pick one element, say r_1, and compare the pairs $(r_1, r_2), \ldots, (r_1, r_n)$. The function *pairsEcs* does just that, i.e., given R returns such a set of pairs.

Algorithm 3: Relations between variables

---

1 $findRelations(\theta, struct) =$
2   **let** $(struct_{ana}, \sigma, Ex) = analyze(\theta, struct)$
3         $concr_{ana} = \theta(struct_{ana})$
4         $pairs = \bigcup_{l \mapsto t \in concr_{ana}} pairsEcs(compose(concr_{ana}, t))$
5         $eqs = \{struct_{ana}\{\!| \, r_1 \, |\!\} = struct_{ana}\{\!| \, r_2 \, |\!\} \mid (r_1, r_2) \in pairs\}$
6         $ineqs = Ex \cup \{\sigma' \mid l \mapsto t \in struct_{ana},$
7                         $(r, \sigma') \in composeUnder(\theta, struct_{ana}, t),$
8                         $concr_{ana}\{\!| \, l \, |\!\} \not\approx concr_{ana}\{\!| \, r \, |\!\}\}$ **in**
9      $unify(\sigma, eqs) \wedge \bigwedge_{\sigma' \in ineqs} \neg\sigma'$

We formalize the correctness of the decision procedure that has been described. We argue that the algorithm *findRelations* is sound and complete, i.e., the formula ϕ can be used to automatically verify privacy for a message-analysis problem by applying our algorithms. Note that the step of verifying whether ϕ actually excludes models of α can be performed with existing SAT solvers.

Theorem 4 (Correctness of *findRelations*). *Let (α, β) be a message-analysis problem, where struct $= \{\!| \, l_1 \mapsto t_1, \ldots, l_k \mapsto t_k \, |\!\}$ for some $t_1, \ldots, t_k \in \mathcal{T}_\Sigma(fv(\alpha))$ and concr $= \theta(struct)$ for some $\theta \in \Theta$. Let $\phi \equiv findRelations(\theta, struct)$. Then*

$$(\alpha, \beta)\text{-privacy holds} \iff \forall \theta' \in \Theta, \theta' \models \phi$$

5   Conclusions

We have designed a decision procedure for message-analysis problems in (α, β)-privacy with destructor theories. This procedure is not all that different from algorithms for static equivalence of frames [1]: we split in composition and decryption, have a saturation procedure for decryption, and finally check if we can compose a term in one saturated frame in a different way while the other frame gives a different result. However, we do not decide static equivalence, rather, one frame, *struct*, has privacy variables, the other, *concr*, is a ground *instance* of *struct*, and the question is if the intruder can learn something about this instantiation. In particular whatever works in *concr*, must work in *struct*; thus if it works only under some unifier σ, then we rule out all models that are not instances of σ, and vice-versa, if something works in *struct* under σ but not in *concr*, then we rule out all instances of σ.

The fact that the algorithm just returns a substitution that must be the case and a set of substitutions that we can rule out allows for a flexible integration into more complex scenarios. First, we can allow for further variables over finite domains, but that are not part of α. This can be for instance when there are choices that are not themselves relevant for the privacy goals like a session identifier; if the intruder finds them out during analysis, this is not directly a violation of privacy, but if that allows for ruling out some model of α, then it is.

Second, when an agent process can branch on a condition (see for instance the discussion of the AF-protocols in [15]), then the reachable states in general have a form that generalizes message-analysis problems, namely there are several possible frames $struct_i$ and associated conditions ϕ_i, and the intruder knows that

$$((\phi_1 \wedge struct_1 = struct) \vee \ldots \vee (\phi_n \wedge struct_n = struct)) \wedge struct \sim concr .$$

Here, we can apply almost the same algorithms for each $struct_i$ with *concr*, except that here we may rule out all models of $\alpha \wedge \phi_i$, meaning we know $\neg\phi_i$.

For future work, we plan to obtain a fully-fledged analysis tool, i.e., exploring the entire set of reachable states, and consider here in particular symbolic representations to avoid exponential blow-ups.

Further, we want to relax the constraints about the algebraic equations. Instead of using only destructor theories, we want to allow for a larger class of protocols to be machine-checked with the framework described, in particular the properties of exponentiation needed for Diffie-Hellman.

Acknowledgments. Thanks to Luca Viganò and Sébastien Gondron for useful comments. This work has been supported by the EU H2020-SU-ICT-03-2018 Project No. 830929 CyberSec4Europe (cybersec4europe.eu).

A   Proofs

Theorem 1 (Correctness of *composeUnder***).** *Let θ be a substitution, struct be a frame and $t \in \mathcal{T}_\Sigma(\mathcal{V})$. Then*

1. *$\forall (r, \sigma) \in composeUnder(\theta, struct, t), \sigma(struct\{\!| r |\!\}) = \sigma(t)$.*
2. *$\forall r \in \mathcal{R}^c, \exists \tau, \tau(struct\{\!| r |\!\}) = \tau(t) \implies$*
   $(\exists \sigma, (r, \sigma) \in composeUnder(\theta, struct, t)$ and $\tau \models \sigma)$.

Proof (Sketch).

1. The idea is to proceed by induction on the structure of t. For the pairs found by comparing with labels or composing a variable, the property holds trivially. For the additional pairs found with terms $f(t_1, \ldots, t_n)$ composed with a public function, the point is that the pairs returned for the arguments are correct by induction. The property is then verified for composing t because it reduces to mapping the unifiers returned to all arguments.
2. The idea is to proceed by induction on the structure of $r \in \mathcal{R}^c$. For a label, there is a pair (r, ε) returned so the property holds. For a recipe that is a composition, i.e., $r = f(r_1, \ldots, r_n)$ for some f and some $r_1, \ldots, r_n \in \mathcal{R}^c$, the point is that the recipes are paired with MGUs by induction. The property is then verified for r because a substitution τ such that $\tau(struct\{\!| r |\!\}) = \tau(t)$ also unifies the arguments inside the function application, so the algorithm can compute an MGU from the results of the recursive calls.   □

Theorem 2 (Correctness of *analyze***).** *Let θ be a substitution, struct be a frame and $(struct_{ana}, \sigma, Ex) = analyze(\theta, struct)$. Then*

1. *$\forall r \in \mathcal{R}, struct_{ana}\{\!| r |\!\} \approx \sigma(struct\{\!| r |\!\})$.*
2. *$\forall r \in \mathcal{R}, \exists r' \in \mathcal{R}^c_{struct_{ana}}, struct_{ana}\{\!| r' |\!\} \approx \sigma(struct\{\!| r |\!\})$.*
3. *$\forall \theta' \in \Theta, \theta'(struct) \sim \theta(struct) \implies \theta' \models \sigma \wedge \bigwedge_{\sigma' \in Ex} \neg\sigma'$.*
4. *$\forall \theta' \in \Theta, \theta' \models \sigma \implies$*
   $(\theta'(struct) \sim \theta(struct) \iff \theta'(struct_{ana}) \sim \theta(struct_{ana}))$.

Proof. 1. When analyzing $\mathsf{l} \mapsto \mathsf{constr}(t_1, \ldots, t_n)$, the frame is augmented with mappings of the form $\mathsf{destr}(r, \mathsf{l}) \mapsto t_i$ following the destructor theory. Thus, the "labels" added are recipes over the domain of *struct*. These shorthands are correct when applying σ, which is required to compose the keys for decryption steps. The frame $struct_{ana}$ is the frame $\sigma(struct)$ with shorthands.

2. We proceed by induction on the structure of r. We consider the occurrence of a destructor destr such that no subrecipe for the arguments of destr contains destructors.

   - If the destructor is applied to a label and the decryption is successful, then a shorthand $m = \mathsf{destr}(r_k, l) \mapsto t'$ has been added in the frame, i.e., $\sigma(struct\{\!| \, m \, |\!\}) \approx t'$, where r_k is some recipe for the key k such that $\mathsf{destr}(k, t) = t' \in E$.
   - If the destructor is applied to a constructor, i.e., for some $r_k, r_1, \ldots, r_n$, $r = \mathsf{destr}(r_k, \mathsf{constr}(r_1, \ldots, r_n))$, and the decryption is successful, then the recipe can be simplified to one of the r_i yielding the same term.
   - If the decryption is not successful, then we can replace the application of destr by the constant error, which represents failed decryption

   We have covered all cases since the subrecipes do not contain destructors. By induction, we can replace all occurrences of destructors in the recipe, i.e., we can define a constructive recipe r' which is the same as r but all occurrences of destructors and have been replaced by the methods listed above.

3. We first show that the intruder can exclude all models that are not instances of σ. The substitution σ has been built from unification of some σ_i in successful analysis steps, i.e., where $(r_i, \sigma_i) \in composeUnder(\theta, struct, k)$ was a possibility to compose a decryption key k, and $r_i \in compose(\theta(struct), \theta(k))$ is also a recipe for the corresponding key $\theta(k)$ in $\theta(struct)$. It suffices to show that $\theta' \models \sigma_i$ for all σ_i. From Theorem 1 follows that σ_i is the MGU under which k can be derived in θ, i.e., $\theta'(struct\{\!| \, r_i \, |\!\}) \not\approx \theta'(k)$ for any θ' that is not an instance of σ_i. Since the intruder can see that r_i produces the correct decryption key in $\theta(struct)$, all models that are not consistent with σ_i can be excluded.

   We next show that all models that are instances of a substitution $\sigma' \in Ex$ can be excluded by the intruder as well. The substitution σ' has been found during analysis of some mapping $l \mapsto t$ where the key k can be composed in the current $struct$ under some unifier but $\theta(k)$ cannot be composed in $\theta(struct)$. There exists $(r_k, \sigma') \in composeUnder(\theta, struct, k)$ for some recipe r_k. There is a destructor destr for the decryption under consideration. We define the recipe $r = \mathsf{destr}(r_k, l)$ for this decryption step. The decryption fails in $\theta(struct)$, so $\theta(struct\{\!| \, r \, |\!\}) \approx \theta(struct\{\!| \, \mathsf{error} \, |\!\})$. Since $\theta'(struct) \sim \theta(struct)$, we also have that $\theta'(struct\{\!| \, r \, |\!\}) \approx \theta'(struct\{\!| \, \mathsf{error} \, |\!\})$. However, the decryption is successful in $struct$, so $\sigma'(struct\{\!| \, r \, |\!\}) \not\approx \sigma'(struct\{\!| \, \mathsf{error} \, |\!\})$. Therefore, θ' is not an instance of σ', because if it were there would be a pair of recipes, namely (r, error), to distinguish the frames.

4. Let $\theta' \in \Theta$ such that $\theta' \models \sigma$. Using property 1. and the fact that $\theta' \models \sigma$, we have that for any recipe r, $\theta'(struct_{ana}\{\!| \, r \, |\!\}) \approx \theta'(struct\{\!| \, r \, |\!\})$. This also holds in particular for θ. Therefore, $\theta'(struct) \sim \theta(struct)$ if and only if $\theta'(struct_{ana}) \sim \theta(struct_{ana})$ because any pair of recipes distinguishing $\theta'(struct)$ and $\theta(struct)$ would also distinguish the analyzed frames, and vice-versa. $\qquad \square$

Theorem 3 (Termination of *analyze***).** *Let θ be a substitution and struct be a frame. Then the call analyze(θ, struct) terminates.*

Proof. By definition, *analyze* calls *analyzeRec*, so what we really want to show is that the call to *analyzeRec* terminates. We now consider that the frame *struct* has been split into three frames N, H, D and denote with σ and Ex the unifier and the set of substitutions passed as arguments to *analyzeRec*, respectively. The size of a term $t \in \mathcal{T}_\Sigma(\mathcal{V})$ is defined as 1 for a variable and $size(f(t_1, \ldots, t_n)) = 1 + \sum_{i=1}^{n} size(t_i)$ for a function application. We abuse the notation and write $size(N \cup H)$ to mean the sum of the size of all terms in $N \cup H$. We consider the tuple $(size(N \cup H), \#N)$. When analyzing the mapping $l \mapsto t \in N$:

- If the decryption of t fails, $l \mapsto t$ is removed from N and put in H. Then $size(N \cup H)$ stays the same but $\#N$ has decreased by 1.
- If the decryption of t succeeds, $l \mapsto t$ is removed from N and put in D. The new terms from the analysis and the terms that were on hold are put in N. Then $size(N \cup H)$ has decreased by at least 1 (t is not present anymore but some of its subterms might be).

The lexicographic order on $(\mathbb{N}, \leq) \times (\mathbb{N}, \leq)$ forms a well-order and the sequence of tuples for the recursive calls is a strictly decreasing sequence bounded by $(0, 0)$, so such a sequence is finite and the call terminates. □

Theorem 4 (Correctness of *findRelations*). *Let (α, β) be a message-analysis problem, where $struct = \{\! | l_1 \mapsto t_1, \ldots, l_k \mapsto t_k | \!\}$ for some $t_1, \ldots, t_k \in \mathcal{T}_\Sigma(fv(\alpha))$ and $concr = \theta(struct)$ for some $\theta \in \Theta$. Let $\phi \equiv findRelations(\theta, struct)$. Then*

$$(\alpha, \beta)\text{-privacy holds} \iff \forall \theta' \in \Theta, \theta' \models \phi$$

Proof. Let $(struct_{ana}, \sigma, Ex) = analyze(\theta, struct)$. First, recall that we have (α, β)-privacy holds $\iff \forall \theta' \in \Theta, \theta'(struct) \sim \theta(struct)$. We show that $\forall \theta' \in \Theta, \theta'(struct) \sim \theta(struct) \iff \theta' \models \phi$. The models that are not instances of σ can already be excluded and violate the privacy of α because $\phi \models \sigma$. We now consider $\theta' \in \Theta$ such that $\theta' \models \sigma$.

- If $\theta'(struct) \not\sim \theta(struct)$: then $\theta'(struct_{ana}) \not\sim \theta(struct_{ana})$ from Theorem 2, so there exists a pair of recipes (r_1, r_2) that distinguishes the frames. From Theorem 2, we can assume without loss of generality that r_1, r_2 are constructive. Moreover, either one the recipes is a label (or from a shorthand) or both recipes have the same constructor at the top-level and one pair of the recipes for the arguments distinguishes the frames. So we can further assume that r_1 is a label (or from a shorthand). This justifies the fact that *findRelations* will perform a check for this pair of recipes.
  - If $\theta'(struct_{ana}\{\! | r_1 | \!\}) \not\approx \theta'(struct_{ana}\{\! | r_2 | \!\})$ and for the concrete observation $\theta(struct_{ana}\{\! | r_1 | \!\}) \approx \theta(struct_{ana}\{\! | r_2 | \!\})$: then θ' cannot be an instance of the substitution σ unifying, among others, the following equation: $struct_{ana}\{\! | r_1 | \!\} = struct_{ana}\{\! | r_2 | \!\}$. The algorithm returns ϕ such that $\phi \models \sigma$, so $\theta' \not\models \phi$.
  - If $\theta'(struct_{ana}\{\! | r_1 | \!\}) \approx \theta'(struct_{ana}\{\! | r_2 | \!\})$ and for the concrete observation $\theta(struct_{ana}\{\! | r_1 | \!\}) \not\approx \theta(struct_{ana}\{\! | r_2 | \!\})$: then θ' is an instance of some substitution σ' found when checking inequations. The algorithm returns ϕ such that $\phi \models \neg\sigma'$, so $\theta' \not\models \phi$.

- If $\theta'(struct) \sim \theta(struct)$: then $\theta'(struct_{ana}) \sim \theta(struct_{ana})$ from Theorem 2. For every $t \in \mathcal{T}_\Sigma$ and $(r_1, r_2) \in pairsEcs(compose(\theta(struct_{ana}), t))$, we have by definition of $compose$ that $\theta(struct_{ana}\{\!| r_1 |\!\}) \approx \theta(struct_{ana}\{\!| r_2 |\!\})$. Since $\theta'(struct_{ana}) \sim \theta(struct_{ana})$, then $\theta'(struct_{ana}\{\!| r_1 |\!\}) \approx \theta'(struct_{ana}\{\!| r_2 |\!\})$. Therefore, $\theta' \models \sigma$, where σ unifies all equations found from calling $compose$ on terms in $\theta(struct_{ana})$.

Let $ineqs$ be the set of substitutions Ex found during analysis union with the substitutions found by the $findRelations$ algorithm. If θ' were an instance of some $\sigma' \in ineqs$, then $\theta'(struct_{ana}) \not\sim \theta(struct_{ana})$ and thus $\theta'(struct) \not\sim \theta(struct)$ following Theorem 2. This would contradict the assumption, so $\theta' \models \neg\sigma'$. Therefore, $\theta' \models \sigma \wedge \bigwedge_{\sigma' \in ineqs} \neg\sigma'$ which is exactly $\theta' \models \phi$. □

References

1. Abadi, M., Cortier, V.: Deciding knowledge in security protocols under equational theories. In: Díaz, J., Karhumäki, J., Lepistö, A., Sannella, D. (eds.) ICALP 2004. LNCS, vol. 3142, pp. 46–58. Springer, Heidelberg (2004). https://doi.org/10.1007/978-3-540-27836-8_7
2. Abadi, M., Fournet, C.: Private authentication. Theoret. Comput. Sci. **322**(3), 427–476 (2004)
3. Baader, F., Nipkow, T.: Term Rewriting and All That. Cambridge University Press, Cambridge (1998)
4. Basin, D., Dreier, J., Sasse, R.: Automated symbolic proofs of observational equivalence. In: 22nd ACM SIGSAC Conference on Computer and Communications Security, pp. 1144–1155. ACM (2015)
5. Bernhard, D., Cortier, V., Pereira, O., Smyth, B., Warinschi, B.: Adapting helios for provable ballot privacy. In: Atluri, V., Diaz, C. (eds.) ESORICS 2011. LNCS, vol. 6879, pp. 335–354. Springer, Heidelberg (2011). https://doi.org/10.1007/978-3-642-23822-2_19
6. Blanchet, B.: Modeling and verifying security protocols with the applied pi calculus and ProVerif. Found. Trends Priv. Secur. **1**(1–2), 1–135 (2016)
7. Boutet, A., et al.: Contact tracing by giant data collectors: opening Pandora's box of threats to privacy, sovereignty and national security. University works (2020). https://hal.inria.fr/hal-03116024
8. Comon-Lundh, H., Cortier, V.: Computational soundness of observational equivalence. In: 15th ACM Conference on Computer and Communications Security, pp. 109–118. ACM (2008)
9. Cortier, V., Delaune, S.: A method for proving observational equivalence. In: 2009 22nd IEEE Computer Security Foundations Symposium, pp. 266–276. IEEE (2009)
10. Cortier, V., Dupressoir, F., Drăgan, C.C., Schmidt, B., Strub, P.Y., Warinschi, B.: Machine-checked proofs of privacy for electronic voting protocols. In: 2017 IEEE Symposium on Security and Privacy, pp. 993–1008. IEEE (2017)
11. Genesereth, M., Hinrichs, T.: Herbrand logic. Technical report, LG-2006-02, Stanford University (2006)
12. Gondron, S., Mödersheim, S., Viganò, L.: Privacy as reachability. Technical report, DTU (2021). http://www2.compute.dtu.dk/~samo/abg.pdf
13. Mödersheim, S.A., Groß, T., Viganò, L.: Defining privacy is supposed to be easy. In: McMillan, K., Middeldorp, A., Voronkov, A. (eds.) LPAR 2013. LNCS, vol.

8312, pp. 619–635. Springer, Heidelberg (2013). https://doi.org/10.1007/978-3-642-45221-5_41

14. Iovino, V., Vaudenay, S., Vuagnoux, M.: On the effectiveness of time travel to inject COVID-19 alerts. Cryptology ePrint Archive, Report 2020/1393 (2020)

15. Mödersheim, S., Viganò, L.: Alpha-beta privacy. ACM Trans. Priv. Secur. **22**(1), 1–35 (2019)

16. Moran, M., Wallach, D.S.: Verification of STAR-vote and evaluation of FDR and ProVerif. In: Polikarpova, N., Schneider, S. (eds.) IFM 2017. LNCS, vol. 10510, pp. 422–436. Springer, Cham (2017). https://doi.org/10.1007/978-3-319-66845-1_28

17. Vaudenay, S., Vuagnoux, M.: Analysis of SwissCovid (2020). https://lasec.epfl.ch/people/vaudenay/swisscovid/swisscovid-ana.pdf

Systems Security

TLS Beyond the Broker: Enforcing Fine-Grained Security and Trust in Publish/Subscribe Environments for IoT

Korbinian Spielvogel[✉], Henrich C. Pöhls, and Joachim Posegga

Passau Institute of Digital Security, University of Passau, 94032 Passau, Germany
office@sec.uni-passau.de

Abstract. Message queuing brokers are a fundamental building block of the Internet of Things, commonly used to store and forward messages from publishing clients to subscribing clients. Often a single trusted broker offers secured (e.g. TLS) and unsecured connections but relays messages regardless of their inbound and outbound protection. Such mixed mode is facilitated for the sake of efficiency since TLS is quite a burden for MQTT implementations on class-0 IoT devices.

Such a broker thus transparently interconnects securely and insecurely connected devices; we argue that such mixed mode operation can actually be a significant security problem: Clients can only control the security level of their own connection to the broker, but they cannot enforce any protection towards other clients.

We describe an enhancement of such a publish/subscribe mechanism to allow for enforcing specified security levels of publishers or subscribers by only forwarding messages via connections which satisfy the desired security levels. For example, a client publishing a message over a secured channel can instruct the broker to forward the message exclusively to subscribers that are securely connected. We prototypically implemented our solution for the MQTT protocol and provide detailed overhead measurements.

1 Introduction

Internet of Things (IoT) environments often rely on the exchange of messages between plentiful devices; the multitude of possible communication flows has led to the introduction of message passing systems, better known as publish/subscribe systems or message *brokers*. Quite obviously, a secure connection between message senders (*publishers*) and message receivers (*subscribers*) is important for many application areas. The security of such systems clearly also relies on the security of the message exchange facilitated by the broker [23]. Since IoT devices are quite heterogeneous and have very different capabilities, e.g. some are not always online or have limited computational or battery power [13], devices might also have very different needs in terms of their security goals/requirements in terms of confidentiality or origin authentication of

© Springer Nature Switzerland AG 2021
R. Roman and J. Zhou (Eds.): STM 2021, LNCS 13075, pp. 145–162, 2021.
https://doi.org/10.1007/978-3-030-91859-0_8

messages. A proper IoT system design should therefore allow devices to specify security needs and enforce them towards other devices.

The role of the message broker is to facilitate data exchange between loosely coupled endpoints by providing message queuing, which decouples sending devices from receiving ones. Thus, there is usually no direct relationship between the publisher and the subscriber and one must rely on the broker to enforce a given security level. We implemented such a broker as a prototype, based on the Message Queuing Telemetry Transport (MQTT) protocol, one of the most common protocols in the IoT [21]. MQTT enables efficient communication even with limited computational power and constrained resources [3]. Essentially, the broker allows clients to publish (send) messages belonging to a specific category, usually referred to as *topic*. A published message is then stored and forwarded by the broker to all clients that signalled their interest by subscribing to that message's topic. The participating entities are usually referred to as *publishers* and *subscribers*. If messages contain privacy-sensitive data, then exchanging these messages without suitable protection can easily be a significant security problem [9]. Furthermore, many devices autonomously send information to the manufacturer's servers which allows for insights into the physical activities at the location where the devices are in use [15].

Two attacks are possible with message queuing systems that do not secure the communication between their senders and receivers (see Fig. 1), which is the case with a plain usage of the MQTT protocol: Firstly, confidentiality can be compromised and unauthenticated third parties can read arbitrary messages. Second, unauthenticated third parties might even create their own messages and inject them into the system, thus compromising integrity. The MQTT protocol is known to have several critical security issues in its default configuration, i.e.: if implemented/configured without additional security mechanisms [1]. These problems have mainly arisen over time, as the protocol at the time of development had other objectives than security, simply because it was not considered to be significant at that time [22] as one relied on physical security or other protection mechanisms. This has changed significantly over time. Application areas like automotive, smart home, logistics or transportation sectors, where MQTT is widely used, now consider security as one of the primary objectives. Compromising integrity and confidentiality of messages by third parties in the message queuing system can therefore have fatal consequences [11].

The standard solution here is to enable encryption and authentication between the clients (subscribers and publishers) and the broker based on the well established[1] and scrutinised [6,7] transport layer security (TLS) protocol. The clients can then authenticate the broker and the broker can authenticate the clients using certificates or usernames and passwords. The client's secure connection will then end at the broker, which is generally seen as trusted. However, some IoT clients are too restricted to use TLS-secured connections, either not for all interactions, or not at all; many message queuing systems allow clients to connect over secured (e.g. using TLS) as well as non-secured connections to

---

[1] See https://transparencyreport.google.com/ or https://telemetry.mozilla.org/.

a broker. Such a broker might then relay messages between clients connected with a different level of security and forward a message received over TLS via an non-encrypted connection (see Fig. 1). The securely connected client of a broker cannot enforce secure connections on other clients and prevent forwarding over insecure connections as shown in case 2 and 3 of Fig. 1. One could isolate non-secured connected devices from securely-connected ones, but this would either disable sensible message flows, or require many more devices to use TLS, which is costly in terms of compute power or run-time.

The rest of this paper is organised as follows: We propose a solution that enables hybrid security levels among connected clients, so clients can connect over secured as well as non-secured connections; we achieve this by extending the trusted broker to enforce a certain level beyond the initial connection on a fine-grained, per message or per topic, policy. A thorough analysis of the problem underlying the MQTT protocol is presented in Sect. 2; we compare our novel, broker-enforced solution to related work in Sect. 3. The solution was prototyped for MQTT, and we argue in Sect. 4 that the concept of an expansion to enforce security levels beyond the broker does generally not require to change the existing clients. Adjustments to the MQTT clients would of course allow optimisations in signalling the intended security level. We measured the overhead of TLS, which is saved when the client could decide to not facilitate a TLS connection for certain messages or topics: Sect. 2.3 presents measurements of the overhead in runtime of TLS for a device from the smallest class[2] of IoT devices [14], i.e. a Wemos D1 mini with the ESP8266EX chip running at 80/160 MHz and only 50 kB of RAM and up to 16 MB external SPI flash [8]. In Sect. 5 we discuss how our approach relates to prior work, like end-to-end or multi-lateral security and conclude in Sect. 6.

2   Problem: No Differentiation of Incoming or Outgoing Security Goals

We will start with recalling some details of the MQTT protocol and its entities before we describe the general problem of the missing differentiation between the security goals of clients in hybrid broker environments in Sect. 2.4.

2.1   MQTT Protocol and Its Entities

An MQTT client is in principle any device that speaks MQTT over a TCP/IP stack, i.e. that runs an MQTT library and can connect to an MQTT broker via a network. Furthermore, MQTT clients are distinguished between MQTT publisher and MQTT subscriber. Whether a client is a publisher, a subscriber or even both depends on whether the client sends messages (publisher) or receives messages (subscriber). The messages here are assigned to a certain topic, which

---

[2] Class-0 is defined as the group of IoT devices with less than 10 KB RAM (Data size) and less than 100 KB ROM (Code size) [14].

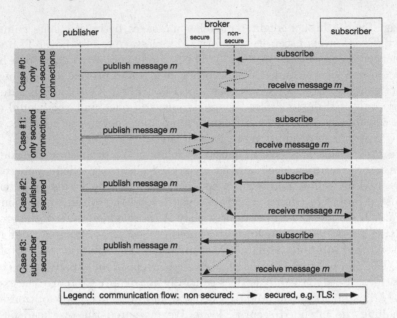

Fig. 1. The four different cases of message forwarding when relaying messages between clients connecting secured and non-secured to the broker

categorizes the messages according to their subject. In MQTT, the term "topic" refers to a UTF-8 string that can consist of several different levels which are separated by a forward slash ("/") [25].

For example, a smart thermometer located in the kitchen of a house could act as an MQTT publisher and send the current temperature of the kitchen as an MQTT message. The corresponding topic for this would be, for example, "home/kitchen/temperature". In turn, another device, such as a home owner's mobile phone, could act as an MQTT subscriber, monitoring the important values of the house, such as temperature, humidity, electricity etc. To do so, the MQTT subscriber would have to subscribe to the topic "home" to receive all messages that have "home" as the first topic-level.

At this point, it should be noted that in the remaining parts of the paper we will use the term "TCP client" as a synonym for any MQTT client that uses plain TCP as the underlying transport protocol and does not implement any additional security measurements to address the vulnerabilities of MQTT. Any client that uses TLS in addition to TCP will be referred to as a "TLS client".

The MQTT Broker is certainly the most important component of the MQTT protocol. It constitutes the interface between the MQTT clients and manages the exchange of messages between them. The MQTT broker thereby ensures that the messages of a certain topic sent by an MQTT publisher are forwarded to the MQTT subscribers which have subscribed to this topic. In addition, the broker also handles the management of the persistent sessions as well as the authentication and authorization of the clients. Since this component is often directly exposed to the Internet, it is particularly important to ensure security, scalability, monitoring and failure resistance of the broker [25].

The minimum requirement for an MQTT system to be functional and useful at the same time is to include (i) a central broker, which forwards the incoming messages of the publishers to the respective subscribers (ii) a subscriber, that receives messages of at least one topic, and (iii) a publisher, that sends a message to that topic. The subscriber and the publisher may also be the same client.

For simplicity the message flow between one publisher, one broker and one subscriber in Fig. 1 shows only the message and implicitly assumes that publisher and subscriber use the same topic. Moreover, Fig. 1 is simplified by having only one publisher and only one subscriber; in general the publish/subscribe architecture is best fitting if there are one-to-many or even many-to-many relations, e.g. m subscribers are listening to the messages of n publishers.

In reality the MQTT brokers and the protocol are built to scale up to large amounts of clients, subscribers as well as publishers [3,16]. Last but not least, Fig. 1 is simplified in respect to the MQTT protocol itself, as MQTT would actually require an initial handshake (CONNECT message) and has acknowledgment messages that indicate the successful reception of commands for connection, subscription and publication (CONACK, SUBACK and PUBACK).

2.2   Trust Assumptions Among Subscribers, Publishers and Brokers

In a publish/subscribe message queuing system the clients trust the broker to process the messages correctly, i.e. the publisher trusts the broker to forward the message to all interested subscribers. Subscribers trust the broker to deliver them all messages of their indicated interest, e.g. the topic they subscribed to.

To increase the security each client can secure the connection to the broker. As discussed this can be done using the MQTT protocol over TLS. Current implementations of MQTT brokers allow to enable TLS and once configured the broker enforces TLS for all clients and strictly rejects all other connection types, such as plain TCP. Devices with even fewer resources than the client in our experiments (e.g., Class-0 IoT devices as defined by [14]) could thus become excluded from the system, as they are not able to allocate sufficient resources for performing a full TLS handshake and are therefore not TLS-capable. For MQTT in particular, it is also conceivable that many of the devices do not require security-sensitive message exchanges and thus have no need for a secure communication channel with the broker. Hence, it would be an unnecessary additional consumption of already rather scarce resources if these devices all had to use TLS. This is why the broker could be deployed in a hybrid or mixed mode, supporting both secured and non-secured connections of its clients.

Table 1. Time to establish an initial connection between client and MQTT broker. Time measured from connection establishment (= sending `CONNECT`) till the `CONNACK` packet is received. TLSv1.2 with ECC (Curve25519) 256 bit keys and ciphersuite ECDHE-ECDSA-AES256-GCM-SHA384. MQTT broker is Eclipse Mosquitto (version 1.4.10) on Rasperrypi 3b+. Number of measurements: 500

	Insecure connection	TLS connection
Average time	9.54 ms	3207.53 ms
Standard deviation	3.69 ms	153.57 ms
Minimum time	4.00 ms	3162.00 ms
Maximum time	40.00 ms	5271.00 ms

2.3   Hybrid or Mixed Mode Brokers and TLS on Small Devices

To not limit the connection to TLS-capable devices only –as discussed above– many MQTT brokers, such as HiveMQ or Mosquitto, allow the configuration of multiple so-called listeners. Each listener enables the specification of one out of several different connection types [12]. For instance, it is possible to configure a broker such that it accepts connections from clients using both plain TCP (port 1883) and TLS (port 8883) simultaneously. A client can then decide which connection type is most suitable for its purposes. Providing the possibility for clients to choose the connection type independently is particularly useful for clients with unreliable network connections, limited available bandwidth or highly limited resources. After all, in some cases it is more important to have a reliable, but possibly insecure connection in order to be able to transfer all data reliably [12].

The performance in terms of runtime for a TLS connection in comparison to a non-secured connection are shown in Table 1. On average, it takes roughly 335 times longer (more than 3 s) to establish a connection using TLS. The work of King and Awad [14] even observed a delay of up to 24 s for certain IoT devices, even though their test setup used DTLS, which is a more efficient and resource-saving version of TLS. For many systems, such a performance loss is intolerable.

2.4   Problem: No Enforcement of Incoming or Outgoing Clients' Security Goals Beyond the Broker

We have identified the following problems of clients wanting to use mixed-mode brokers. By mixed-mode brokers we refer to brokers offering non-secured as well as secured connections to their clients, but relaying messages based on the clients topics and not taking into account the security level of their client's connection. For simplicity we differentiate only two security levels: non-secured and secured. In practice 'secured' means to send MQTT messages over a TLS connection while 'non-secured' uses just TCP. Thus, we either protect a message's confidentiality and integrity, or not. It would be straightforward to extend our proposed solution to more than two and thus more fine grained security levels.

1st problem:

Client subscribing via a secured connection to a mixed-mode broker has no information about the security level of the connection of publishers, i.e. from a subscriber's perspective the received message is looking the same in case 1 (published secured) and case 3 (published non-secured) of Fig. 1.

2nd problem:

Client publishing via a secured connection to a mixed-mode broker can not enforce the security level of the connection of subscribers, i.e. from a publisher's perspective the sent message could either flow to the subscriber like in case 1 (secured) or as in case 2 (non-secured) of Fig. 1.

Thus, in a mixed-mode environment there is a risk that the confidentiality or integrity of the message is only protected from the publisher to the broker, or only from the broker to the subscriber – but it is never enforced beyond. More flexibility would allow a client to enforce security levels beyond the broker if the application demands it, but also allow to not enforce this where needed:

1st scenario:

Publisher wants to extend security level enforcement beyond the broker to the subscribers

2nd scenario:

Subscriber wants to extend security level enforcement beyond the broker to the publishers

3rd scenario:

Publisher relaxes the security level for future communication beyond the broker to the subscribers

4th scenario:

Subscriber relaxes the security level for future communication beyond the broker to the publishers

This flexibility is currently not enforceable within the existing publish/subscribe model and not found in existing implementations.

3   Related Work

The Message Queue Telemetry Transport protocol is a data transfer protocol developed to transfer data at the lowest possible cost. Additional mechanisms for protecting confidentiality and integrity were neglected accordingly [24]. It replaces the typical end-to-end connection between devices in such a way that data producers and data users are decoupled. It is the origin of the Client-to-Broker architecture particularly used in the modern IoT [10]. The latest MQTT specification [3] defines the protocol as follows: *"MQTT is a Client Server publish/subscribe messaging transport protocol. It is light weight, open, simple, and designed so as to be easy to implement. These characteristics make it ideal for use in many situations, including constrained environments such as for communication in Machine to Machine (M2M) and Internet of Things (IoT) contexts where a small code footprint is required and/or network bandwidth is at a pre-mium.".* The protocol in general runs over TCP/IP or over any other network protocol that provides ordered, lossless and bi-directional connections [2].

As shown in the previous chapters, the MQTT protocol includes a number of vulnerabilities in its default state. Many other authors have therefore analyzed the protocol for its vulnerabilities and presented methods to address these vulnerabilities. Andy et al. [1] analyzed the number of freely available MQTT brokers with the help of Shodan. In addition, they demonstrated how attackers can violate the goals of data privacy, authentication, and data integrity in MQTT-based systems based on numerous scenarios. As a security measure against these numerous attack vectors, they propose the implementation of a security mechanism - specifically, the use of TLS. Harsha et al. [11] also examined the possible attacks on MQTT based systems. In addition to the attacks already mentioned by Andy et al. [1], they illustrate how MQTT specific features such as wildcards can be exploited to subscribe to all topics simultaneously without knowing the specific topic name. Thus, they demonstrate how an attacker can disclose a maximum amount of information from an MQTT based system. Furthermore, the authors prove that the integrated authentication mechanism of MQTT in the CONNECT message (= username and password authentication) is ineffective without additional protection mechanisms to ensure confidentiality, since the credentials are transmitted in plaintext and thus freely accessible to all attackers who are able to read or intercept network packets.

To address these vulnerabilities, Harsha et al. [11] suggest the use of TLS or any mechanism for the encryption of the payload in combination with Access Control Lists (ACL) which define the access policies for a certain topic, i.e. which client can interact in which way with which topic. Finally, the authors demonstrated that TLS in combination with ACL can mitigate all of their defined attack-scenarios that previously violated the goals of confidentiality, authentication and integrity. Closest to our approach is the TLS-proxy and firewall approach that was presented by Vučnik et al. [26]. The authors implement a proxy that enforces TLS encrypted MQTT traffic for certain clients while allowing a non-secured plain TCP connection from others, e.g. those connected via the local network as local clients are seen as trustworthy. Their approach does not allow the clients to request the broker-mediated protection beyond the broker on a fine grained level of topics or messages, but just enforces it based on physical network location. It would be subject to future work to enhance our approach to take the physical network position into account when our broker is making the decision to forward messages.

4   Broker to Enforce Security Levels Beyond the Broker

As we have presented the clients are in need to be able to specify the security levels that they would want to see enforced. In Fig. 2 we have shown the intervention of the broker when the publishing client would like to enforce its security level of requiring secured connections beyond its own connection to the broker.

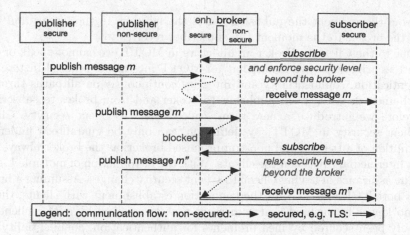

Fig. 2. Our proposal: trusted enhanced broker enforces publisher's security level

To enforce this the message *m'* shown in Fig. 2 is no longer forwarded by the broker to a subscriber that connected only over a non-secured channel. The same would hold true for the enforcement of the security level of a subscriber, i.e. for a secure subscriber the broker would not forward –and thus the subscriber would not receive messages– published by non-secured publishers, which is depicted for message *m'* in Fig. 3. We have termed the request to uphold the security level of the client to other clients beyond the broker as follows: *broker-mediated client-to-client* security.

4.1   Client-to-Client Security Mediated by the Broker

In the existing publish/subscribe model the brokers are trusted to forward messages. In our solution the extended broker must be additionally trusted to enforce the clients security level. In a conventional MQTT system with a broker that only offers one type of connection, the clients are always aware of the achieved security goals when it comes to the connection of other clients, since each client has the same committed conditions which can then also be expected from other clients. In the case the broker only allows TCP connections the publisher sends the MQTT message in plaintext to the broker, which then distributes the message in plaintext to the subscribers. Both publisher and subscriber have an insecure connection to the broker and therefore do not expect any security measures to be implemented on the path from client to client by any means. In the case of TLS enforcement of the broker, a publisher sends the MQTT message over a secure communication channel to the broker. The broker in turn forwards the message to the corresponding subscribers also over a secure communication channel. TLS thereby ensures the security goals authentication, confidentiality and integrity of the message during the communication of client and broker. All participating clients therefore can expect these security goals to be continuously guaranteed, i.e. from the moment the publisher sends the message to the broker and then from the broker to the moment the subscriber receives it.

Due to the Client-to-Broker architecture in MQTT, we cannot speak of end-to-end security when we mean that an MQTT message is secured in terms of authentication, confidentiality and integrity continuously on all paths throughout the network, i.e., from publisher to broker and from broker to subscriber. Therefore we introduce a new term, called Client-to-Client security. Client-to-Client security in MQTT, by definition, can only be guaranteed under the assumption of a trusted and non-compromised broker, as the broker always acts as an intermediary between the clients. With the introduction of multiple Listeners, the assurance of having Client-to-Client security changes. Assuming a broker offers both TCP and TLS for the connection establishment with clients, then it can no longer be ensured that a message sent or received by a TLS client has actually been secured by measurements for authentication, confidentiality and integrity continuously throughout all paths through the network, since TCP clients can also interact with TLS clients, as previously discussed in Sect. 2.4. This security problem occurs on the interaction of a TLS publisher with a TCP subscriber (as depicted in case 0 of Fig. 1) or a TCP publisher with a TLS subscriber (case 3 of Fig. 1) by the help of the broker, the message is transmitted insecurely over the network at least one time and therefore violates the security goal of Client-to-Client security.

Thus, we speak of broker-mediated client-to-client security for the remainder of this work.

4.2   Enforcement of the Same Level of Client-to-Client Security Between Clients by an Enhanced Broker

For an enforcement by a trustworthy broker, it is upfront important for the broker to detect a conflict between the interests of a publisher and the ones of the current and future subscribers. First, the broker needs to identify and retain the security level of the client by inspecting incoming message on publish requests (PUBLISH) or subscription requests (SUBSCRIBE). Second, the broker needs to detect the conflicts between the security levels and act accordingly on every message forwarding action. We enhanced the broker to check the MQTT protocol field User Properties, in which our modified client can signal its wish for enforcement of its own security level beyond the broker. While this requires a small modification on the client side, one could also work with unmodified clients and just assume their intention for a certain security level from their current connection type. For example messages like PUBLISH or SUBSCRIBE when received over a secured connection, e.g. TLS, would result in the broker assuming that they want to have an enforcement of their security level beyond the broker. The latter would then only require the clients to switch from a secure to a non-secure connection and vice-versa depending on their desired enforcement.

When a broker receives a PUBLISH message the broker must decide whether the message may be forwarded. We consider the following cases based on the MQTT protocol and TLS or plain TCP connected clients:

1. **Securely connected publisher sends message and requests to enforce Client-to-Client Security:**
   If the MQTT publisher is connected via TLS and has informed the MQTT broker that Client-to-Client security should be enforced by including the respective `User Properties` in the `CONNECT` or `PUBLISH` message, then the broker checks whether the subscribers meet the requirements of Client-to-Client security, i.e. whether they have implemented mechanisms for securing authentication, confidentiality and integrity, before the `PUBLISH` message is forwarded to the subscribers. If a subscriber fulfils these requirements, e.g. when the subscriber is also connected to the broker via TLS, the broker forwards the `PUBLISH` message to this subscriber. All subscribers that do not meet the requirements e.g. if they are connected via plain TCP, will be denied access to this `PUBLISH` message.

2. **Non-Secure Publisher sends message and subscriber has requested to enforce Client-to-Client Security:**
   If the MQTT publisher is connected via plain TCP, the broker checks whether there are any MQTT subscribers that have the requirement to enforce Client-to-Client security and are connected to the broker via TLS. The `PUBLISH` message will thus not be delivered to these clients. All other subscribers – all TCP subscribers and the TLS subscribers that have not specified the requirement for Client-to-Client security– will receive the message.

3. **In all other cases,** the MQTT `PUBLISH` message can be directly forwarded to the subscriber in the usual way.

4.3 Possibility to Extend to the Security Goals

Note, it is possible to define more fine-grained security goals. For the sake of simplicity this work only discusses two distinct level of security, secured (e.g.

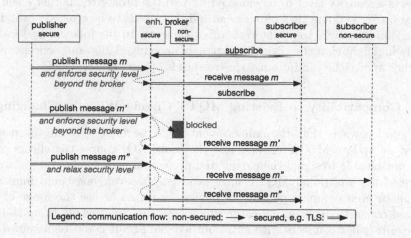

Fig. 3. Our proposal: trusted enhanced broker enforces subscriber's security level

via TLS) and non-secured (e.g. plain TCP) connections. However, our approach can be extended to contain any types of security parameters which would allow to be compared against each other in order to let the broker derive a security level that is sufficient for both clients. For example, one could be technically far more specific what type of TLS protection is required by specifying the exact list of TLS cipher suites to be used, e.g. specify that ephemeral Diffie-Hellman shall be used with an RSA algorithm using a certain key length and a certain hashing algorithm like TLS_ECDHE_ECDSA_WITH_AES_256_GCM_SHA384. This could be used to provide integrity of messages only via choosing non-encrypting TLS ciphersuites. But it could also be extended to take into account the level of security protection by other means, e.g. integrity protection by signatures on the message level directly [18], but it seems to be preferably to favour ECDSA over RSA for less resource consumption [4] on IoT devices. Another extension could be to segregate communication by network location, e.g. from outside a trusted network, or when transmitted via VPN. This is left as future work, but our framework is extensible in this respect. Sole requirement is that the broker remains able to compare the security goals to identify the minimum level to make a decision which messages to forward to whom in order to achieve client-to-client security.

5   Broker-Mediated Enforcement in Relation to Other General Security Concepts

We have presented an enhancement of the broker, that is extended to be trusted to only selectively forward messages in order to uphold a requested security level by one corresponding client (publisher or subscriber) also beyond the broker to other corresponding clients. We have termed this broker-mediated client-to-client security in order to highlight the following: i) each corresponding client requests a security level to be enforced beyond the broker to another client and ii) the broker is doing the enforcement and thus needs to be trusted beyond just forwarding messages to all interest correspondents. In the following we want to briefly highlight that the client could remain unchanged, how our concept relates to other approaches and discuss the overheads of our enhancements.

5.1   Compatibility to Existing MQTT Clients Without Changing

The good news is that the enhancement could be used without the need to adjust or update MQTT clients, just the broker. Of course the clients would then not be able to signal their requested protection level freely, as they are not aware of the additional MQTT flags/headers. However, one could implement default or even complex policies for devices or topics or use the usage of TLS secured connections as an indicator which level the client wants to uphold, e.g. if the subscriber connects with extra burden via TLS it could be assumed that it wants to listen only to authentic incoming messages coming from secured connections. For increased interconnection, one could also assume that legacy clients would not want to uphold their own security level beyond the broker, leaving the problem still unsolved for legacy clients.

5.2 Comparison to Other Approaches

Multilateral Security. The notion "multilateral security" was already established in the 1990s [19] and early 2000s [5,17,20] and is defined as follows: *"Multilateral security considers different and possibly conflicting security requirements of different parties and strives to balance these requirements. It means taking into consideration the security requirements of all parties involved. It also means considering all involved parties as potential attackers"* [20]. In a later publication [17], the term was narrowed down to the following requirements:

1. Each party has its particular protection goals.
2. Each party can formulate its protection goals.
3. Security conflicts are recognized and compromises negotiated.
4. Each party can enforce its protection goals within the agreed compromise.

Besides, it is also clarified that the security properties must be dynamically adaptable [17] and that *"Multilateral Security does not necessarily enable every participant to enforce all of her individual security goals, but at least it provides transparency of the security of an action for all parties involved"* [5]. So, while the definitions and formulations of the various authors differ, they basically all state the same essential requirements. Our solution achieves the requirements 1–3, as each client can identify its security goals and the broker recognises conflicts between these stated goals and if possible enforces them. When discussing requirement number 4 one could treat the combination of a client and a trusted and enhanced broker as a single party. Broker and publisher can then enforce the security level desired by the publisher beyond the broker towards other subscribers; and broker and subscriber together can enforce it towards publishers. If one would treat the broker as an individual party in the above meaning, then requirement 4 can not be fulfilled by publishers nor subscribers alone and thus requirement no. 4 could not be met.

End-to-End Security. The term end-to-end security applied to the publisher subscriber interaction would mean that the broker is only able to break availability by maliciously dropping messages, but the clients would be capable of upholding confidentiality and integrity [4,18] of messages exchanged even if the broker is malicious and reads or modifies messages. This would allow clients to put less trust into the broker, e.g. broker could be honest (forward messages) but be curious (break confidentiality) or even actively tamper with the message as end-to-end means that the client on the other end of the communication will notice. This is different to the broker-mediated client-to-client security as it requires a more trusted and enhanced broker. However, client-to-client removes the burden of having to maintain individual keys and trust relation among clients.

Other Network Security Notions. As discussed in the related work section, there are approaches to place a transparent TLS proxy and a firewall to secure MQTT brokers. Vučnik et al.'s approach that ensures traffic traverses through the proxy and not directly by placing the firewall and proxy in front of a plain MQTT server [26]. As discussed our approach is more versatile and different as we allow the clients to relax their own security level which would not be possible with the transparent TLS proxy. However, following the idea and borrowing network security terms, one could describe our proposed solution as a firewall inside the broker to separate or segregate the message flows. For clarity we decided to not mix existing, clearly defined terminologies and decided to call it broker-mediated client-to-client security.

5.3   Overheads in Prototypical Implementation

In the context of this paper, we developed a first prototype of an MQTT broker that, as described in Sect. 4, takes into account the desired security levels of the clients and, if necessary, performs operations to enforce them even beyond the broker. For the implementation we chose the programming language Python 3.8.5, as one of our main goals was to design the code as comprehensible as possible, so that other developers can adopt the concepts for their own purposes, e.g. for the extension of existing MQTT brokers such as HiveMQ or Mosquitto.

In our conducted experiments to determine the resulting overhead of our approach, we considered two different aspects: (1) the overhead per MQTT message and (2) the computational overhead on the side of the broker, which arises from the enforcement process. Our observations regarding the message size are the following: (1) if the broker implicitly determines and enforces the desired security level of the clients based on their connection types (secured or non-secured), no additional information has be to included in the various MQTT messages and (2) if the MQTT clients should be able to indicate their desired security levels to the broker, it requires a minimum of 7 additional bytes (in the User Properties field of the MQTT message, which was introduced in MQTT version 5). This User Property field either has to be added once when the connection to the broker is established (i.e. in the CONNECT message) to define the security-level for all subsequent PUBLISH/SUBSCRIBE messages or alternatively it can also be added in each PUBLISH/SUBSCRIBE message individually to enable an even more fine-grained definition of security levels. With an extension to the current MQTT specification i.e. with the introduction of a new, dedicated identifier for security-levels in the MQTT message, we would even be able to reduce the overall message overhead to 2 additional bytes (1 byte for the identifier and 1 byte for the security-level).

In order to determine the resulting computational overhead, we measured the time it takes on the broker-side to forward an incoming PUBLISH message to a subscriber. The time is measured from the receipt of the message to the transmission of the message to the subscriber. We measured this for normal broker behavior, i.e. messages are forwarded without any enforcement of security levels beyond the broker, as well as for our extended broker behavior i.e. security levels of the clients are enforced beyond the broker. Our 500 simulation runs show that there are no significant performance differences between these two approaches (median 109 ms for the normal behavior and 111 ms for the extended behavior).

Here, it should be noted that this is only a prototype, which focuses purely on functionality and does not implement any optimizations. It is therefore conceivable that there may well be greater differences in the case of performance optimizations. In the current state of our research, however, we could not observe any significant performance differences.

6   Conclusion and Future Work

In this paper we have shown the importance of security aspects in publish/subscribe based message queuing systems and pointed out the existence of a fundamental problem in today's systems if they are deployed allowing mixed levels of security in their connection to the clients. We have exemplified the problem, as well as our solution, with real implementations of TLS and plain TCP connections to an MQTT broker. The resulting problem of clients being unable to control the enforcement of security levels beyond the broker can either be solved by strictly isolating non-secured from secured clients, or it requires all devices the burden of constantly being connected over TLS. The former hinders a multitude of possible communication flows that might be totally acceptable and intended. For the latter, we (and other works) have demonstrated an impact on smaller devices which makes it impossible in many environments to enforce TLS on all clients.

Even though there are many available security mechanisms that address these problems, there are still more than 150,000 MQTT systems freely accessible via the Internet[3].

There are reasonable justifications for an MQTT based system to neglect the usage of those security mechanisms, especially the usage of TLS. However, TLS is able to mitigate many and most importantly the most severe attack vectors. We have found that one of the main reasons for neglecting the usage of TLS, is the immense negative impact of TLS on the duration of the connection establishment between the MQTT client and the MQTT broker - the connection establishment using plain TCP takes 10 ms on average, while the TLS connection establishment takes 3208 ms. This performance loss occurs, as handling the additional computational overhead of TLS often poses a challenge for the resource constrained IoT devices. As a response, we have presented our broker-mediated enforcement to make the use of TLS in MQTT-based systems more fine-grained and thus the extra effort spent for TLS more tolerable. In our concept, which we have prototypically implemented, an MQTT broker can be configured to accept multiple connection types, such as TCP and TLS, simultaneously. As a result, TLS can be enforced exclusively on devices that are in need of TLS protection, rather than enforcing it on all devices, which currently is the state-of-the-art.

---

[3] https://www.shodan.io, search query 'mqtt', Accessed: 17.01.2021.

Or it can be enforced for certain topics or messages only. In this paper, we have subsequently presented and defined a new security model for message queuing publish/subscribe systems that follows the approach of multilateral security. Our enhanced broker enforces what we termed Client-to-Client security, i.e. a continuous protection of authentication, confidentiality and integrity of the message on all ways throughout the network mediated by the broker from the publisher to the subscriber or vice versa. It allows the clients to define their security on a fine-grained level (e.g. per subscribed topic or per published message). Furthermore, we have provided a first implementation for MQTT brokers and MQTT clients that successfully realizes multilateral security in MQTT based systems. By extending the OASIS MQTT specification, we would be able to improve the method of transferring the client's security goals significantly with respect to the overhead of Multilateral Security (from a minimum of 7 bytes to fixed 2 bytes). Overall, however, with the current state of research of Multilateral Security in MQTT based systems, a new level of security can be achieved.

In future work we will try to integrate the enhanced functionality into established MQTT brokers such as Mosquitto or HiveMQ. Based on these results, further techniques can be developed to improve the overall performance of enforcement of security-levels beyond the broker.

It is also important to clarify whether current smart devices are even capable of supporting the indication of their desired security-levels, i.e. whether these devices support MQTT version 5 and if it is possible to specify the necessary User Properties, or whether the enforcement beyond the broker can only be realized in practice through enforcement based on the connection types; as noted in Sect. 5.1 our solution would not require changes on the clients' MQTT or communication stack.

Another aspect to be clarified is how the full trust of the MQTT client into the MQTT broker can be relaxed: Among the possibilities it would be conceivable to use homomorphic encryption to hide specific information of an MQTT message, that should not be revealed to the MQTT broker.

Finally, it is worth investigating whether well-established light-weight alternatives to the TLS protocol can lead to improvements that are worth the reduced security offered by light-weight cryptography.

References

1. Andy, S., Rahardjo, B., Hanindhito, B.: Attack scenarios and security analysis of MQTT communication protocol in IoT system. In: 2017 4th International Conference on Electrical Engineering, Computer Science and Informatics (EECSI), pp. 1–6, September 2017. https://doi.org/10.1109/EECSI.2017.8239179
2. Banks, A., Briggs, E., Borgendale, K., Gupta, R. (eds.): MQTT Version 3.1.1. Organization for the advancement of structured information standards, Woburn, USA, October 2014. http://docs.oasis-open.org/mqtt/mqtt/v3.1.1/os/mqtt-v3.1.1-os.html. Latest version: http://docs.oasis-open.org/mqtt/mqtt/v3.1.1/mqtt-v3.1.1.html

3. Banks, A., Briggs, E., Borgendale, K., Gupta, R. (eds.): MQTT Version 5.0. Organization for the advancement of structured information standards, Woburn, USA, March 2019. https://docs.oasis-open.org/mqtt/mqtt/v5.0/os/mqtt-v5.0-os.html. Latest version: https://docs.oasis-open.org/mqtt/mqtt/v5.0/mqtt-v5.0.html

4. Bauer, J., Staudemeyer, R.C., Pöhls, H.C., Fragkiadakis, A.: ECDSA on things: IoT integrity protection in practise. In: Lam, K.-Y., Chi, C.-H., Qing, S. (eds.) ICICS 2016. LNCS, vol. 9977, pp. 3–17. Springer, Cham (2016). https://doi.org/10.1007/978-3-319-50011-9_1

5. Clauß, S., Köhntopp, M.: Identity management and its support of multilateral security. Comput. Netw. **37**(2), 205–219 (2001)

6. Cremers, C., Horvat, M., Scott, S., van der Merwe, T.: Automated analysis and verification of TLS 1.3: 0-RTT, resumption and delayed authentication. In: 2016 IEEE Symposium on Security and Privacy (SP), pp. 470–485 (2016). https://doi.org/10.1109/SP.2016.35

7. Davis, H., Günther, F.: Tighter proofs for the SIGMA and TLS 1.3 key exchange protocols. In: Sako, K., Tippenhauer, N.O. (eds.) ACNS 2021. LNCS, vol. 12727, pp. 448–479. Springer, Cham (2021). https://doi.org/10.1007/978-3-030-78375-4_18

8. Espressif Documentation: ESP8266EX Datasheet V6.6 (2020). https://www.espressif.com/en/support/documents/technical-documents. Accessed 15 July 2021

9. Fragkiadakis, A., Oikonomou, G., Pöhls, H.C., Tragos, E.Z., Wójcik, M.: Securing communications among severely constrained, wireless embedded devices. In: Aziz, B., Arenas, A., Crispo, B. (eds.) Engineering Secure Internet of Things Systems. The Institute of Engineering and Technology, October 2016. http://www.theiet.org/resources/books/security/secIoT.cfm

10. Götz, C.: MQTT: Protokoll für das Internet der Dinge, April 2014. https://m.heise.de/developer/artikel/MQTT-Protokoll-fuer-das-Internet-der-Dinge-2168152.html. Accessed 03 Feb 2021

11. Harsha, M.S., Bhavani, B.M., Kundhavai, K.R.: Analysis of vulnerabilities in MQTT security using Shodan API and implementation of its countermeasures via authentication and ACLs. In: 2018 International Conference on Advances in Computing, Communications and Informatics (ICACCI), pp. 2244–2250, September 2018. https://doi.org/10.1109/ICACCI.2018.8554472

12. HiveMQ Documentation - Listeners (n.d.). https://www.hivemq.com/docs/hivemq/4.5/user-guide/listeners.html/. Accessed 01 Mar 2021

13. Kaspersky Lab: Internet of Things: What Is IoT? IoT Security, December 2018. https://www.kaspersky.com/resource-center/definitions/what-is-iot. Accessed 27 Jan 2021

14. King, J., Awad, A.: A distributed security mechanism for resource-constrained IoT devices. Informatica **40**, 133–143 (2016)

15. Klement, F., Pöhls, H., Spielvogel, K.: Towards privacy-preserving local monitoring and evaluation of network traffic from IoT devices and corresponding mobile phone applications. In: IEEE 3rd Workshop on Internet of Things Security and Privacy (WISP 2020) Held in Conjunction with Global IoT Summit 2020 (GIOTS 2020), pp. 1–6. IEEE, June 2020. https://doi.org/10.1109/GIOTS49054.2020.9119507

16. Mishra, B., Kertesz, A.: The use of MQTT in M2M and IoT systems: a survey. IEEE Access **8**, 201071–201086 (2020). https://doi.org/10.1109/ACCESS.2020.3035849

17. Pfitzmann, A.: Multilateral security: enabling technologies and their evaluation. In: Wilhelm, R. (ed.) Informatics. LNCS, vol. 2000, pp. 50–62. Springer, Heidelberg (2001). https://doi.org/10.1007/3-540-44577-3_4

18. Pöhls, H.C.: JSON Sensor Signatures (JSS): end-to-end integrity protection from constrained device to IoT application. In: Proceedings of the Workshop on Extending Seamlessly to the Internet of Things (esIoT) at the IMIS-2012 International Conference (IMIS 2015), pp. 306–312. IEEE, July 2015. https://doi.org/10.1109/IMIS.2015.48. Accessed Sept 2017
19. Rannenberg, K.: Recent development in information technology security evaluation - the need for evaluation criteria for multilateral security. In: Proceedings of the IFIP TC9/WG9.6 Working Conference on Security and Control of Information Technology in Society on Board M/S Illich and Ashore, pp. 113–128. North-Holland Publishing Co., Amsterdam (1993)
20. Rannenberg, K.: Multilateral security a concept and examples for balanced security. In: Proceedings of the 2000 Workshop on New Security Paradigms, NSPW 2000, New York, NY, USA, pp. 151–162. Association for Computing Machinery (2001). https://doi.org/10.1145/366173.366208
21. Skerrett, I.: Why MQTT has become the de-facto IoT standard, October 2019. https://dzone.com/articles/why-mqtt-has-become-the-de-facto-iot-standard. Accessed 10 Feb 2021
22. The HiveMQ Team: Introducing the MQTT Protocol - MQTT Essentials: Part 1, January 2015. https://www.hivemq.com/blog/mqtt-essentials-part-1-introducing-mqtt/. Accessed 12 Apr 2021
23. The HiveMQ Team: Introducing the MQTT Security Fundamentals, April 2015. https://www.hivemq.com/blog/introducing-the-mqtt-security-fundamentals/. Accessed 24 Jan 2021
24. The HiveMQ Team: TLS/SSL - MQTT Security Fundamentals, May 2015. https://www.hivemq.com/blog/mqtt-security-fundamentals-tls-ssl/. Accessed 12 Apr 2021
25. The HiveMQ Team: Client, Broker/Server and Connection Establishment - MQTT Essentials: Part 3, July 2019. https://www.hivemq.com/blog/mqtt-essentials-part-3-client-broker-connection-establishment/. Accessed 14 Feb 2021
26. Vučnik, M., Švigelj, A., Kandus, G., Mohorčič, M.: Secure hybrid publish-subscribe messaging architecture. In: 2019 International Conference on Software, Telecommunications and Computer Networks (SoftCOM), pp. 1–5 (2019). https://doi.org/10.23919/SOFTCOM.2019.8903868

Root-of-Trust Abstractions for Symbolic Analysis: Application to Attestation Protocols

Georgios Fotiadis[1]([✉]) [iD], José Moreira[2]([✉]) [iD], Thanassis Giannetsos[3]([✉]) [iD], Liqun Chen[4] [iD], Peter B. Rønne[1] [iD], Mark D. Ryan[2], and Peter Y. A. Ryan[1] [iD]

[1] SnT & DCS, University of Luxembourg, Esch-sur-Alzette, Luxembourg
{georgios.fotiadis,peter.roenne,peter.ryan}@uni.lu
[2] School of Computer Science, University of Birmingham, Birmingham, UK
{j.moreira-sanchez,m.d.ryan}@cs.bham.ac.uk
[3] Ubitech Ltd., Digital Security and Trusted Computing Group, Athens, Greece
agiannetsos@ubitech.eu
[4] Surrey Centre for Cyber Security, University of Surrey, Guildford, UK
liqun.chen@surrey.ac.uk

Abstract. A key component in building trusted computing services is a highly secure anchor that serves as a Root-of-Trust (RoT). There are several works that conduct formal analysis on the security of such commodity RoTs (or parts of it), and also a few ones devoted to verifying the trusted computing service as a whole. However, most of the existing schemes try to verify security without differentiating the internal cryptography mechanisms of the underlying hardware token from the client application cryptography. This approach limits, to some extent, the reasoning that can be made about the level of assurance of the overall system by automated reasoning tools. In this work, we present a methodology that enables the use of formal verification tools towards verifying complex protocols using trusted computing. The focus is on reasoning about the overall application security, provided from the integration of the RoT services, and how these can translate to larger systems when the underlying cryptographic engine is considered perfectly secure. Using the Tamarin prover, we demonstrate the feasibility of our approach by instantiating it for a TPM-based *remote attestation* service, which is one of the core security services needed in today's increased attack landscape.

Keywords: Trusted computing · Remote attestation · TPM modelling · Formal verification · Tamarin prover · SAPiC

1 Introduction

In the last years, academia and industry working groups have made substantial efforts towards realizing next-generation smart-connectivity *Systems-of-Systems*. These systems have evolved from local, standalone systems into safe and secure

© Springer Nature Switzerland AG 2021
R. Roman and J. Zhou (Eds.): STM 2021, LNCS 13075, pp. 163–184, 2021.
https://doi.org/10.1007/978-3-030-91859-0_9

solutions ranging from cyber-physical end devices, to edge servers and cloud facilities. The core pillar in such ecosystems is the establishment of trust-aware *service graph chains*, comprising both resource-constrained devices, running at the edge, but also container-based technologies. The primary existing mechanism to establish trust is by leveraging the concept of trusted computing, which addresses the need for verifiable evidence about a system and the integrity of its trusted computing base. To this end, related specifications provide the foundational concepts, such as *measured boot, sealed storage, platform authentication* and *remote attestation*.

An essential component in building such trusted computing services is a highly secure anchor (either software- or hardware-based) that serves as a Root-of-Trust (RoT), providing cryptographic functions, measuring and reporting the behavior of running software, and storing data securely. Examples include programmable Trusted Execution Environments (TEEs), and fixed-API devices, like the Trusted Platform Module (TPM) [25]. Such components are considered inherently secure elements and implement hardened protections (e.g., tamper-proof or side-channel protections), because any vulnerability on them can compromise the security assurance of the overall system. This sets the challenge ahead: *Because such RoTs by definition are trusted, all internal operations including handling of cryptographic data can be idealized. However, this does not directly translate to the overall application security that leverages such RoTs.*

Thus, formal verification of protocols and interfaces has become a fundamental process to identify bugs or misuse cases when building complex interacting systems, as several earlier works have shown, e.g., [6,22]. There are two noteworthy difficulties when considering formal verification in these settings. First, the inherent fact that protocol verification is an undecidable problem for unbounded number of protocol executions and unbounded size of the terms. And second, the additional difficulty faced by verification tools when considering protocols with non-monotonic mutable global states, which may provoke numerous false attacks or failure to prove security; see [7]. Trusted computing protocols fall into both categories, because the non-volatile memory of the RoTs can be regarded as a state that may change between executions of the protocol.

Indeed, several works on symbolic verification of hardware RoTs that are part of other high-level functionalities take into account the usage of persistent state [2,7]. Some notable examples in the context of the TPM are the works by Shao et al., which cover specific subsets of TPM functionalities, such as Enhanced Authorization (EA) [22] or HMAC authorization [21], identifying misuse cases. Also, Xi et al. [31] and Wesemeyer et al. [30] conduct formal analysis and verification of the Direct Anonymous Attestation (DAA) protocol of the TPM. On the other hand, Delaune et al. [8], propose a Horn-clause framework where they prove its soundness and use ProVerif to approximate the TPM internal state space, helping to address non-termination issues.

A recurrent characteristic when formally verifying the aforementioned scenarios is that there is usually no distinction between the cryptography used for self-consumption of the RoT (e.g., the mechanism it uses for secure storage) and cryptography that is provided specifically for the overall application. This has the inherent drawback that reasoning about the security of a large application or service forces reasoning about the internals of the security device itself, thus, limiting the scope of the reasoning that automated analysis tools can achieve.

Contribution. The main objective of the present work is to propose a methodology for proving security in scenarios based on services that make use of RoTs, by idealizing the internal functionalities of the security device, except those that provide explicit cryptographic functionalities for the service being offered. In order to illustrate our methodology, we concentrate on a class of remote attestation services based on the TPM. Even though we focus on a particular case of attestation, we build an abstract model for a subset of TPM primitives sufficient to implement the core functionalities of generic attestation services. From the perspective of formally verifying RoT-based applications, this model represents a means of reasoning about security and privacy (of offered services) without being bogged down by the intricacies of various crypto primitives considered in the different platforms. We conduct our analysis in the symbolic model of cryptography (Dolev-Yao adversary [9]) using the Tamarin prover [4] and its front-end SAPiC [15]. We define a number of security properties relevant for the considered scenario, and successfully verify them within this framework.

2   Background

In this section we summarize specific notions related to RoT, TPM and remote attestation that will be needed in our discussion to follow. For more details, we refer the reader to [3, 12, 20, 25–27].

The TPM as a Root of Trust. The Trusted Computing Group (TCG) splits the responsibility of the RoT into three categories: measurement, storage and reporting [25, §9.4]. The RoT for measurement is usually the first piece of BIOS code that is executed on the main processor during boot, and starts a chain of measurements. The RoT for storage and reporting are responsibilities assigned to the TPM, typically implemented as a tamper-resistant hardware embedded in a *host* device. The TPM and the host device form a *platform*.

A *measurement chain of trust* is a mechanism that allows to establish trust from the low-level RoT for measurement to a higher-level object, e.g., the OS. Each component in the chain measures the next component, and these measurements are checked against reference values, typically provided by the platform manufacturer, before passing control to the next component. For instance, the RoT will measure the (remaining part of) the BIOS, the BIOS will measure the bootloader, and so on. Each component in the chain updates the TPM's Platform Configuration Registers (PCRs), which are a set of special registers that store the representation of the measurements as a hash chain.

The TPM contains an embedded key pair known as the Endorsement Key (EK) generated and certified by the platform manufacturer. The private part of the EK never leaves the TPM. This key pair uniquely identifies the platform. If this key pair is used to sign platform measurements, it will compromise the platform privacy. Therefore, the TPM offers mechanisms to generate an arbitrary number of Attestation Keys (AKs) that can be used to attest the platform state by signing the PCR contents. These AKs are generated in such a way that it can be ensured to an external verifier that the signature was generated by a legitimate TPM, without revealing the identity of that TPM.

Moreover, the TPM offers mechanisms to restrict access to TPM commands and objects by defining *authorization policies*. Most notably, in TPM 2.0, the Enhanced Authorization (EA) mechanism allows to define flexible, fine-grained authorization policies by combining a number of assertions through logical connectors. For instance, a system administrator could create a TPM key and associate with it a policy that allows the usage of that key when (i) the PCRs are in a given state, *or* (ii) a password is provided *and* the user is physically present. The authorization policy is stored, within the TPM object, as a hash chain called `authPolicy`. An *authorization session* is the mechanism used to pass in authorization values or policies, and to maintain state between subsequent commands. To load or use a TPM object a session must be created, and the user will indicate what assertions must be checked. The TPM checks the assertions and updates the session attribute `policyDigest` (a hash chain) if they succeed. If the `policyDigest` of the session matches the `authPolicy` of a given object, then access to that object is granted. We refer the reader to [25, §19.7] for the complete details, and to Appendix A for specific illustration purposes.

Remote Attestation. It is a mechanism to provide evidence of the integrity status of a platform [12,20]. It is typically realized as a challenge-response protocol that allows a third party (*verifier*) to obtain an authentic and timely report about the state of an untrusted, and potentially compromised, remote device (*prover*). The TPM allows implementing privacy-preserving remote attestation protocols. Remote attestation services are currently used in a variety of scenarios, ranging from attestation for isolated execution environments based on the –now outdated– Intel's Trusted Execution Technology [13], to more modern approaches used together with Intel's Software Guard Extensions, e.g., [14,29].

From a high-level perspective, a remote attestation protocol requires that the user first creates an AK that will be used to sign attestation reports (*quotes*). A quote is essentially composed of the contents stored in selected PCRs (which reflect the platform state) signed with the AK. As commented above, the user has the ability to create as many AKs as they wish, but each AK is required to be certified by a third party called the Privacy Certification Authority (PCA). The certification process, detailed in Sect. 4, implies that the PCA knows the relationship between EK and AKs, but the PCA is trusted not to reveal this information, which would break the anonymity of the platform.

We also note that the TCG has an alternative method for performing remote attestation without revealing the EK to a trusted third party, which is known as Direct Anonymous Attestation (DAA) [5]. However, DAA works by design only in conjunction with the TCG specification for TPMs. Since the aim in this paper is to formalize the notion of secure remote attestation in a more general context, we focus on the first approach, i.e., attestation using a PCA. Such protocols represent most of the real-world applications and they do not modify the core characteristics of the remote attestation service. Further, we argue that the formalization methods that we present here can be used as the basis for other hardware-based remote attestation instances, not only TPMs.

The Tamarin Prover and SAPiC. For our modelling approach we have chosen the Tamarin prover [4,17] and its front-end SAPiC [15]. SAPiC allows modelling protocols in (a dialect of) the applied pi-calculus [1], and converts the processes specification into multiset rewrite rules (MSRs) that can be processed by Tamarin. Security properties can be expressed as first-order logic formulas. Everything that SAPiC does can be expressed in MSRs in Tamarin, but it provides an encoding (e.g., for locks, reliable channels, state handling) which is likely more concise than an ad-hoc modelling a user would come up with using MSRs. Hence, SAPiC has a better chance for termination. We present a brief description of the SAPiC syntax in Appendix B; see [4,15] for the complete details.

Tamarin and SAPiC have already been used successfully for modelling TPM functionalities in existing works, e.g., [21,22,30], and they offer a convenient syntax for modelling protocols with global state. However, as mentioned above, it is rather challenging to model protocols with arbitrarily mutable global state, as it is required in the scenario presented in this paper. Therefore some technical alternatives and manual intervention have been adopted in order to define a realistic adversary. See Sect. 5 below.

3   A Methodology for Modelling Protocols with RoTs

The key idea in our modelling approach is to consider a further layer of abstraction within the traditional symbolic model of cryptography [9], and idealize the internal functionalities of the RoT, except those providing cryptography to a consumer application (like hashing, asymmetric encryption or signatures), capturing their intended semantics rather than their implementation. That is, in addition to the assumption of "perfect cryptography" from the symbolic model (e.g., a ciphertext can only be decrypted by providing the correct key), we abstract and idealize any of the cryptography operations that the RoT uses for self consumption and are not intended to take part in a client application. Consider, for example, the limited amount of non-volatile memory of the RoT. This has the side effect that it needs to use encryption to offload memory contents securely to the host; an ancillary operation unrelated to the client application.

To achieve this, we propose replacing such self-consumption cryptographic functionalities of the RoT with non-cryptographic mechanisms, for example, using a combination of strong access control with channels not visible to the adversary where honest parties interact (private channels). We call this approach the *idealized model of cryptography*, which in addition to restricting the adversary

Table 1. Assumptions considered in the three models.

Computational	Symbolic	Idealized
Messages are bitstrings, and the cryptographic primitives are functions from bitstrings to bitstrings	Messages are terms in an algebra on cryptographic primitives, defined as function symbols	Messages are terms in an algebra on cryptographic primitives, defined as function symbols. Cryptography operations of the RoT for self consumption are abstracted
The adversary is any probabilistic Turing machine with a running time polynomial in a security parameter	The adversary is restricted to compute only using these primitives	The adversary is restricted to compute only using these primitives, and to interact with the RoT only through its interface
Cryptography is implemented securely with overwhelming probability in the security parameter	Cryptography is implemented securely	Cryptography is implemented securely. Cryptographic operations of the RoT that are not exposed to the application are assumed to be secure

capability in computing terms using only cryptographic function symbols, it also idealizes the internal operations of the RoT, assuming they are "perfect." We provide a comparison of the assumptions considered in the computational, symbolic and idealized models in Table 1.

Such an idealized model will enable the reasoning about (and comparing) different TPM services under various adversarial models and for different security guarantees, excluding any possible implications from the leveraged cryptographic primitives. Further, this approach simplifies the modelling of complex protocols, such as the attestation procedure that we study in the paper, and hence it gives the chance to automated analysis tools to be more likely to terminate. From the perspective of formally verifying trusted hardware components, this approach can provide a means of reasoning about security and privacy (of offered services) without being bogged down by the intricacies of various crypto-related primitives considered in the different platforms. On the downside, the idealized approach that we present here is not suitable for capturing potential vulnerabilities stemming from the TPM internal cryptography [21,22], nor it can identify timing attacks, as those presented in [18]. However, this is something well studied in the literature, when it comes to the non-perfect secrecy of the TPM's crypto primitives, thus, in this paper we opted for focusing on idealized models that have a direct impact on real-world applications.

Thus using this approach, one has to prove or assume two facts. First, the particular RoT under analysis implements securely those high-level functionalities that are part of a certain application or service. This can be proved under some model of cryptography which might require significant effort, but this effort will be required to be done only once. Second, that the system is secure when we use an idealized version of the RoT instead of the real device. This task indeed cannot be reused, and needs to be done for each application or service considered. Idealizing cryptography used internally in a RoT allows to carry out an analysis of the cryptography that is relevant to the application itself more concisely, where this analysis can be supported by the use of a more broadly accessible set of tools than those used so far to analyze such applications. Further, it allows to address more complex protocols and larger use cases and compositions of Systems-of-Systems with current formal verification technologies.

The overall overview of our methodology is as follows:

i. Identify and select a subset of RoT functionalities that apply to the service.
ii. Obtain an idealized model, and identify the best approach to model them. Assume or prove security of the idealized functionalities.
iii. Model the application-specific scenario using the idealized device.
iv. Define and model the set of security properties to be considered.

The strategy of idealizing as much of the cryptography as possible should make the task of proving that an application or a system is secure, for some specific notion of security, more manageable. Therefore, simplifying the RoT internal cryptographic components is a worthy consideration. To illustrate our methodology, we focus on an attestation protocol based on TPMs. We describe the complete scenario in Sect. 4 and we instantiate our methodology in Sect. 5.

4   Remote Attestation Using a PCA

The goal of the TPM-based remote attestation protocol presented in this section is to establish a secure communication channel between a Client and a Service Provider (SP), while ensuring the trust status of the Client. The protocol is based on [11], and it is a generic version of a network management protocol presented in [23,24]. There are four devices that participate in the protocol: the Client, a TPM embedded in the Client, the PCA Server, and the SP. See Fig. 1.

Notation. For an entity A, we denote A_{pub} and A_{priv} its public and private keys, respectively. We denote $cert_A(x)$ a certificate for object x issued by entity A, and $sign_A(y)$ a signature of y using private key A_{priv}. Also, for a TPM key k we denote k_{pub} and k_{priv} its public and private key parts, $k_{authPolicy}$ its EA policy, k_h its TPM object handle [25, §15], and k_{name} its name (a unique identifier computed as a hash of its public data [25, §16]). For clarity of exposition, we omit session management objects and parameters in the description of the protocol.

First of all, the Client receives the PCA certificate, signed with the SP key and initializes the TPM by extending the PCR to the current firmware/software values. In order to achieve the establishment of a secure communication channel between the Client and the SP the following phases are executed: (a) The Client

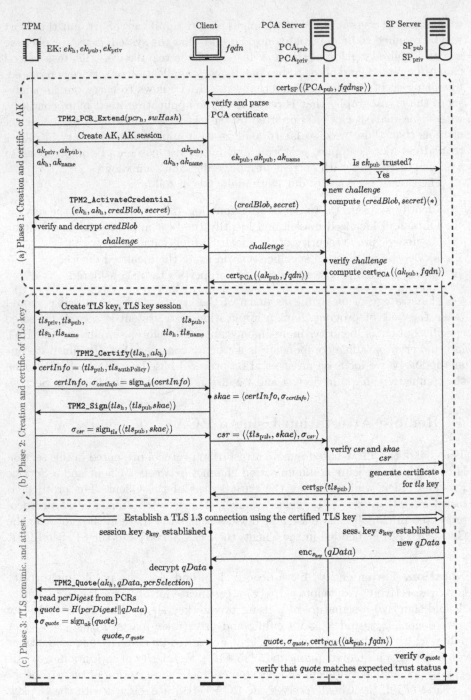

Fig. 1. Remote attestation protocol using a PCA. (*) The PCA can compute *credBlob* and *secret* on its own, or by calling the convenience command `TPM2_MakeCredential`(ek_{pub}, *challenge*, ak_{name}) on a local TPM.

creates an AK using the TPM and this AK is certified by the PCA. (b) The Client creates a TLS key using the TPM, which is certified by the PCA and signed by the SP. (c) Finally, the Client uses the TLS key to establish a secure communication channel with the SP for exchanging encrypted messages and attestation quotes. The three phases are described in detail below.

Phase 1: Creation and Certification of AK. In the first step, the Client creates an AK via the TPM, which is certified by the PCA in a similar way as in [11]. This initial AK is not bound to a PCR state through EA, because authorization for the AK will be accomplished with the certificate that will be issued by the PCA. The AK certification sub-protocol works as follows. Upon receiving the EK, the AK and a desired fully-qualified domain name (FQDN), the PCA creates a random *challenge* and protects it using the TPM command $\texttt{TPM2\_MakeCredential}(ek_{\text{pub}}, challenge, ak_{\text{name}})$, which outputs the values:

- *secret*: a random *seed* encrypted with ek_{pub},
- *credBlob*: encrypt-then-MAC of the *challenge* using keys derived from *seed*.

The Client receives this pair of values and uses the TPM to execute:

$$\texttt{TPM2\_ActivateCredential}(ek_{\text{h}}, ak_{\text{h}}, credBlob, secret)$$

which retrieves the *challenge* after performing some validation checks. Then, the Client sends it to the PCA. If the *challenge* matches, the PCA is convinced that the AK and EK are bound to a legitimate TPM and issues the AK certificate $\text{cert}_{\text{PCA}}(\langle ak_{\text{pub}}, fqdn \rangle)$. See Fig. 1(a).

Phase 2. Creation and Certification of the TLS Key. In this phase, the Client creates a TLS signing key using the TPM, which is bound to PCR state through EA. At this point, the PCRs have already been extended with appropriate firmware/software measurements using a succession of $\texttt{TPM2\_PCRExtends}$.

Let $tls_{\text{priv}}, tls_{\text{pub}}$ be the generated TLS key pair. The Client executes the command $\texttt{TPM2\_Certify}(tls_{\text{h}}, ak_{\text{h}})$, which attests the TLS key, in order to vouch that it is protected by a genuine, but unidentified TPM. This attestation is a signature $\sigma_{certInfo}$ by the AK over information that describes the key, which we abstract as the tuple $certInfo = \langle tls_{\text{pub}}, tls_{\text{authPolicy}} \rangle$. The signed tuple, plus some additional information, is known as Subject Key Attestation Evidence (SKAE), and it is an X.509 certificate extension [28], $skae = \langle certInfo, \sigma_{certInfo} \rangle$.

Next, the Client creates a Certification Signing Request (CSR) for the TLS key. The CSR is composed of the message $\langle tls_{\text{pub}}, skae \rangle$ and the signature on this message with the private part of the TLS key. This is done using the command:

$$\sigma_{csr} = \texttt{TPM2\_Sign}(tls_{\text{h}}, \langle tls_{\text{pub}}, skae \rangle).$$

The value $csr = \langle \langle tls_{\text{pub}}, skae \rangle, \sigma_{csr} \rangle$ is sent to the PCA, which verifies both csr and $skae$ signatures, using tls_{pub} and the AK certificate, and forwards CSR to the SP. The SP issues $\text{cert}_{\text{SP}}(tls_{\text{pub}})$, which is sent to the Client. See Fig. 1(b).

Phase 3. TLS Communication and Device Attestation. The last step is where the secure communication channel between the Client and the SP is established. The Client and the SP execute the TLS 1.3 protocol [19] using the TLS key that was created in the previous step, to establish a common symmetric encryption session key s_{key}. The SP encrypts some random data $qData$ with s_{key} and sends the ciphertext to the Client. Upon receipt, the Client decrypts the ciphertext obtaining $qData$. For the attestation part, the Client executes:

$$(quote, signature) = \mathtt{TPM2\_Quote}(ak_h, qData, pcrSelection),$$

to quote the PCR contents $pcrDigest$ referenced in $pcrSelection$, where $quote = H(pcrDigest \parallel qData)$ and $signature = \mathrm{sign}_{ak_{priv}}(quote)$. The AK certificate and the pair $(quote, signature)$ are sent to the SP, which verifies the signature and the PCR values that reflect the trust status of the platform. See Fig. 1(c).

5   Application of the Modelling Methodology

In this section, we apply the modelling methodology, specifically Steps i.–iii., discussed in Sect. 3, to the use case presented in Sect. 4. We address the verification of security properties (Step iv.) in Sect. 6. Recall that the objective is to come up with high-level abstractions of the relevant RoT commands that will allow us to model the functionalities of the trusted component not directly related to the cryptographic operation needs of the target application.

Adversarial Model. We consider the usual Dolev-Yao model [9] for an adversary sitting between the Client and the two servers (PCA, SP). This is because we assume that there is a trusted infrastructure supporting the interactions between the two servers and it is not a viable target for the adversary. Consequently, we consider three processes in our model: the Client, the TPM and the Server, representing both the PCA and the SP. The adversary is allowed to monitor and interfere in the communication between the Client and the Server. However, the communication between the Client and the TPM is treated independently. More precisely, we allow the adversary a certain degree of control over the communication channel between the Client and the TPM. For instance, the adversary can behave as a *passive adversary*, in order to capture more relaxed trust assumptions, such as the case where the Client has malware installed for monitoring the interactions between the (host) Client and the TPM, but not for intercepting or querying the TPM (using the TPM as an oracle).

Assuming near zero-trust assumptions for the Client requires additional validation of several processes that are executed in the host to protect against fully compromised Clients that try to either manipulate the parameters given to the TPM or use the TPM as a "crypto engine," that is, send falsified data (which can be considered as part of the attestation) to the TPM to be signed. This essentially considers a Dolev-Yao adversarial model which allows an adversary to both monitor and modify all interactions between the Client and the TPM.

The critical operation to verify is the management of the policies depicting the correct PCR values to which the use of the TLS key is bounded to. A compromised host can either create a false policy or bound the correct policy to a wrong representation of the PCR values, resulting in the incorrect use of the TLS key. Such verification proofs can be done using the TPM's certification functionality and validated by a trusted entity, such as the PCA. PCR values representing the "correct" state of the Client should be circulated by the PCA, and signed under its private key, as part of the answer to the TPM2_ActivateCredential command. Since the certification of the TPM has already been included in the described models, for simplicity, we have excluded the further modelling of such additional proofs, thus considering only attackers that can monitor but cannot modify the interactions between the Client and the TPM.

i. **Identify and select a subset of RoT functionalities.** Since the focus is on attestation services, instead of modelling all the TPM commands and functionalities, we concentrate on a specific subset of commands that are common in most reference scenarios and application domains in relation with this service. Such commands are related to object creation, authorization sessions, EA, PCR extension, remote attestation, and cryptographic operations. Concretely, the commands that we consider are:

- Key and session management: TPM2_StartAuthSession, TPM2_PolicyPCR, TPM2_PCRExtend, TPM2_Create
- Attestation: TPM2_MakeCredential, TPM2_ActivateCredential, TPM2_Sign, TPM2_Certify, TPM2_Quote

These commands provide TPM functionalities that are crucial in establishing chains of trust in generic heterogeneous environments. Our intuition is that the models that we will describe for these commands will serve as both a basis for reasoning about the security of a wide set of TPM-based applications and for reasoning about the security of the TPM's mechanisms themselves.

ii. **Obtain an idealized model.** Our models for the TPM commands mentioned above are presented in Fig. 2 using SAPiC syntax (see Appendix B). The cryptographic operations that we need to abstract are the creation of hash chains, which are used for updating PCR and policy digest values, secure storage, as well as object and session management in general. Note that we do not need to model the command TPM2_MakeCredential, as it does not rely on TPM internal secrets. We describe our modelling key points below.

- **Modelling hash chains.** PCR values are the results of measurements of a platform or software state. When the command TPM2_PCRExtend(pcr_h, v) is executed, the TPM extends the contents of the PCR referenced by pcr_h as $pcrDigest = H(pcrDigest \parallel v)$. Applying TPM2_PCRExtend iteratively, a single digest is obtained, representing the sequence of measurements of the platform state. An object can be *sealed* to a PCR value, meaning that it can only be accessed when the PCR has been appropriately extended to that particular value. As such, the *actual* semantics to get access to the object

```
let StartAuthSession =
  in('TPM2_StartAuthSession');
  new ~sₕ;
  lock 'device';
  insert ⟨'policyDigest', ~sₕ⟩, nil;
  out(~sₕ);
  unlock 'device'

let Create =
  in(⟨'TPM2_Create', authPolicy⟩);
  new ~kₕ;
  new ~kₚᵣᵢᵥ;
  lock 'device';
  let kₚᵤᵦ = pk(~kₚᵣᵢᵥ) in
  insert ⟨'authPolicy', ~kₕ⟩, authPolicy;
  insert ⟨'privPart', ~kₕ⟩, kₚᵣᵢᵥ;
  insert ⟨'pubPart', ~kₕ⟩, kₚᵤᵦ;
  out(⟨~kₕ, kₚᵤᵦ⟩);
  unlock 'device'

let Sign =
  in(⟨'TPM2_Sign', kₛₕ, kₕ, m⟩);
  lock 'device';
  lookup ⟨'policyDigest', kₛₕ⟩ as kₚd in
  lookup ⟨'authPolicy', kₕ⟩ as kₐₚ in
  if kₚd = kₐₚ then
    lookup ⟨'privPart', kₕ⟩ as kₚᵣᵢᵥ in
    out(signₖₚᵣᵢᵥ(m));
    unlock 'device'
  else
    unlock 'device'

let Certify =
  in(⟨'TPM2_Certify', kₛₕ, kₕ, akₕ⟩);
  lock 'device';
  lookup ⟨'policyDigest', kₛₕ⟩ as kₚd in
  lookup ⟨'authPolicy', kₕ⟩ as kₐₚ in
  if kₚd = kₐₚ then
    lookup ⟨'pubPart', kₕ⟩ as kₚᵤᵦ in
    lookup ⟨'privPart', akₕ⟩ as akₚᵣᵢᵥ in
    out(signₐₖₚᵣᵢᵥ(⟨kₚᵤᵦ, kₐₚ⟩));
    unlock 'device'
  else
    unlock 'device'
```

```
let PCR_Extend =
  in(⟨'TPM2_PCR_Extend', value⟩);
  lock 'device';
  lookup 'PCR' as pcr_list in
  insert 'PCR', ⟨value, pcr_list⟩;
  unlock 'device'

let PolicyPCR =
  in(⟨'TPM2_PolicyPCR', sₕ⟩);
  lock 'device';
  lookup 'PCR' as pcr_list in
  lookup ⟨'policyDigest', sₕ⟩ as pd_list in
  insert ⟨'policyDigest', sₕ⟩,
         ⟨pcr_list, 'TPM_CC_PolicyPCR', pd_list⟩;
  unlock 'device'

let ActivateCredential =
  in(⟨'TPM2_ActivateCredential', kₛₕ, kₕ, akₛₕ, akₕ, credBlob⟩);
  lock 'device';
  lookup ⟨'policyDigest', akₛₕ⟩ as akₚd in
  lookup ⟨'authPolicy', akₕ⟩ as akₐₚ in
  if akₚd = akₐₚ then
    lookup ⟨'pubPart', akₕ⟩ as aₚᵤᵦ in
    lookup ⟨'privPart', kₕ⟩ as kₚᵣᵢᵥ in
    if verifyCredential(akₚᵤᵦ, kₚᵣᵢᵥ, credBlob) = true then
      let challenge = activateCredential(akₚᵤᵦ, kₚᵣᵢᵥ, credBlob) in
      out(challenge);
      unlock 'device'
    else
      unlock 'device'
  else
    unlock 'device'

let Quote =
  in(⟨'TPM2_Quote', kₛₕ, kₕ, qData⟩)
  lock 'device';
  lookup 'PCR' as pcr_list in
  lookup ⟨'policyDigest', kₛₕ⟩ as kₚd in
  lookup ⟨'authPolicy', kₕ⟩ as kₐₚ in
  if kₚd = kₐₚ then
    lookup ⟨'privPart', kₕ⟩ as kₚᵣᵢᵥ in
    out(signₖₚᵣᵢᵥ(⟨qData, pcr_list⟩));
    unlock 'device'
  else
    unlock 'device'
```

Fig. 2. Idealized TPM commands (sketch). See Appendix B for an overview of the SAPiC syntax.

is performed by comparing a digest value stored in the object blob with a PCR hash value. However, the *intended* semantics is that the object can only be accessed if a certain number of PCR extensions have been executed with corresponding specified values. Therefore, in our idealized approach, we need to find an alternative description for the PCR extension that captures that intended semantics. The idea is to keep a record of all PCR extensions in a list pcr_{list} as global, mutable state, and append each new digest provided by the client to this list. More concretely, the idealization of the process of extending a value v_n to pcr_{list}, translates to:

$$\text{append}(v_n, pcr_{list}) \Rightarrow pcr_{list} = (\underbrace{v_1, v_2, \ldots, v_{n-1}}_{\text{previous } pcr_{list}}, v_n)$$

Then, the adversary cannot gain access to a TPM object that is sealed to PCR, unless he extends the pcr_{list} with the corresponding values in the intended order, and not only any combination of extensions leading to the same hash value. We apply the same idea to the case of policy digests, which consists of hash chains similar to PCRs.

- **Usage of equational theories.** We model cryptographic equational theories as usual, e.g., for the signature generation and verification we use the Tamarin built-in function symbols `pk/1`, `sign/2` and `verify/3` satisfying $verify(sign(m, k), m, pk(k)) = true$. On the other hand, the command `TPM2_MakeCredential`, discussed above, is used to protect a randomly generated value *challenge*, with (a variation of) the encrypt-then-MAC scheme. The seed for the symmetric keys is encrypted with the public part of the EK. The command `TPM2_ActivateCredential` will retrieve the value *challenge* after being provided with the appropriate private keys and execute some internal checks. These commands can be abstracted by the equational theory with function symbols `pk/1`, `makeCredential/3`, `activateCredential/3` and `verifyCredential/3`. For an object name n and a private key k it must be satisfied that:

$$verifyCredential(n, k, makeCredential(pk(k), challenge, n)) = true$$
$$activateCredential(n, k, makeCredential(pk(k), challenge, n)) = challenge.$$

The first equation verifies the correctness of the blob, hence emulates the HMAC operation. The second retrieves the *challenge*, which models the symmetric decryption process.

- **Secure storage and object management.** As a resource-constrained device, the TPM offers the possibility of offloading memory contents into the host in the form of an encrypted blob. The object can then be loaded again if appropriate authorization is provided. We idealize this functionality by assuming that the TPM has unlimited memory space. This is achieved by using as many memory cells as objects or sessions are required. Therefore, we do not model the command `TPM2_Load`, and assume that objects are readily available through their handles after invoking `TPM2_Create`. In a real scenario a user might want to offload memory objects (e.g., when the TPM is switched off). But if a security property holds without offloading memory objects it will also hold when these objects are offloaded, since the adversary will have access to less objects. The communication to/from the TPM needs to be carefully addressed, since if this channel is made fully available to the adversary it would be an overestimation of his capabilities: he could detach, interact with and reattach the TPM at his will at any time. Therefore we need to implement access control (e.g., through private channels) when using some critical commands. This is discussed below.

iii. **Model the application-specific scenario using the idealized device.** As commented above, in our model we aggregate the PCA and the SP servers depicted in Fig. 1 as a single Server process. The main purpose is to capture the communication between the three processes (Client, TPM, Server) in a way that

let Client = (//sending TPM command   let TPM = (//receiving TPM command
let tpm_send_cmd =   let tpm_recv_cmd =
   ⟨CmdCode, $param_1, \ldots param_k$⟩ in   ⟨CmdCode, $param_1, \ldots param_k$⟩ in
event TPM_SendCmd(tpm_send_cmd);   in(tpm_recv_cmd);
out(tpm_send_cmd);   event TPM_RecvCmd(tpm_recv_cmd);
P) Q) //TPM processess command here.

Fig. 3. Tamarin templates for sending/receiving TPM commands

replicates the real-world interactions and modes of operation, to the best possible extent, according to the proposed adversarial model. Modelling the channel between the Client and the TPM as a "standard" private channel in applied pi-calculus caused various technical difficulties for the tool in completing the proofs. For this reason, we have considered several strategies in SAPiC that allow the adversary to observe, but not interfere in that channel:

- **Tamarin restrictions.** Used in order to limit the capabilities of the adversary. We use the templates for sending/receiving TPM commands depicted in Fig. 3, and the following restriction on the execution traces:

$$\forall c, i. \text{ TPM\_RecvCmd}(c)@i \qquad \text{(RestrictionTPMCommand)}$$
$$\Rightarrow ((\exists j. \text{ TPM\_SendCmd}(c)@j \land (j < i))$$
$$\land \neg(\exists k. \text{ TPM\_RecvCmd}(c)@k \land \neg(k = i)))$$

This ensures that in order for a TPM to receive and process a message, an (injective) TPM call must have been executed by the Client process. This forbids an external adversary from calling the TPM arbitrarily, but it allows an internal (e.g., malware) adversary access to the TPM.
- **Usage of the public channel.** Whenever it is possible, we output the response of the TPM to the public channel (e.g., when it produces public keys). To some extent, this could overestimate the capabilities of the adversary, as it assumes that he can always listen to the communication channel between the TPM and the Client. Still, the adversary does not have access to internal secrets such as the EK or private parts of the objects. That is, in most cases, we can assume that the output of the TPM is available to the adversary to prove the security properties we are interested in.
- **Direct usage of multiset rewrite rules.** The SAPiC calculus has an advanced feature which allows direct access to the multiset rewrite system of Tamarin. In order to emulate asynchronous message transfers between the Client and the TPM, we perform the following updates in Fig. 3:

    replace out(tpm_send_cmd) with [ ]─[ ]↦[CmdNameIn(tpm_send_cmd)]
    replace in(tpm_recv_cmd)   with [CmdNameIn(tpm_send_cmd)]─[ ]↦[ ]

The state fact CmdNameIn(tpm_send_cmd) is produced by the Client, consumed by the TPM process, and it is not available to the adversary at any time point. A similar approach can be devised for the TPM outputs, i.e., the TPM produces a state fact that is consumed by the Client process.

Source Code. Our model is split in three parts, corresponding to the three phases of the protocol from Sect. 4, namely AK certification, TLS certification and attestation. The SAPiC models are available at [10].

6   Verification

We address our last step (Step iv.) by describing a number of high-level security properties, defined for the protocol that is presented in Sect. 4. These properties are expressed as first-order logic formulas using Tamarin lemmas [4] and they focus on achieving integrity, confidentiality and attestation in the different phases. The notation "$Ev(p_1, \ldots, p_n)@t$" below stands for an execution of event with name "Ev" and parameters $p_1, \ldots, p_n$, executed at time t.

Sanity-Check Properties. We model a number of properties to guarantee the existence of execution traces that reach the end of each possible branch in the protocol. Whereas these reachability properties do not encode any security guarantee in particular, they are required in order to ensure a non-trivial verification of the remaining correspondence properties. That is, a property of the form Event2 $\Rightarrow$ Event1 will be trivially satisfied if Event2 is never reached. Therefore, for a given party A we define a number of events $AFinish\_i()$, where i ranges over the number of branches of the process that defines party A. We then define the following collections of exists-trace lemmas (one for each branch):

$$\exists t_1. \ AFinish\_i()@t_1. \qquad \text{(Reachability)}$$

Availability of Keys at Honest Processes. We define a number of properties that ensure that all honest parties have initial access to the trusted key material required, so that they can build a chain of trust and successfully complete each phase of the protocol. This property can be treated as a premise in our models. We define the event $HasKey(label, pid, k)$, where $label$ is the key identifier (e.g., 'EK', 'AK'), pid is a unique process identifier, and k is the key value. This event is launched at the start of each entity process. Therefore, we require:

$$\forall label, pid_1, pid_2, k_1, k_2, t_1, t_2. \ (pid_1 \neq pid_2) \land HasKey(label, pid_1, k_1)@t_1 \land$$
$$HasKey(label, pid_2, k_2)@t_2 \Rightarrow (k_1 = k_2). \qquad \text{(KeyAvailability)}$$

Key Freshness. This property ensures that the created key material is not reused as a new key during the execution of the protocol. This applies both to asymmetric keys (e.g., AK public and private parts), as well as to symmetric keys (e.g., session keys). We define the event $GenerateKey(label, tid, k)$, where $label$ is the key identifier, tid stands for thread execution of the principal process, and k is the value of the generated key. The property is captured by the lemma:

$$\forall label, tid_1, tid_2, k, t_1, t_2. \ GenerateKey(label, tid_1, k)@t_1 \land$$
$$GenerateKey(label, tid_2, k)@t_2 \Rightarrow (tid_1 = tid_2). \qquad \text{(KeyFreshness)}$$

Key Secrecy. This property ensures that the sensitive key material, namely private or symmetric session keys, is not available to the adversary. Similarly, we define the lemma SecretKey($label, k$), where $label$ is the key identifier and k represents its value. This event is launched after the corresponding key material has been created in each processes. This is modeled through the lemma:

$$\forall label, k, t_1. \text{ SecretKey}(label, k)@t_1 \Rightarrow \neg(\exists t_2. \ K(k)@t_2), \qquad \text{(KeySecrecy)}$$

where $K(\dots)$ is the event fact denoting adversary knowledge.

Authentication. We consider the agreement property from Lowe's hierarchy [16] in the parameters exchanged in each phase of the protocol. Whenever it is possible (e.g., for a session key), we also require injective, mutual agreement. As customary, we encode this property through the usage of the events ARunning($id_A, id_B, pars$) and BCommit($id_B, id_A, pars$), where the former is placed on the party A being authenticated, and the latter is placed in party B, to whom the authentication is being made. The placement of these events has some flexibility, but not all placements are correct. The ARunning event must be placed *before* party A sends its last message, and the BCommit event must be placed *after* party B receives and verifies the last message sent by A. The variable $pars$ capture the set of parameters which are being agreed. The corresponding lemma has the following form in its injective version:

$$\forall id_A, id_B, pars, t_1. \text{ BCommit}(id_B, id_A, pars)@t_1 \Rightarrow$$
$$((\exists t_2. \text{ ARunning}(id_A, id_B, pars)@t_2 \land (t_2 < t_1)) \land$$
$$\neg(\exists id'_B, id'_A, t_3. \text{ BCommit}(id'_B, id'_A, pars)@t_3 \land \neg(t_3 = t_1))). \quad \text{(Agreement)}$$

In case the agreement is mutual, we require an additional lemma where the roles of A and B are reversed.

Transfer of Information as Generated. Such lemmas ensure that information generated at different stages in the protocol, such as certificates or attestation reports, are received at the destination process as generated by the process of origin. We model this property through the events GenerateValue($label, v$) and ReceiveValue($label, v$), executed at the sender and receiver side respectively:

$$\forall label, v, t_1, t_2. \text{ ReceiveValue}(label, v)@t_1 \Rightarrow$$
$$(\exists t_2. \text{ GenerateValue}(label, v)@t_2 \land (t_2 < t_1)).$$
$$\text{(CorrectTransfer)}$$

No Reuse of Key. This property ensures that a specific key is used only once in its intended context. We consider this property mainly used for single-use session keys. We therefore define the event UseKey($label, k$) and lemma

$$\forall label, k, t_1, t_2. \text{ UseKey}(label, k)@t_1 \land \text{UseKey}(label, k)@t_2 \Rightarrow (t_1 = t_2).$$
$$\text{(NoKeyReuse)}$$

Table 2. Summary of verified properties in SAPiC/Tamarin

Property	Phase 1		Phase 2		Phase 3	
	Objects	Steps	Objects	Steps	Objects	Steps
Reachability	–	37	–	103	–	18
KeyAvailability	EK, AK, PCA_{pub}	1378	AK, TLS, SP_{pub}	537	AK, SP_{pub}	24
KeyFreshness	AK	4	TLS	4	s_{key}, $qData$	4
KeySecrecy	EK, AK, PCA_{priv}	12	TLS_{priv}, SP_{priv}	10	AK, s_{key}	6
Agreement	$cert_{PCA}(AK)$, *challenge*	403	AK, TLS, *swHash*	2987	s_{key} *qData*	2237
CorrectTransfer	$cert_{PCA}(AK)$	383	CSR	406	*quote*	9
NoKeyReuse	n/a	n/a	n/a	n/a	s_{key}	8
Corrupted	n/a	n/a	n/a	n/a	–	1699

No Attestation of Corrupted Client. This property signifies that a Client that is in a corrupted (untrusted) state will not be able to perform a successful attestation. Note that the PCR value of the Client's TPM will be extended to an expected reference value only if its configuration is in a trusted state. SAPiC offers a non-deterministic branching construct which we use to model the fact that the Client might be in a trusted or untrusted state, but the remaining parties in the model do not know a priori which one. We define the event Corrupted(id_A), which is launched at the beginning of the corrupted branch, and reuse the event ServerCommit(id_B, id_A, *pars*), launched after a successful verification of the Client attestation report. We express this property as follows

$$\forall id_A, t_1.\ \text{Corrupted}(id_A)@t_1 \Rightarrow$$
$$\neg(\exists id_B, pars, t_2.\ \text{ServerCommit}(id_B, id_A, pars)@t_2 \wedge \neg(t_1 < t_2))).$$
$$\text{(Corrupted)}$$

Table 2 summarizes the results of our analysis using SAPiC/Tamarin: the objects to which each property is related, and the number of proof steps taken to prove the corresponding lemmas. The simulations have been executed in a VM 3 cores, 4 GB RAM on Intel(R) Core(TM) i5-4570 @ 3.20 GHz. The tool has been able to successfully verify them as expected, showing the feasibility of our approach in abstracting the functionalities of the TPM as a RoT for reporting.

7 Conclusion

In this paper, we introduce a new formal verification methodology, in which our focus is to idealize the internal functionalities of the RoT in such a way that we exclude the cryptographic actions carried out by the RoT and replace them with non-cryptographic approaches. This idealized model of cryptography allows for a more effective verification process, especially when complex protocols and extensive use case scenarios are considered. We formalized the notion of secure remote attestation towards trust aware service graph chains, in "Systems-of-Systems," and verified Tamarin lemmas showing that our models satisfy the three key security properties that entail secure remote attestation and execution: integrity, confidentiality, and secure measurement. Furthermore, in order to model this service, we also considered additional TPM processes such as the creation of TPM keys, the Enhanced Authorization (EA) mechanism, the management of the Platform Configuration Registers (PCRs), and the creation and management of policy sessions. We argue that the included TPM commands cover a wide range of TPM-based applications and hence they can serve as a baseline for modelling additional TPM functionalities, in various application domains in the literature. Finally, we believe that our methodology of idealizing the cryptography can be used as an extensible verification methodology that enables rigorous reasoning about the security properties of a RoT in general.

Acknowledgements. We would like to thank François Dupressoir and Robert Künnemann for useful discussions. We would also like to thank the anonymous reviewers for their insightful comments. This work was partially supported by the European Union's Horizon 2020 Research and Innovation programme under grant agreements No. 779391 (FutureTPM) and No. 952697 (ASSURED), and by the UK Engineering and Physical Sciences Research Council (EPSRC) under grant EP/R012598/1.

A   Create a TPM Key with PCR Policy

We show a simplified example on the usage of EA. We note that, for clarity, we are omitting many details on TPM internals and TPM objects; see [3, 25–27]. In brief, the user executes the command TPM2_StartAuthSession(TRIAL) in order to initiate a fresh trial session. The TPM creates a handle $trial_{sh}$ for this session, initiates the policy digest $trial_{pd}$ to zero and returns $trial_{sh}$ to the user. The user executes the command TPM2_PolicyPCR($trial_{sh}, pcr_h, swHash$), which asks the TPM to update the policy digest of the trial session as:

$$trial_{pd} = H(trial_{pd}\|\text{'TPM\_CC\_PolicyPCR'}\|swHash),$$

where $H(\ )$ is a hash function. The user executes TPM2_PolicyGetDigest($trial_{sh}$) in order to obtain $trial_{pd}$ and calls TPM2_Create($trial_{pd}$). The TPM will create a new object (key) $k = (key_{priv}, key_{pub})$ with authorization policy $key_{ap} = trial_{pd}$ and returns to the user the protected object blob. Now the user creates a policy session s with TPM2_StartAuthSession(EA) and the TPM sets $s_{pd} = nil$ and returns the handle s_h to the Client. Then, the Client executes the command TPM2_PolicyPCR($s_h, pcr_h, swHash$) in order to update the policy digest s_{pd}, and then TPM2_Load($s_h, objectBlob$) and obtains k_h, k_{pub}, k_{name}. This procedure is summarized in Fig. 4.

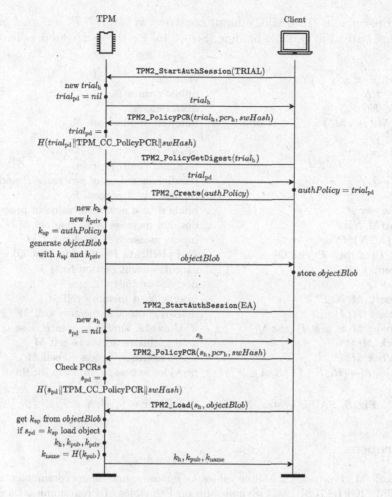

Fig. 4. Create a TPM key with PCR policy

B SAPiC Syntax

Figure 5 describes the SAPiC syntax. The syntax allows to define a protocol as a process. It is then translated into a set of Tamarin MSRs that adhere to the semantics of the calculus, which is a dialect of the applied pi-calculus [1]. The calculus comprises an *order-sorted term algebra* with infinite sets of publicly known names PN, freshly generated names FN, and variables $\mathcal{V}$. It also comprises a signature Σ, i.e., a set of function symbols, each with an arity. Messages are elements from a set of terms $\mathcal{T}$ over PN, FN, and $\mathcal{V}$, built by applying the function symbols in Σ. Events in SAPiC are similar to Tamarin action facts, and they annotate specific parts of the process to be used to define security properties. We denote $\mathcal{F}$ the set of Tamarin action and state facts. As opposed to the applied pi-calculus [1], SAPiC's input construct in (M, N); P performs pattern matching instead of variable binding. See [4,15] for the complete details.

$\langle M, N \rangle ::= x, y, z \in \mathcal{V}$	variables
$\mid p \in PN$	public names
$\mid n \in FN$	fresh names
$\mid f(M_1, \ldots, M_k)$ s.t. $f \in \Sigma$ of arity k	function application
$\langle P, Q \rangle ::=$	processes
$\mid 0$	terminal (null) process
$\mid P \mid Q$	parallel execution of processes P and Q
$\mid !P$	replication of process P
$\mid$ new $\sim n; P$	binds n to a new fresh value in process P
$\mid$ out$(M, N); P$	outputs message N to channel M
$\mid$ in$(M, N); P$	inputs message N to channel M
$\mid$ if $Pred$ then P [else Q]	P if predicate $Pred$ holds; [else Q]
$\mid$ event $F; P$	executes event (action fact) F
$\mid P + Q$	non-deterministic choice
$\mid$ insert $M, N; P$	inserts N at memory cell M
$\mid$ delete $M; P$	deletes content of memory cell M
$\mid$ lookup M as x in P [else Q]	if M exists, bind it to x in P; else Q
$\mid$ lock $M; P$	gain exclusive access to cell M
$\mid$ unlock $M; P$	waive exclusive access to cell M
$\mid [L] -\![A]\!\rightarrow [R]; P \quad (L, R, A \in \mathcal{F}^*)$	provides access to Tamarin MSRs

Fig. 5. SAPiC syntax. Notation: $n \in FN, x \in \mathcal{V}, M, N \in \mathcal{T}, F \in \mathcal{F}$.

References

1. Abadi, M., Fournet, C.: Mobile values, new names, and secure communication. In: ACM SIGPLAN-SIGACT Symposium on Principles of Programming Languages (POPL), London, UK, pp. 104–115. ACM, January 2001
2. Arapinis, M., Phillips, J., Ritter, E., Ryan, M.D.: StatVerif: verification of stateful processes. J. Comput. Secur. **22**(5), 743–821 (2014)
3. Arthur, W., Challener, D.: A Practical Guide to TPM 2.0: Using the Trusted Platform Module in the New Age of Security. Apress, Berkeley (2015)
4. Basin, D., Cremers, C., Dreier, J., Meier, S., Sasse, R., Schmidt, B.: Tamarin prover (v. 1.6.1), August 2021. https://tamarin-prover.github.io
5. Brickell, E.F., Camenisch, J., Chen, L.: Direct anonymous attestation. In: ACM Conference on Computer and Communications Security (CCS), Washington, DC, pp. 132–145. ACM, October 2004
6. Chen, L., Ryan, M.: Attack, solution and verification for shared authorisation data in TCG TPM. In: Degano, P., Guttman, J.D. (eds.) FAST 2009. LNCS, vol. 5983, pp. 201–216. Springer, Heidelberg (2010). https://doi.org/10.1007/978-3-642-12459-4_15
7. Cheval, V., Cortier, V., Turuani, M.: A little more conversation, a little less action, a lot more satisfaction: global states in ProVerif. In: IEEE Computer Security Foundations Symposium (CSF), Oxford, UK, pp. 344–358, July 2018

8. Delaune, S., Kremer, S., Ryan, M.D., Steel, G.: Formal analysis of protocols based on TPM state registers. In: IEEE Computer Security Foundations Symposium (CSF), Cernay-la-Ville, France, pp. 66–80. IEEE, June 2011
9. Dolev, D., Yao, A.: On the security of public key protocols. IEEE Trans. Inf. Theory **29**(2), 198–208 (1983)
10. Fotiadis, G., et al.: Repository for SAPiC/Tamarin models, October 2021. https://github.com/jmor7690/stm2021-rot-abstractions
11. Goldman, K.: Attestation protocols. Technical report, IBM, December 2017
12. Goldman, K., Perez, R., Sailer, R.: Linking remote attestation to secure tunnel endpoints. In: ACM Workshop on Scalable Trusted Computing (STC), Alexandria, VA, pp. 21–24. ACM, November 2006
13. Greene, J.: Intel trusted execution technology: hardware-based technology for enhancing server platform security (2013)
14. Hongwei, Z., Zhipeng, K., Yuchen, Z., Dangyang, W., Jinhui, Y.: TSGX: defeating SGX side channel attack with support of TPM. In: Asia-Pacific Conference on Communications Technology and Computer Science (ACCTCS), Shenyang, China, pp. 22–24. IEEE, April 2021
15. Kremer, S., Künnemann, R.: Automated analysis of security protocols with global state. J. Comput. Secur. **24**(5), 583–616 (2016)
16. Lowe, G.: A hierarchy of authentication specifications. In: IEEE Computer Security Foundations Workshop (CSFW), Rockport, MA, pp. 31–43. IEEE, June 1997
17. Meier, S., Schmidt, B., Cremers, C., Basin, D.: The TAMARIN prover for the symbolic analysis of security protocols. In: Sharygina, N., Veith, H. (eds.) CAV 2013. LNCS, vol. 8044, pp. 696–701. Springer, Heidelberg (2013). https://doi.org/10.1007/978-3-642-39799-8_48
18. Moghimi, D., Sunar, B., Eisenbarth, T., Heninger, N.: TPM-FAIL: TPM meets timing and lattice attacks. In: USENIX Security Symposium (USENIX Security), pp. 2057–2073. USENIX Association, August 2020
19. Rescorla, E.: The transport layer security (TLS) protocol version 1.3. RFC 8446, RFC Editor, August 2018. https://www.rfc-editor.org/rfc/rfc8446.txt
20. Sailer, R., Zhang, X., Jaeger, T., van Doorn, L.: Design and implementation of a TCG-based integrity measurement architecture. In: USENIX Security Symposium (USENIX Security), San Diego, CA. USENIX Association, August 2004
21. Shao, J., Qin, Y., Feng, D.: Formal analysis of HMAC authorisation in the TPM2.0 specification. IET Inf. Secur. **12**(2), 133–140 (2018)
22. Shao, J., Qin, Y., Feng, D., Wang, W.: Formal analysis of enhanced authorization in the TPM 2.0. In: ACM Symposium on Information. Computer and Communications Security (ASIA CCS), Singapore, pp. 273–284. ACM, April 2015
23. The FutureTPM Consortium: FutureTPM use case and system requirements. Deliverable D1.1, FutureTPM, June 2018
24. The FutureTPM Consortium: Demonstrators implementation report - first release. Deliverable D6.3, FutureTPM, April 2020
25. Trusted Computing Group (TCG): Trusted Platform Module Library Specification, Part 1: Architecture (Family "2.0", Level 00, Revision 01.59), November 2019
26. Trusted Computing Group (TCG): Trusted Platform Module Library Specification, Part 2: Structures (Family "2.0", Level 00, Revision 01.59, November 2019
27. Trusted Computing Group (TCG): Trusted Platform Module Library Specification, Part 3: Commands - Code (Family "2.0", Level 00, Revision 01.59), November 2019
28. Trusted Computing Group (TCG) - Infrastructure Work Group: Subject Key Attestation Evidence Extension (Version 1.0, Revision 7), June 2005

29. Weiser, S., Werner, M.: SGXIO: generic trusted I/O path for Intel SGX. In: ACM Conference on Data and Application Security and Privacy (CODASPY), New York, NY, pp. 261–268. ACM, March 2017

30. Wesemeyer, S., Newton, C.J.P., Treharne, H., Chen, L., Sasse, R., Whitefield, J.: Formal analysis and implementation of a TPM 2.0-based direct anonymous attestation scheme. In: ACM Asia Conference on Computer and Communications Security (ASIA CCS), Taipei, Taiwan, pp. 784–798. ACM, October 2020

31. Xi, L., Feng, D.: Formal analysis of DAA-related APIs in TPM 2.0. In: Au, M.H., Carminati, B., Kuo, C.-C.J. (eds.) NSS 2014. LNCS, vol. 8792, pp. 421–434. Springer, Cham (2014). https://doi.org/10.1007/978-3-319-11698-3_32

Towards Decentralized and Provably Secure Cross-Domain Solutions

Joud Khoury$^{(\boxtimes)}$, Zachary Ratliff, and Michael Atighetchi

Raytheon BBN, Cambridge, MA 02138, USA
{joud.khoury,zachary.ratliff,michael.atighetchi}@raytheon.com

Abstract. Cross-Domain Solutions (CDS) are widely deployed today for secure and timely sharing of information across security domains. Content filters are a key function of the CDS used to mitigate data threats. CDS's today are centralized and trusted and their deployments are being increasingly consolidated at the enterprise. This centralization and reliance on always-on connectivity to the enterprise introduces risk to timely and secure information sharing at the tactical edge. In this work, we take a step towards decentralizing the CDS functionality by distributing its security relevant components across untrusted tactical edge devices while still providing guarantees on the integrity of the end-to-end filtering pipeline. We instantiate a proof-of-concept decentralized CDS for bitmap image filtering and we demonstrate two alternative designs with similar trust assumptions but different performance tradeoffs. Both designs are based on *verifiable computation*. Our most performant system is able to filter a 250×250 pixel image in 15 s, $20\times$ faster than a strong baseline, and is able to scale to much larger images ($13\times$ larger scale than baseline within the available memory budget). We discuss ongoing and future work enhancing the expressiveness, performance, and security of the design.

1   Introduction

Cross-Domain Solutions (CDS) are widely deployed by the Department of Defense (DoD) for secure and timely sharing of information across security domains to support joint, interagency, and multinational mission operations. A transfer CDS filters and passes information flows between different security domains to protect against a wide range of data threats. Filters are a critical component of a CDS, performing a variety of functions such as data verification, inspection, sanitization, cleansing, and transformation to mitigate threats. Examples of such filtering include removing potential malware from the data via

Approved for public release (PA); distribution unlimited. PA Case No: AFRL-2021-1484

This material is based upon work supported by the United States Air Force under Contract No. FA8750-20-C-0200. Any opinions, findings and conclusions or recommendations expressed in this material are those of the author(s) and do not necessarily reflect the views of the United States Air Force.

© Springer Nature Switzerland AG 2021
R. Roman and J. Zhou (Eds.): STM 2021, LNCS 13075, pp. 185–203, 2021.
https://doi.org/10.1007/978-3-030-91859-0_10

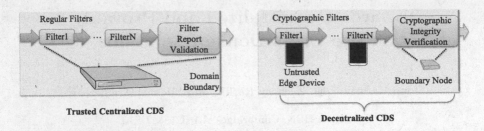

Fig. 1. A decentralized CDS distributes security relevant components over low assurance devices while providing end-to-end provable guarantees of the integrity of the filtering pipeline. This enables secure cross-domain information sharing at the tactical edge where access to a centralized enterprise or tactical CDS may not be available.

normalization, removing particular parts of the data via redaction, or transforming the data to new forms (e.g., reducing precision of coordinates or imagery or converting between protocols). The CDS ensures that the filtered data complies with the security policy. CDSs are widely deployed across the DoD, and are starting to be deployed for securing commercial operational networks [2,19].

Given that software-based CDSs are too complex to be able to prove their security mathematically, significant engineering thought has gone into successfully building CDSs that are secure by design, as defined for example by the National Security Agency's (NSA) Raise The Bar (RTB) strategy [17]. The pillars of the RTB strategy are the least privilege and least knowledge, and the Redundant, Always Invoked, Independent Implementations, and Non-Bypassable (RAIN) principles. Briefly, these principles ensure that failure of a single security-relevant component (e.g., a filter or a domain separation component) results in contained damage and does not compromise the whole CDS.

As a result, CDS platforms used by the DoD today are trusted. Their centralized and protected implementations (software and configurations) contribute to the high level of trust placed in them. Additionally, the community has started to consolidate CDS deployments on the enterprise, to gain a better picture of all existing network cross-connects. We argue that such centralization of the CDS and reliance on always-on connectivity to the enterprise introduce risk to mission success especially in Disconnected, Intermittent, Limited bandwidth (DIL) tactical environments where connectivity is intermittent.

In this work, we describe how to decentralize the CDS by distributing its security relevant components across existing low-assurance tactical edge devices while still providing the desired high-assurance guarantees required of CDSs (Fig. 1). A decentralized CDS capability complements today's enterprise and tactical CDSs enabling secure cross-domain information sharing when access to the enterprise or single-device tactical CDSs is not available. Decentralization additionally protects against the centralized CDS becoming a single point of failure or compromise. The resulting Decentralized CDS (DCDS) can initially support a limited and well-defined subset of information flows that are necessary for effective operations in disconnected tactical environments.

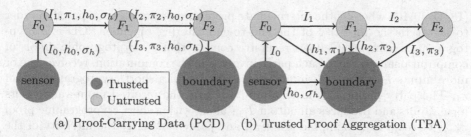

(a) Proof-Carrying Data (PCD)   (b) Trusted Proof Aggregation (TPA)

Fig. 2. Two instantiations of a decentralized CDS filtering pipeline with three filters F_0, F_1, F_2. Sensor produces and signs images that get filtered on the way to a domain boundary (the verifier). Each filter acts as a prover generating a proof of the integrity of its local computation. The domain boundary accepts and passes the filtered images if and only if the cryptographic proof(s) π_i associated with the filtered content is/are valid; (a) proofs are recursively composed using proof carrying data and the domain boundary only needs the last proof π_3, or (b) all intermediate proofs are aggregated at the domain boundary.

A key technical challenge with decentralization is ensuring end-to-end correctness and security of the CDS filtering pipeline despite individual components of the pipeline being untrusted. Today's enterprise and tactical CDSs employ trusted operating systems and/or trusted hardware, ensuring system integrity using mechanisms such as Trusted Platform Module based trusted boot, Mandatory Access Control, Discretionary Access Control, and OS-level integrity monitoring. The strategic combination of these security mechanisms provides the basis for building the trusted filtering pipelines adhering to the RAIN principles. When decentralizing the CDS such that its components run on different edge platforms, we can no longer assume the platforms are trusted yet we must still ensure the integrity of the end-to-end filtering pipeline.

With the help of advanced cryptography and specifically *verifiable computation*, we instantiate a proof-of-concept filtering pipeline where different filters reside on different *untrusted* edge platforms, and the end-to-end integrity of the pipeline is provably guaranteed. Specifically, in our DCDS setting, a *sensor* produces and signs content (imagery in this case). The content is passed through a pipeline of compute nodes each of which performs permissible filtering on the content before forwarding it to the next node in the pipeline. The filtered content arrives at a trusted *domain boundary* (the verifier), which verifies the authenticity and integrity of the final result, i.e., it verifies that the final transformed content is a compliant transformation of the original content and is authentic, before passing the content across the domain boundary.

As shown in Fig. 2, we describe two alternative decentralized CDS architectures with similar trust assumptions but different performance tradeoffs. A key theme in our design is that every (untrusted) filtering node must furnish a cryptographic *proof* of correctness of its local filtering computation. The first architecture (Fig. 2(a)) is implemented as an application of Proof-Carrying Data

(PCD) [9,10], whereby the intermediate proofs are recursively composed in order to attest to the integrity of the end-to-end filtering pipeline. PCD is a cryptographic scheme that allows recursive composition of cryptographic proofs of computational integrity. Each party involved in the computation, receives one or more inputs I_i where each input is associated with a short cryptographic proof π_i. The party performs a local computation on the received inputs and on its local inputs and produces an output I_{i+1} along with a short cryptographic proof π_{i+1}. Given a cryptographic proof π_i, any party can verify the integrity of the full computation history up to step $i-1$. Verification is public and is very fast, on the order of milliseconds, and proofs are very short on the order of hundreds of bytes. In this PCD setting, the trusted domain boundary receives a single proof that attests to the authenticity and integrity of the entire end-to-end distributed filtering computation.

The second architecture (Fig. 2(b)) is implemented using a Trusted Proof Aggregator (TPA). Each filtering node at step i performs a local computation on the input I_i and forwards the output I_{i+1} to the next node in the pipeline for additional filtering. Additionally, node i produces a tuple (h_{i+1}, π_{i+1}) corresponding to a hash and a cryptographic proof, that it forwards to the domain boundary. The domain boundary node aggregates and checks each of the individual proofs to verify the integrity of the end-to-end filtering computation. Our TPA architecture exploits the fact that the boundary node must be trusted regardless of whether we use PCD or other designs, since the boundary node ultimately makes the decision on whether to pass content across the boundary or not. This insight allows us to aggregate the proof verification at the trusted boundary node using simple proof chaining. Proof chaining is simpler and admits a set of optimization that enhance its performance relative to the recursive proof composition design. Proof verification is a lightweight operation that can be efficiently lowered to hardware on the boundary node (such as an FPGA) and placed along with other hardware-based functions such as the diode responsible for one way transfers.

We use filtering of bitmap images as the example data type in this paper since most bitmap image formats such as JPEG, PNG, GIF, and TIFF can be converted into raw bitmaps without losing information, and in fact this is a common normalization step used by CDSs today for filtering images [17]. We implement bitmap filtering adhering to NSA's Inspection and Sanitization guide for Bitmaps [11], filtering both header and pixel data. Our most performant implementation takes around 15 s to filter a 250×250 pixel image for a single step of the pipeline. This is 20× faster than the baseline PCD system. Our optimizations reduce the total number of constraints by 30× allowing scaling to 13× larger images than baseline within the same memory budget. Finally, we significantly reduce the end-to-end latency of the pipeline by having the filtering nodes prove in parallel. This means our speedups relative to baseline increase with the depth of the pipeline. Our predicates can be used to filter text documents, not just images, by treating characters as pixels.

Our work makes the following novel contributions:

- Design, implementation, and performance evaluation of two alternative architectures for decentralizing the CDS that achieve provable end-to-end authenticity and integrity guarantees with different performance tradeoffs; to our knowledge, this is the first application of verifiable computation to decentralizing cross domain solutions.
- Implementation and optimization of compliance predicates for bitmap filtering. Our optimizations collectively deliver 20× speedups over prior work for image authentication from PCD [18] at the 250×250 image size, and 13× image scaling. In addition, the end-to-end latency of our filtering pipeline is very weakly dependent on the pipeline's depth.

The rest of the paper is organized as follows. Relevant background on cryptographic protocols is presented in Sect. 2. We present the two DCDS designs in Sect. 3, followed by the implementation details in Sect. 4, and the optimizations in Sect. 5. We evaluate the performance of the design in Sect. 6. Finally, related and future work is presented in Sect. 7 before concluding.

2   Background

We review the definitions of arithmetic circuits, preprocessing zk-SNARKs, and proof carrying data, and we refer the reader to [6] for details.

2.1   Arithmetic Circuit Satisfiability in Field $\mathbb{F}$

An $\mathbb{F}$-arithmetic circuit $C : \mathbb{F}^n \times \mathbb{F}^h \to \mathbb{F}^l$ is defined by the relation $\mathcal{R}_C = \{(x, a) : C(x, a) = 0\}$. Here a is called the witness (auxilliary input) and x is the public input and the output is 0. The language of the circuit is defined by $\mathcal{L}_C = \{x : \exists a, C(x, a) = 0\}$. Here $x \in \mathbb{F}^n$ (i.e., x is represented as n field elements), $a \in \mathbb{F}^h$, and the output in $\mathbb{F}^l$. A hashing circuit for example takes the (private) input/witness a and its hash x, and asserts that $H(a) = x$.

2.2   Preprocessing zk-SNARK

A preprocessing *zero-knowledge succinct non-interactive argument of knowledge* (pp-zk-SNARK or simply zk-SNARK) for $\mathbb{F}$-arithmetic circuit satisfiability comprises three algorithms (G, P, V), corresponding to the *Generator*, the *Prover*, and the *Verifier*.

$G(\lambda, C) \to (\mathsf{pk}, \mathsf{vk})$ Given a security parameter λ and the $\mathbb{F}$-arithmetic circuit C, sample a keypair comprising a public proving key pk and a public verification key vk.

$P(\mathsf{pk}, x, a) \to (\pi)$ Given the public prover key pk and any $(x, a) \in \mathcal{R}_C$, generate a succinct proof π attesting that $x \in \mathcal{L}_C$

$V(\mathsf{vk}, x, \pi) \to b \in \{0, 1\}$ checks that π is a valid proof for $x \in \mathcal{L}_C$.

The zk-SNARK is the basic cryptographic building block we use to instantiate both CDS architectures.

2.3   Proof Carrying Data (PCD)

Proof carrying data allows distributed computation among mutually-untrusted parties [6,9]. Each party receives s input messages each of size n from other parties $z_{in} \in \mathbb{F}^{s \cdot n}$, adds its local input $z_{\text{loc}} \in \mathbb{F}^{n_l}$ of size n_l to it, and produces an output $z \in \mathbb{F}^n$ along with a succinct proof which is sent to downstream parties in the computation graph. Here s is referred to as the *arity*.

A *compliance predicate* $\prod$ defines the valid local computation performed at each party. Given a message z and a proof, the goal of PCD is to ensure $\prod$-compliance i.e., that every local party's computation along the sequence of computations that produced z satisfies $\prod$. The predicate $\prod$ is represented as an $\mathbb{F}$-arithmetic circuit with inputs $(z, z_{in}, z_{\text{loc}}, b_{\text{base}})$ where $b_{\text{base}} \in \mathbb{F}$ denotes whether the local party is the base party i.e., has no predecessors in the computation graph.

A PCD system comprises algorithms (*Generator, Prover, Verifier*), corresponding to the generator, prover, and verifier.

Generator$(\lambda, \prod) \rightarrow (\text{pk}, \text{vk})$ Given a security parameter λ and the compliance predicate $\prod$ expressed as a $\mathbb{F}$-arithmetic circuit, sample a keypair comprising a public proving key pk and a public verification key vk.

Generator$(\text{pk}, z_{in}, \pi_{in}, z_{\text{loc}}, z) \rightarrow (z, \pi_{out})$ Given the public prover key pk, a set of input messages z_{in} with corresponding compliance proofs π_{in}, local input z_{loc}, and output z, generate a succinct proof π_{out} attesting that z is $\prod$-compliant.

Verifier$(\text{vk}, z, \pi) \rightarrow b \in \{0, 1\}$ checks that z is $\prod$-compliant.

Appendix A reviews an instantiation of PCD from zk-SNARK and elaborates on the performance of such system in terms of circuit size and prover algorithm space and time complexity.

3   Decentralized CDS Designs

We present two designs for a DCDS filtering pipeline. The first is a direct application of PCD whereby integrity proofs are recursively composed as content gets transformed along the filtering pipeline, while the second design relies on a *trusted aggregator* to perform the proof composition. In our simplified transfer CDS scenario, the domain boundary node must be trusted as it ultimately has to make the decision on whether to pass filtered content across the domain boundary. This is true regardless of the design, whether centralized or decentralized. We leverage this inherent trust assumption in order to design the trusted aggregator, which significantly enhances the efficiency of the filtering pipeline while providing similar assurances.

3.1 DCDS from Recursive Proof Composition

Our PCD design is inspired by [18], where the authors implement a compliance predicate for image authentication under a set of permissible transformations. Figure 2(a) presents a high level overview of the approach. Consider an existentially unforgeable signature scheme $S = (G_S, S_S, V_S)$ with private signing key v_s and public verification key p_s (e.g., ECDSA), and let H be a collision-resistant hash function. The sensor produces an image I_0, hashes it to $h_0 = H(I_0)$, signs the hash using its private signing key v_s to produce σ_h, and sends the tuple (I_0, h_0, σ_h) to a successor filtering node F_0. Filter F_0 performs a *permissible* filtering computation on the input image I_0 (e.g., redaction, cropping, rotation, scaling, and so on) as defined by the compliance predicate $\prod$, generates the filtered output image I_1 along with cryptographic proof π_1, and forwards the tuple $(I_1, \pi_1, h_0, \sigma_h)$ to the next filter in the pipeline, and so on. Finally, the domain boundary node checks the authenticity of the image and the integrity of the end-to-end filtering pipeline simply by checking the last proof π_3. Verifying π_3 ensures that the filtered image I_3 has a *permissible provenance* i.e., I_3 is the output of a set of $\prod$-compliant computations on an original input image whose hash is h_0, and that σ_h is a valid signature of h_0 under v_s.

The compliance predicate $\prod(z_{in}, z_{loc}, z_{out}, b_{base})$ for image authentication, i.e., the local computation that each node must perform, is shown in Algorithm 1. The base filtering node (which has no inputs, and has the original signed image from the sensor, and has $b_{base} = 1$) verifies in the PCD that $h_{in} = H(I_{in})$ is a valid hash of the original image $I_{in} = I_0$. The base node, and every successor filtering node along the way, verify that $h_{in} == h_{out}$, i.e., the hash is passed through the computation unchanged, and verify that the output image $I_{out} == F(I_{in}, \gamma)$ is a valid filtering transformation of the input image I_{in} according to $z_{loc} = (F, \gamma)$ where F is the filtering transformation identifier and γ is metadata for the transformation such as size for cropping or scaling factor.

The domain boundary verifies that,

- the PCD proof is valid, i.e., $Verifier(vk, z_{in}, \pi_{in}) == 0$ which ensures that I_{in} is a permissible provenance and it is authentic, and
- the signature σ_h is a valid signature of h_{in} under p_s where p_s is the public verification key, and this step as in [18] is performed *outside-the-PCD* for efficiency reasons as this avoids having to implement signature verification in the PCD. More formally, it checks $V_S(p_s, h_{in}, \sigma_h) == 0$

With this scheme, only the base node runs the hashing functionality in the PCD. An efficient hashing circuit from [18] from subset-sum exists already (it is required for the PCD system itself). A hash fits in one element, and the ECDA 384-bit signature fits in two elements (recall each element is 298 bits). The security of this design follows directly from [18]. We describe the implementation of the bitmap filtering transformation F in more detail in Sect. 4, and the performance optimizations in Sect. 5.

Algorithm 1. Compliance Predicate $\prod(z_{in} = (I_{in}, h_{in}, \sigma_{in}), z_{\text{loc}} = (F, \gamma), z_{out} = (I_{out}, h_{out}, \sigma_{out}), b_{\text{base}})$

1: **if** b_{base} **then**   ▷ i.e., base case
2:     **return** $F \in \mathcal{F}$ and $F(I_{in}, \gamma)$==I_{out} and h_{in}==$H(I_{in})$
3: **else**
4:     **return** $F \in \mathcal{F}$ and $F(I_{in}, \gamma)$==I_{out} and h_{out}==h_{in}
5: **end if**

3.2   DCDS from Proof Aggregation

Our proof aggregation DCDS design is shown in Fig. 2(b) and provides similar assurances. Our instantiation of the proof aggregation is however more efficient primarily because of using a more efficient hashing circuit and parallelization as we shall describe in Sect. 5.4 and Sect. 5.5. As with the PCD design, the sensor produces an image I_0, hashes it to $h_0 = H(I_0)$, signs the hash using its private signing key v_s to produce σ_h. It sends the tuple (h_0, σ_h) directly to the boundary node (the verifier), and it sends the image I_0 to the successor filtering node F_0. Each filtering node i in the pipeline uses pp-zk-SNARK prover algorithm to generate a proof π_{i+1} attesting to the following statements:

1. $h_i == H(I_i)$
2. $I_{i+1} == F_i(I_i)$
3. $h_{i+1} == H(I_{i+1})$

Formally, node i computes $P(\text{pk}, (h_i, h_{i+1}), (I_i, I_{i+1})) \rightarrow (\pi_{i+1})$, where the hashes are the public input and the images are the private witness. Node i directly sends the tuple (π_{i+1}, h_{i+1}) to the domain boundary. Notice that both the proof and the hash are very small on the order of hundreds of bytes, incurring little extra communication cost. The last filtering node in the pipeline (node 2 in Fig. 2(b)) additionally sends its output filtered image (I_3) to the domain boundary.

Given the final transformed image I_n (for an n step pipeline) and all the intermediate hashes and proofs $((h_n, \pi_n), \ldots, (h_1, \pi_1), h_0, \sigma_h)$, the boundary node verifies the following conditions:

- $h_n == H(I_n)$, this is performed outside the SNARK
- $V(\text{vk}, (h_i, h_{i+1}), \pi_{i+1}) == 0, \forall i \in [0, n-1]$
- $V_S(p_s, h_0, \sigma_h) == 0$, i.e., σ_h is a valid signature of h_0 under the public verification key p_s; this is also performed outside the SNARK

The boundary node passes the filtered image across the boundary if and only if all these conditions are met.

The security of this scheme follows from the following facts. If $H(I_n) == h_n$ and $V(\mathsf{vk}, (h_{n-1}, h_n), \pi_n) == 0$, then I_n must equal $F_n(I_{n-1})$ for some I_{n-1}. Similarly, recursively verifying each of the proofs proves there is some original image I_0 from which I_n is derived according to a sequence of valid filters F_i. If in addition σ_h is a valid signature on h_0, the domain boundary can prove that I_0 is authentic (produced by the sensor with possession of the signing key).

4   Implementation

We implement, optimize, and evaluate bitmap (BMP) image filtering for both the recursive proof composition and proof aggregation DCDS designs. We evaluate the implemented compliance predicate in terms of the total number of image pixels $N = w \times h$, where w and h are the width and height of the image. Our C++ implementation is built on top of libsnark [3].

In general, a BMP file consists of five main parts; a file header, image header, color table, pixel array, and an International Color Consortium (ICC) color profile. The image header is the most complex from a compatibility standpoint due to the varying versions. However, the BITMAPINFOHEADER format introduced in Windows 3.0 is the most commonly used format for compatibility reasons and is the focus of this work. We disregard bitmaps with the optional ICC color profile since these are less common and are only supported under version 5 image headers. And we only consider uncompressed bitmaps with 24 bit color depths, as these are most common in practice.

Bitmap Inspection and Sanitization. We implement a compliance predicate $\prod$ adhering to the National Security Agency's Inspection and Sanitization guide (ISG) for Bitmaps [11]. The ISG provides an analysis on various elements that are contained within the BMP file structure and how they can be a cause for concern for either hiding sensitive data or attempts to exploit a system. We implement a majority of the recommendations for mitigating these threats.

File Header Compliance The file header is a 14-byte structure that stores general information about the BMP. It begins with the magic bytes 0x424D, and then defines the file size, reserved bytes, and offset address of the pixel data.

Image Header Compliance The BMP Info Header image header type is 40 bytes and contains general information about the size, compression type, number of planes, resolution, and bit count of the BMP. The ISG outlines data *attack* and data *hiding* concerns with BMP image headers. Most attacks are prevented though the zeroing out of unused fields, or ensuring that default values are used. Our compliance predicate ensures the size of the image header is 40 bytes, the colors used value equals 0 (no color table present), the colors important value equals 0 (default value indicating that all colors are required), compression value equals 0 (compression not used), number of planes equals 1 (only supported value for BMP files), and that the width and height fields correspond to the size of the image.

Color Table The Microsoft Developer Network (MSDN) states that the color table is optional in Bitmaps with ≥ 8 bit color depths. Additionally, the NSA's inspection and sanitization guide for BMP files recommends removing the color table in BMP files with 24 bit color depths. For this reason, we only consider BMP files without a color table present.

Bitmap Pixel Filtering In addition to filtering the headers of the BMP file, our compliance predicate filters the BMP pixels. We implement a simple compliance predicate (filter) for *redaction* which performs any of the following: identity transformation, blacking out of image pixel regions, and/or cropping the images in a single compliance predicate.[1] The transformation is defined by a $w \times h$ redaction matrix R of boolean values. The constraints over R require that $R_{i,j} \times I_{i,j} = O_{i,j}$ where I is the input pixel matrix, and O is the output pixel matrix. The booleanity of R is enforced by requiring $R_{i,j} \times (1 - R_{i,j}) = 0$. This simple compliance predicate can simultaneously do *cropping*, *black-out boxes*, and *identity* transformations using only $2N$ multiplication gates.

5 Baseline and Optimizations

We implement several optimizations and evaluate their performance against a strong baseline. We show a $20\times$ speedup in prover time over the state-of-the-art [18], allowing us to filter over large 900×900 images. We describe the baseline and each of the optimizations next.

5.1 PCD Baseline

The baseline is based on the state-of-the-art image authentication from PCD [18]. Given that the source code of [18] is not publicly available, we implemented our BMP filtering predicate within libsnark's [3] PCD implementation which uses BCTV14 [6] pp-zk-SNARK for recursive proof composition over the MNT4 and MNT6 cycles of elliptic curves. Following [18], we also use the subset-sum hash function for hashing field elements, and we implement digital signatures outside the PCD. We verified that the number of constraints in our baseline circuit closely match those reported in [18].

5.2 Switching to Groth16

We switch to the Groth16 proving system [16] from BCTV14 [6], and implement the Groth16 verifier circuit in the PCD. The Groth16 proving system has faster verification and size-optimal proofs for pairing-based arguments. Faster verification and smaller proofs naturally imply less computation in the proof verification

---

[1] We also added other useful transforms (e.g., downscaling the image by a some factor) which we do not describe here for simplicity but they are part of the codebase.

portion of the prover's circuit as there are fewer input wires and fewer gates. As a concrete comparison, Groth16 proofs consist of only 2 $\mathbb{G}_1$ elements and 1 $\mathbb{G}_2$ element compared to BCTV's proofs of 7 $\mathbb{G}_1$ elements and 1 $\mathbb{G}_2$ element. The smaller Groth16 proofs result in a verification savings of 9 fewer pairings and 4 fewer pairing-product equations used for verifying proofs.

More importantly, the Groth16 prover requires fewer multi-exponentiations compared to BCTV14. Groth16 uses $5m - 2n$ less exponentiations in $\mathbb{G}_1$ and $m - n$ less exponentiations in $\mathbb{G}_2$, where $m \geq n$ represent the number of wires and n the number of multiplication gates respectively. We also use the asymmetric bilinear map construction for efficiency. Asymmetric elliptic curves are more practically and efficiently realizable for higher security levels [12]. Note that the savings in exponentiations mainly apply to dense R1CS statements. In other words, if the majority of R1CS constraints involve wires that carry a 1 or a 0, then the multi-exponentiations become cheap, in which case Groth16 doesn't help reduce the prover cost.[2] This is indeed the case for our prover's circuit since the majority of the constraints are due to *booleanity*, the unpacking of field elements to bits for hashing. However, when combined with our second optimization (next section) which significantly reduces the booleanity constraints, the savings become more noticeable.

5.3   Reducing Booleanity Constraints

The PCD hashing circuit hashes the bit representation of the string vk$\|z$ where vk is the verification key and z is the input message which includes the image in our application. Unpacking of these field elements to bits in order to hash them is very expensive. The overall size of the main PCD circuit C_{pcd} is $|\prod| + s \cdot 89412 + (1 + s) \cdot N \cdot 298 + 11925$ gates, where s is the arity (number of incoming messages to each node) and N is the input size (see Appendix A and [6] § 5 for details). The term $11920 + (1 + s) \cdot N \cdot 298$ costs around 10 million gates for even a small 128×128 image where $N = 16384$ pixels or field elements each is 298 bits (the arity $s = 1$).

The binary representation of the verification key is 11920 bits (gates). On the other hand, the binary representation of the inputs z costs $(1 + s) \cdot N \cdot 298$ gates since each element of the input is represented with $\lceil \log r_4 \rceil = 298$ bits (gates). However, since we know that each element of the input message (a raw pixel) is represented with fewer than 32 bits, we can truncate the input before hashing it. We unpack each pixel f to its binary representation and enforce $f = \sum_{i=1}^{32} b_i \cdot 2^{i-1}$ for each bit b_i of f. Implicit in this constraint is that the 266 most significant bits of f must equal 0 if it holds, thereby avoiding the booleanity checks on those values. This optimization reduces the booleanity gates by a factor of $298/32 = 9.3\times$. For a 128×128 image, the resulting circuit is reduced from 10 million to about 1 million gates. It also reduces the number of variables (wires in the circuit) and accordingly the proving key size by about $6\times$.

---

[2] In this case FFTs dominate the prover's cost, and the cost of FFTs in both BCTV14 and Groth16 are the same.

Table 1(b) shows the significant improvements resulting from these first two optimizations. Specifically, at the 250×250 image size, we see around $9\times$ reduction in number of constraints in the circuit (from 37.8M to 4.3M), $5\times$ reduction in prover time, and $6.6\times$ reduction in peak memory utilization at the prover.

5.4   Algebraic Hash Functions

In both the PCD and proof aggregation settings, the vast majority of the compliance predicate's constraints are due to the hashing of input and output images. Even with the booleanity optimization, the booleanity constraints continue to dominate the cost of our circuit. Traditional hashing algorithms such as SHA are complex and not well-suited for SNARK applications since they require converting $\mathbb{F}_p$ elements to bits, incurring a non-trivial $\lceil \log(p) \rceil$ multiplication gates per field element cost. This roughly amounts to 1 constraint per bit per field element and dominates our circuit's overall cost. For this reason, recent work has proposed algebraic hash functions whose domain is $\mathbb{F}_p$ [15].

We instantiate the Poseidon hash function [15] over $\mathbb{F}_p$ and analyze the performance benefits. First, we observe that Poseidon achieves on the order of 0.3 constraints per bit, compared to the subset-sum's cost of 1 constraint per bit (due to the unpacking of bits from $\mathbb{F}_p^m$). However, our booleanity optimization from earlier reduced the cost from 1 constraint per bit to around 0.1 constraints per bit. We observe that rather than truncating the field elements for the algebraic hashing gagdet, we can instead pack multiple pixels into a single field element. For the BN254 curve, we are able to squeeze 7 pixels into a single 254 bit field element. We use a pixel packing gadget that ensures for a field element $X \in \mathbb{F}_p$ and a set of pixel values f, $\sum_{i=0}^{6} 2^{32i} \cdot f[i] == X$.

We implement the Poseidon hashing for the proof aggregation setting only, since integrating it into PCD is non trivial and beyond the scope of this paper. The results are shown in Table 1(c), showing an additional $3\times$ reduction in number of constraints in the circuit translating to $5\times$ speedups in prover time at the 250×250 image size. Note that the difference in performance between Table 1(c) and Table 1(b) is primarily because of the Poseidon hashing, i.e., we expect the two sets of results to be close once Poseidon is integrated into PCD. This is because the number of constraints for PCD's unique verification circuit (the V component of C_{pcd}) are very small relative to the number of constraints due to the compliance predicate (the $\prod$ component of C_{pcd}).

5.5   Reducing Pipeline Latency

The end-to-end latency of the DCDS filtering pipeline is defined as the time from image publication at the sensor until the filtered content crosses the boundary (or fails). As shown in Fig. 2, this latency depends on the depth of the pipeline, the number of filtering steps in our example. In a naive instantiation of the DCDS pipelines of Fig. 2 whereby each filter generates the proof and forwards the output(s) to the next filter in the pipeline, the end-to-end latency t_k for a pipeline of depth k is $O(kt_{prover})$, where t_{prover} is the prover time (the time each filter needs in order to produce a proof over its computation). For example, Table 1(b) (Table 1(c)) show the prover time to be 62 s (15 s) for a 250×250 image. Multiplying these numbers by the depth of the pipeline can get expensive.

We make t_k independent of k in the proof aggregation setting of Fig. 2(b) i.e., $t_k \approx O(t_{prover})$. When a filter node F_i receives its input image I_i, it *natively* executes the equivalent traditional filtering software to produce the filtered output image I_{i+1}. Let t_{F_i} denote this native execution latency, and note that this t_{F_i} is orders of magnitude faster than t_{prover}. Node F_i forwards I_{i+1} to the next filtering node in the pipeline. In parallel to the native execution, Node F_i runs the expensive prover algorithm on the input image and forwards (h_{i+1}, π_{i+1}) to the boundary node as described in Sect. 3.2. As soon as F_{i+1} receives I_{i+1} from F_i, it can immediately begin performing its local computation, rather than waiting on F_i to produce (h_i, π_i). For a pipeline of depth k, it can be shown that the end-to-end latency t_k is reduced from $k(t_{prover} + t_{comm} + t_{verifier})$ to $(\sum_{i=0}^{k-1} t_{F_i}) + t_{prover} + k(t_{comm} + t_{verifier})$, where t_{comm} is the one-hop communication latency.

A similar approach can be used to reduce the latency of the PCD setting (Fig. 2(a)). At first glance, it appears that one cannot parallelize the distributed computation since each sequential hop requires a proof of correctness from the previous DCDS node. However, we observe that the majority of the prover's computation is independent of the previous proof, and can accordingly start in parallel. For example, a monolithic prover can split the circuit into two sections (a) and (b) such that (a) corresponds to wire values independent of the previous proof π_{i-1} and (b) corresponds to wire values dependent on π_{i-1}. The prover then applies techniques from [20] to compute a proof π_i by first computing the values associated with (a), and later computing the values associated with (b) when π_{i-1} arrives. It can be shown that the majority of the prover's computation involves wire values *independent* of the previous proof π_{i-1}, and therefore the majority of the distributed PCD computation can be performed in parallel by forwarding native execution output. We leave this PCD Implementation for future work.

6   Performance Evaluation

We evaluate the performance (compute and memory costs) of the designs for a single hop of the filtering pipeline in terms of the prover time (time for each filter F_i to produce a proof on its local computation) and peak memory, and verifier time (time for the boundary node to verify a single proof π_{i+1}), for different image sizes. The prover's memory footprint includes loading the proving key $\prod$ corresponding to the compliance predicate pk, where the size of the proving key in MB is denoted by $|\text{pk}|$, and $|\prod|$ is the size of the compliance predicate in terms of number of R1CS constraints. Table 1 shows the performance results of three

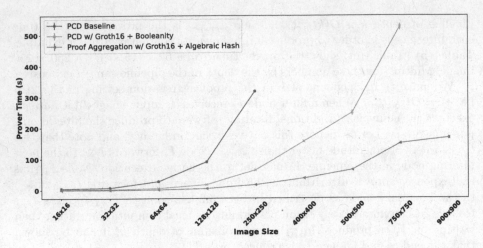

Fig. 3. Comparison of baseline, optimized PCD, and aggregation designs in terms of prover's time (seconds) for different image sizes. The x-axis is quadratic.

different systems on an AWS c5.18xlarge instance with 72 cores and 144 GB RAM. Table 1(a) shows the results for the baseline PCD system of Sect. 5.1. The baseline prover algorithm runs out of memory for images larger than 250×250 pixels. At the 250×250 image size, the filtering predicate has more than 37M constraints and takes the prover more than 5 min and around 100 GB of memory to generate a proof! The proof size $|\pi|$ is 2988 bits.

Table 1(b) shows enhanced performance of the baseline PCD system when incorporating the Groth16 and Booleanity optimizations described in Sect. 5. The optimizations result in $5\times$ speedup in prover time at the 250×250 image size, and the reduction in prover memory allow increasing the image size by $9\times$ before running out of memory. The proof size is reduced to 1493 bits.

Table 1(c) shows the performance of the proof aggregation system with comparable assurances, including Groth16 and algebraic hash optimizations from Sect. 5. At the 250×250 image size, the optimized proof aggregation system delivers $20\times$ speedups in prover time. Additionally, proof verification time is constant (independent of the input image size) since constant-size hashes make up the public input of the circuit. In this proof aggregation design however, the aggregator must verify k proofs for a depth k pipeline each on the order of 5 ms as shown in Table 1(c). The $30\times$ reduction in number of R1CS constraints further enables scaling to large 900×900 image sizes, a $13\times$ larger scale than baseline. The proof size is 1019 bits.

Finally, Fig. 3 compares the three proof systems in terms of prover time showing the relative speedups attained and the resulting increase in image scale. Note that the x-axis in the figure is quadratic, and the scaling is linear in pixels.

Table 1. Performance of the DCDS proof system for a single hop computation on an AWS c5.18xlarge instance with 72 cores and 144 GB RAM. $|\prod|$ is the number of R1CS constraints in the DCDS circuit which contains the predicate. Generator, prover, verifier times are in seconds. $|\pi|$ is the proof size in bits, and Mem is prover's memory in GB. The table compares three systems: (a) unoptimized PCD based proof system, (b) Optimized PCD based proof system, and (c) optimized proof aggregation based proof system. The 250 × 250 image size results are highlighted for comparison.

Image Size	$\lvert\prod\rvert$	|pk| (MB)	Generator	Prover	Verifier	Mem	$\lvert\pi\rvert$ (bits)
(a) PCD Baseline							
64×64	2,780,396	750.0	80.32	27.67	0.062	12.37	2988
128×128	10,153,196	2,740.8	281.21	90.18	0.096	30.79	2988
250×250	37,822,796	10,351.6	686.77	316.70	0.220	99.48	2988
(b) PCD w/ Groth16 + Booleanity optimizations							
64×64	353,783	82.7	11.35	5.73	0.025	6.11	1493
128×128	1,189,367	289.7	37.28	17.12	0.043	8.24	1493
250×250	4,325,255	1,073.6	119.01	62.72	0.107	15.66	1493
400×400	10,928,055	2,782.4	246.59	154.66	0.246	31.88	1493
500×500	17,109,255	4,274.8	379.63	246.81	0.377	46.56	1493
750×750	38,325,255	9,698.1	706.07	524.71	0.822	98.74	1493
(c) Proof Aggregation w/ Groth16 + Algebraic hash optimizations							
64×64	85,227	14.4	2.29	1.41	0.005	5.78	1019
128×128	338,655	57.3	7.98	4.75	0.005	7.41	1019
250×250	1,289,571	212.5	18.96	15.98	0.005	14.02	1019
400×400	3,301,043	569.5	50.40	36.63	0.005	26.87	1019
500×500	5,157,987	850.0	69.23	63.45	0.005	39.17	1019
750×750	11,604,043	1,936.3	182.29	147.78	0.005	81.59	1019
900×900	16,709,987	2,747.6	248.07	165.70	0.005	114.89	1019

7 Related and Future Work

To our knowledge, this is the first design and implementation of a CDS filtering pipeline based on verifiable computation. Furthermore, we are not aware of any work on decentralizing the CDS architecture across several potentially untrusted devices. Our work is inspired by PhotoProof [18], which describes an image authentication proof-of-concept library using the proof-carrying data scheme of [6]. PhotoProof demonstrated the feasibility of distributed image filtering, however, PhotoProof's ability to scale to larger images was largely limited due to the unavailability of modern algebraic hashing techniques [1,15] and optimized proof systems [16].

In terms of future work, we identify the following three thrusts:

Expressiveness, Performance, and Security. The ability to efficiently filter more complex data types is critical for CDS adoption and for mission enablement. In addition to bitmap filtering, we implemented filters for redacting text documents that use the same principles as the BMP filters discussed here (treating characters in the document like pixels), and we plan to continue enhancing the expressiveness and efficiency of these predicates. Additionally, we plan to experiment with newer constructions of PCD based on accumulation schemes [8], which realize recursive proof composition without the sublinear-time verification requirement. These constructions may permit higher levels of security avoiding for example the limitations inherent to PCD constructions from cycles of elliptic curves [6], while additionally providing post-quantum security properties.

Confidentiality Protection The present DCDS design is primarily concerned with protecting the integrity of the filtering pipeline even when computed on low assurance devices. A filtering node in the current design sees the plaintext input images as well as the witness, both of which may need to be confidential. We plan to extend the design such that the filtering nodes are able to perform a *verifiable computation* over *encrypted data* keeping both the input and the witness private from the filtering node. This problem is akin to verifiable and private delegation of computation [13]. However, these protocols require ideas from fully-homomorphic encryption (FHE) and verifiable computations simultaneously and are currently expensive. We are experimenting with simpler partially homomorphic schemes that are efficient and suffice for some of the desired computations.

Hardware Acceleration To support filtering of information flows that require low latency, the prover time must be further reduced. Consider for example the pp-zk-SNARK prover's optimized algorithm is defined [5] (see § 4.3 and Fig. 10-b in [5]). There are two main operations the prover runs: computing the coefficients h of a polynomial $H(z)$, and computing the proof π using 8 large multi-scalar multiplications of the form $\alpha_1 P_1 + \ldots + \alpha_n P_n$ where P_i are elements of group G_1 (or G_2) and α_i are scalars. Both of these sets of operations can directly benefit from hardware acceleration. We will investigate using GPU or FPGA implementations of FFTs over big integers and multi-scalar multiplications. We expect this may lead to up to two orders of magnitude speedups for large circuits.

8   Conclusion

This paper presents a first step towards building decentralized and provably secure cross domain solutions, allowing secure composition of CDS components (such as content filters) running on untrusted edge devices. A decentralized CDS capability complements today's enterprise and tactical CDS enabling secure cross-domain information sharing when access to the enterprise or single-device tactical CDSs is not available, such as with the disconnected, intermittent, and limited tactical edge. We show that instantiating such a decentralized capability can be made practical, for the simple image filtering predicates considered in this paper. We expect the active research efforts for enhancing the practicality of verifiable computations will render this paradigm increasingly more practical in the future.

A   From zk-SNARK to PCD

A PCD system (*Generator, Prover, Verifier*) is constructed in [7] using *recursive composition of pp-zk-SNARK* (G, P, V) *proofs.* The main idea behind recursive proof composition is that the new proof system has to prove two things now at each node: (1) *the proof of the previous computation step is valid* **and** (2) *the node performed a valid local computation.* In other words, the pp-zk-SNARK is used to prove that the input proof π_{in} attests to the compliance of z_{in}, **and** the output z is $\prod$-compliant given (z_{in}, z_{loc}). This effectively allows recursion so that the *history* can now be discarded at each step, and hence enables compliance predicate verification only by looking at the proof and data from the last step.

More concretely, in order to construct the recursive PCD proof system, the PCD circuit C_{pcd} must encode the pp-zk-SNARK verification algorithm V in addition to the local computation corresponding to the compliance predicate $\prod$ i.e., one must construct the $\mathbb{F}$-arithmetic circuit C_V corresponding to V as a sub-circuit of C_{pcd}.

A known efficient pp-zk-SNARK verification function uses pairings on elliptic curves [6]. Since, the verification function, the circuit C_V, operates over the base field $\mathbb{F}_q$ of the curve rather than over $\mathbb{F}_r$ over which the NP statement is defined,[3] realizing C_{pcd} in practice is challenging (see [6] for details). For the sake of this discussion, we just mention that C_{pcd} involves a lot more than the local computation. There are two separate PCD circuits, each one on a different elliptic curve, such that the two curves are on a *cycle.* The main PCD circuit C_{pcd} does three things:

1. implements a collision-free hash function that verifies the output hash of vk, z is valid, which involves circuits for bit conversion because the hash function operates over bit strings (this step is required in order to bypass the circular dependency between the two proof systems generated from the two curves on a cycle)
2. verifies the local predicate $\prod(z, z_{in}, z_{loc}, b_{base})$
3. recursively verifies $C_V(vk, z_{in}, \pi_{in})$ for each pair which also involves circuits for bit conversion

Circuit Size. The overall size of the main PCD circuit C_{pcd} is $|\prod| + s \cdot 89412 + (1 + s) \cdot n \cdot 298 + 11925$ gates, where s is the arity (number of incoming messages to each node) and n is the input size (see [6] §5 for details; there is also an auxiliary PCD circuit we don't show here as it has constant cost.). This shows the (additive) dependence of the prover cost on $|\prod|$. Besides the predicate, a main contributor to cost is the booleanity checks which requires expanding into their bit representations each of the input and output messages $((1 + s) \cdot n \cdot 298$ gates), where $\mathbb{F}_r$ is a prime field of 298 bits. For a large input such as a 128×128 image i.e., $n = 16384$ field elements each 298 bits, this term can be large requiring

---

[3] Here q is the size of the base field over which the curve is defined, and r is the order of the group (number of points on the curve).

around 10 million gates even for $s = 1$, far exceeding the cost of the predicate $\prod$. This $\lceil \log r_\alpha \rceil = 298$ blow up factor seems to be inherent to the construction because the collision-resistant hash function operates on binary string inputs (see [6] §4.1), and expanding a field element x to its bit representation requires $\lceil \log r_\alpha \rceil$ constraints to verify $\sum_i b_i 2^i = x$, where b_i is the bit at index i in x's binary representation.

Prover Key Size and Memory. The prover key is made of a large set of group elements. Here, we relate the number of group elements in the proving key to the input and circuit dimensions to understand the effect of circuit complexity on performance. The number of elements in the key depends on the Quadratic Arithmetic Program (QAP) instance [14], which is derived from the Rank-1 Constraint System (R1CS) through an efficient reduction (see [4] Appendix E). Briefly, a R1CS constraint system is expressed as $A \cdot s \odot B \cdot s = C \cdot s$, where s is a vector of $m + 1$ variables (input, intermediate, and output variables) corresponding to the m wires in the arithmetic circuit (an additional special variable, one, is used resulting in $m+1$ variables). And A, B, and C are matrices of dimension $l \times m + 1$ for a system with l constraints corresponding to the l gates of the circuit (each row corresponds to a constraint).

A R1CS constraint system is reduced to a QAP instance with the same number of $m + 1$ variables and whose degree is $d(l)$, where $d(l)$ is some value larger than l selected for an evaluation domain to optimize computations of Lagrange polynomials and FFT/iFFT. The QAP instance is similarly represented with three sets of polynomials A', B', and C' each containing $m + 1$ polynomials each of which is degree $d(l)$. In summary, the resulting proving key contains at most $6m + d(l) + 13$ elements from group $\mathbb{G}_1$ and $m + 4$ elements from group $\mathbb{G}_2$. Reducing m, the number of wires in the circuit, significantly affects performance (key size, memory, generator time, and prover time). The proof always has 7 $\mathbb{G}_1$ elements and 1 $\mathbb{G}_2$ element [5].

References

1. Aly, A., Ashur, T., Ben-Sasson, E., Dhooghe, S., Szepieniec, A.: Design of symmetric-key primitives for advanced cryptographic protocols. IACR Trans. Symmetric Cryptol. **2020**, 1–45 (2020)
2. Australian Cyber Security Centre: Fundamentals of cross domain solutions, June 2020. https://www.cyber.gov.au/acsc/view-all-content/publications/fundamentals-cross-domain-solutions, Accessed 10 Apr 2020
3. Ben-Sasson, E., Chiesa, A., Genkin, D., Kfir, S., Tromer, E., Virza, M.: libsnark, 2014. https://github.com/scipr-lab/libsnark
4. Ben-Sasson, E., Chiesa, A., Genkin, D., Tromer, E., Virza, M.: SNARKs for C: verifying program executions succinctly and in zero knowledge. In: Canetti, R., Garay, J.A. (eds.) CRYPTO 2013. LNCS, vol. 8043, pp. 90–108. Springer, Heidelberg (2013). https://doi.org/10.1007/978-3-642-40084-1_6
5. Ben-Sasson, E., Chiesa, A., Tromer, E., Virza, M.: Succinct non-interactive zero knowledge for a von Neumann architecture. In: USENIX Security 2014, pp. 781–796 (2014)

6. Ben-Sasson, E., Chiesa, A., Tromer, E., Virza, M.: Scalable zero knowledge via cycles of elliptic curves. Algorithmica **79**(4), 1102–1160 (2017)
7. Bitansky, N., Canetti, R., Chiesa, A., Tromer, E.: Recursive composition and bootstrapping for snarks and proof-carrying data. In: Proceedings of the Forty-Fifth Annual ACM Symposium on Theory of Computing, pp. 111–120 (2013)
8. Bünz, B., Chiesa, A., Mishra, P., Spooner, N.: Proof-carrying data from accumulation schemes. IACR Cryptol. ePrint Arch. **2020**, 499 (2020)
9. Chiesa, A., Tromer, E.: Proof-carrying data and hearsay arguments from signature cards. In: ICS, vol. 10, pp. 310–331 (2010)
10. Chiesa, A., Tromer, E.: Proof-carrying data: secure computation on untrusted platforms (high-level description). Next Wave Natl. Secur. Agency Rev. Emerging Technol. **19**(2), 40–46 (2012)
11. Cross Domain Products and Technology Branch of the Information Assurance Directorate: Inspection and Sanitization Guidance for Bitmap File Format. Technical report, Version 1.0, National Security Agency, January 2012
12. Galbraith, S., Paterson, K., Smart, N.: Pairings for cryptographers. Cryptology ePrint Archive, Report 2006/165 (2006). https://eprint.iacr.org/
13. Gennaro, R., Gentry, C., Parno, B.: Non-interactive verifiable computing: outsourcing computation to untrusted workers. In: Rabin, T. (ed.) CRYPTO 2010. LNCS, vol. 6223, pp. 465–482. Springer, Heidelberg (2010). https://doi.org/10.1007/978-3-642-14623-7_25
14. Gennaro, R., Gentry, C., Parno, B., Raykova, M.: Quadratic span programs and succinct NIZKs without PCPs. In: Johansson, T., Nguyen, P.Q. (eds.) EUROCRYPT 2013. LNCS, vol. 7881, pp. 626–645. Springer, Heidelberg (2013). https://doi.org/10.1007/978-3-642-38348-9_37
15. Grassi, L., Khovratovich, D., Rechberger, C., Roy, A., Schofnegger, M.: Poseidon: a new hash function for zero-knowledge proof systems. In: Proceedings of the 30th USENIX Security Symposium. USENIX Association (2020)
16. Groth, J.: On the size of pairing-based non-interactive arguments. In: Fischlin, M., Coron, J.-S. (eds.) EUROCRYPT 2016. LNCS, vol. 9666, pp. 305–326. Springer, Heidelberg (2016). https://doi.org/10.1007/978-3-662-49896-5_11
17. National Cross Domain Strategy and Management Office: Cross Domain Solution (CDS) Design and Implementation Requirements: 2020 Raise the Bar (RTB) Baseline Release. Technical report, NCDSMO-R-00008-003_00, National Security Agency, December 2020
18. Naveh, A., Tromer, E.: Photoproof: cryptographic image authentication for any set of permissible transformations. In: 2016 IEEE Symposium on Security and Privacy (SP), pp. 255–271. IEEE (2016)
19. Smith, S.: Shedding light on cross domain solutions (2015). https://www.sans.org/white-papers/36492/. Accessed 10 Apr 2020
20. Wu, H., Zheng, W., Chiesa, A., Popa, R.A., Stoica, I.: DIZK: a distributed zero knowledge proof system. In: USENIX Security 2018, pp. 675–692 (2018)

Author Index